INTERTEXTS

Reading Pedagogy
in College Writing Classrooms

INTERTEXTS

Reading Pedagogy
in College Writing Classrooms

Edited by

Marguerite Helmers
University of Wisconsin, Oshkosh

 LAWRENCE ERLBAUM ASSOCIATES, PUBLISHERS
2003   Mahwah, New Jersey   London

Lawrence Erlbaum Associates, Inc., Publishers
10 Industrial Avenue
Mahwah, NJ 07430

Cover design by Kathryn Houghtaling Lacey
Original pastel by Deborah DeWit Marchant, 1998

Library of Congress Cataloging-in-Publication Data

Intertexts : reading pedagogy in college writing classrooms,
edited by Marguerite Helmers.

ISBN 0-8058-4227-6 (cloth : alk. paper) — ISBN 0-8058-4498-8 (pbk. : alk. paper)

Copyright information for this volume can be obtained
by contacting the Library of Congress.

Books published by Lawrence Erlbaum Associates are printed on acid-free paper,
and their bindings are chosen for strength and durability.

Printed in the United States of America
10 9 8 7 6 5 4 3 2 1

For Bill, Reader of Music

As you read a book word by word and page by page,
you participate in its creation, just as a cellist playing
a Bach suite participates, note by note, in the creation,
the coming-to-be, the existence of the music.
—Ursula K. LeGuin

Contents

Preface

In the new century, the problem of the teaching of reading promises to develop as an issue that engages the entire curriculum of the university. Teachers of all subject areas will lament that students cannot read as new demands are placed on students, as degree requirements shift and change, as writing itself alters its style and focus, as hypertextual and visual communication dominate the classroom and everyday life. Yet, as is argued here in *Intertexts*, *reading* is not a simple process of absorbing the qualities of the best that has been said from the Great Books that appear on the syllabi in departments of English, but a complex, ever-changing process of situational interaction and self-reflection with words, images, and other readers. In this collection, we hope to establish a series of theoretical and pedagogical questions that will inform discussions about how to teach reading to undergraduates in various curricular settings.

When educators complain that their students "can't read," they are not implying that their students are unable to decode a page of markings; rather, they are looking for something beyond the surface level of reading for meaning. "Attentive" re-readings or "in-depth" readings are terms applied to reading practices that are ideal: valuing rereading, acknowledging that rereadings may hold different interpretations depending on time and place, coming to a knowledge that responses may differ between readings. Reading actively counters the tendencies toward passive consumption and appreciation, argues feminist critic Estella Lauter. An active reading process assumes that reader and text have agency, intention, and a repertoire of persuasive techniques. Although most critics would recognize that the cultural, ideological repertoire of a text affects readers, Lauter takes the argument a step further. By making choices, whether to accept, reject, or argue, the reader affects the reception of the text. Through this dialogic process, both the reader's ideology and the text's representation of the world coexist (Lauter np).

The writers in this book advocate taking the insights of writing theory and pedagogy and applying those theories and practical ideas to reading practice. Certain classroom practices have become accepted as important acts in composition, such as collaboration, the use of journals, the importance of active marking, re-reading and questioning. Conceptions of reader, text, and cultural situation as mutually determinate are essential if composition is to crucially engage reading as a practice that is coeval with writing. Furthermore, as Kathleen McCormick stressed, it is essential for teachers to bring disciplinary assumptions to the fore:

> Whether or not they are conscious of it, however, teachers at all levels are always teaching their students how to read. The different ways students are asked to read imply particular values and beliefs about the nature of texts, the nature of readers as subjects of texts and as subjects in the world, and about meaning and language itself. (7)

Accordingly, the intent of this book is not to "bridge the gap" between the teaching of writing and the teaching of literature, but to argue that any "gap" between reading and writing is a construct. We seek to erase disciplinary deadlock and replace them with renewed commitments to studying the processes of learning and teaching.

The perspectives of the writers in this book span centuries as well as genres and teaching strategies. Certainly, the writers do not always agree on the best methods of teaching. Yet, collectively, their voices stress the need to reinvent English Studies as a discipline that engages textual practices of many styles and at many levels. It is true that this is not a new plea, but with the advent of a new century and the acknowledged changes taking place in university general education and in the teaching faculty, shouldn't it finally be time to support new paradigms of instruction?

It is something of a commonplace in reading instruction to urge students to connect with various types of texts by relating them to personal experience. Kathleen McCormick opens this volume by turning that assumption on its side, asking how students can acquire knowledge about what they *have not* lived. Students often encounter texts that resist them because their lived experience and their textual repertoires do not enable them to make sense of the ideas, the allusions in the text, the historical circumstances that fostered the text's production. In particular, it is the weaker readers in the college classrooms who appear to struggle from an absence of historical and textual backgrounds. In response to this problem, McCormick outlines a plan for symptomatic reading that draws from the work of cultural critics Pierre Machery and Raymond Williams. Her previous works have also introduced symptomatic reading and her experiences as a teacher in Hartford, Connecticut brought her close to many students who read culture in highly different ways than the privileged college students in her classrooms. Here, she invites further discussion by stressing that weaker readers are not lacking in reading strategies, but read in ways that differ from institutionally sanctioned practices (what Williams terms *dominant* ideologies). These readers often have "street knowledge" that is complex and critical. To bridge this gap between the street and the school, McCormick introduces three critical questions for teachers: what are students' histories of reading? how does the media encourage reading? and what are our culture's dominant reading practices?

Lizabeth Rand speaks to the socio-physiological situation of reading instruction by detailing her teaching experiences with adult members of a Seventh Day Adventist Church in Nebraska (chap. 3). These students taught her that reading is a process of socialization into ways of thinking and behaving according to group norms, what the French historian Michel Foucault termed a process of "disciplining." The Adventists construed appropriate "public discourse" as acting, speaking, and writing in ways that imitated Jesus. Rather than censuring the church for injurious brainwashing, however, Rand argues that all teachers of writing and reading can learn from her experiences. Clearly, the Adventists are not alone in being socialized into particular reading practices that alienate them from mainstream values of education. She advocates the use of literacy narratives that specifically ask students to investigate the ways that their upbringing has shaped their responses to various mainstream assumptions and values.

Following Rand's ethnographic description, we engage two dominant theoretical modes of reading practice: classical declamation and reader-response theory. Although the Adventists advocate imitation of Jesus Christ, classical Greek and Roman rhetoricians also advocated imitation of particularly influential speakers. In chapter 4, Nancy Christiansen stresses that misconceptions about the role of imitation in classical education have led contemporary educators to resist its value. Reading involves

an understanding of declamation, the "master genre" that frames all discourse. Declamation is a double-frame, involving argument and drama,
interpretation and performance. To imitate is to read well and to demonstrate an understanding of the "author's motives, attitudes, passions,
strategies, and judgments." Thus, at its best, classical education in the
modern classroom involves active learning and athletic practice.

Patricia Harkin and James Sosnoski may, at first, appear to differ from
Christiansen in their views of teaching argument (chap. 5); however, their
points are much the same. Their critique of three popular argument textbooks emphasizes that the textbook authors fail to acknowledge the extent to which emotion and individualized readings create meaning. Reading theories in textbooks are static and decontextualized. At their best,
the authors of textbooks for first-year composition courses must work
harder to restate the importance of "frameworks for describing how and
why readings differ—from person to person, from context to context,
from culture to culture" (107).

Charles Hill (chap. 6) moves from the familiar world of print culture to
questions of reading and writing in a visual universe. Hill argues that
equal classroom attention should be given to understanding and creating
visual media, pointing to a need in college education to merge the technical possibilities of electronic publishing with the more cognitive processes
of analysis, imitation, creation, and re-creation. As Hill points out, our
neglect of the visual stems largely from our inherited "dislike and disparagement of mass culture, and from our fears that visual and other modes
of communication will overtake, replace, or diminish the importance of
the print medium" (125). A significant problem of pedagogical practice in
English Studies, then, is its resistance to change. Caught in traditional ge-
stalts of print culture, teachers must now realize that the media surrounding them—visual images, video advertisements, hypertext—have *already*
changed the way students construe narrative and page design.

Hypertext itself becomes a powerful way of interrogating traditional
texts, as Marcel Cornis-Pope and Ann Woodlief argue (chap. 7).
Teaching literary criticism to undergraduates, both Cornis-Pope and
Woodlief have discovered that students benefit from the possibilities of
multiple, interactive authorship that hypertext provides. Offering readers their protocols for reading, the authors argue that these questions
are best used in a networked community, for students are best served
when they can *see*—in other words, *read*—multiple interpretations on
the screen. Students discover that their interpretations are related to
others' interpretations, and they return to the text for further re-read-

ings. Thus, they form "a reading community in a nonlinear field," amplifying the point that reading well is itself a nonlinear, recursive, and collaborative process.

The experimental, nonlinear, postmodern aspects of reading are exemplified in linear print form by Mary Ann Cain and George Kalamaras's investigation into their own subjectivity as teachers of writing and reading (chap. 8). Over the years, Cain and Kalamaras have worked to bring their professional identities as poets into full expression as teachers of writing. They argue that the composition classroom should be a *nexus of discourses*, a term they borrow from Stephen North. It is this plurality of voices that they enact in their contribution to this book. Performing their argument that writing is a process of reading and rereading that must set aside powerful and oppressive constraints, Cain and Kalamaras invite dialogue, e-mail messages, reflection and classification into their prose, subtly deconstructing our own expectations for explication of this "topic" reading.

Like Cain and Kalamaras, Mariolina Salvatori teaches us to value ambiguity. Salvatori has a long and distinguished history of working with reading pedagogy from inside the field of composition. In the concluding chapter to this book, she discloses her own experiences with teaching writing. Bringing students in first-year composition into the difficult process of reading poetry, Salvatori finds that she can engage their decoding and interpretive processes by emphasizing their reading difficulties. The "difficulty paper" that she has assigned and refined over many years brings reading-as-process and writing-as-process together in a positive construction of meaning.

We hope that our readers will find our advice to be practical and that teachers and the directors of writing programs will be guided to develop syllabi and assignments by the essays in this book. Ways to refigure the syllabus for first-year composition include including visual design, images, and web-page development to students in writing courses (Hill), preparing online reading communities (Cornis-Pope and Woodlief), and insuring that courses have a multidiscursive texture that draws on a variety of textual products (Cain and Kalamaras). Specific assignments that address the intersections between reading and writing are literacy narratives (Rand), the "double master frame" of declamation (Christiansen), and the difficulty paper (Salvatori). Finally, Harkin and Sosnoski urge program directors and teachers of composition to exercise a healthy skepticism about the textbooks that find their way into our classrooms. The issue is not whether "readers"—as these books are metonymically called—

should be present, but *how* these collections of essays are to be read. Their very physical presence suggests the operation of commercial values: these essays were chosen as significant texts of American culture, marked as worthy of salvage and collection. Ideologically, then, the texts function to circumscribe communities large and small, whether it is to define "America" as a heterogeneous democracy or to empower students to think of themselves as literate agents of the public sphere.

Finally, a word on our omissions. Critical readers will find absences within this text. For one, it is true that in this volume we don't discuss assessment. As a discipline, we need to define what we believe about reading processes and describe what we do to teach reading before we can assess students' progress and our own. It is also true that we do not make particularly fine distinctions between race, class, gender or even "the writer" and "the reader." The contributions of Elizabeth Flynn's and Patrocinio Schweickart's *Gender and Reading* was immensely influential in the field of literary studies; without the insights of the contributors to that book into the difference that historical situation and educational opportunity can make on how texts are interpreted, this book, *Intertexts*, would not be possible. Similarly, once readers are introduced to the foundational gay studies film *The Celluloid Closet*, it is difficult to return to an innocent or naïve reading of cinema that does not consider the sexual orientation of actors and characters. Jacqueline Tobin and Raymond Dobard are just two of several writers who have examined the sophisticated use of non-print codes to free slaves in 19th century America. In *Hidden in Plain View*, they describe African-American quilt makers as the devisors of "visual maps to freedom" (67). Quilts, maps, romance novels, popular film, the images of *Life* magazine or *Jet*, the strands of rap music and the blues, billboards, television commercials, sitcoms, talk shows, mystery novels, poetry: all employ codes that entwine a reader's race, class, and gender with the larger social tapestry of American education.

Although some may see the absence of direct attention to race, class and gender as a failure of our rhetoric to grasp the complexities of the reading situation, it is our hope that far more will see our oversights as an invitation to assert those differences in their own work. We are aware of the history and insights of gender theorists and critics who examine constructions of race and literacy in the United States. At the same time, we are aware that to treat differences between racial and socioeconomic histories with any sensitivity, a much longer, more complex investigation is needed. It is our hope that the area of reading becomes a vibrant topic of discussion and investigation in the university.

WORKS CITED

McCormick, Kathleen. *The Culture of Reading and the Teaching of English.* Manchester, UK: Manchester UP, 1994.

Tobin, Jacqueline, and Raymond Dobard. *Hidden in Plain View: The Secret Story of Quilts and the Underground Railroad.* New York: Doubleday, 1999.

Acknowledgments

There are many people to thank in the development of this book. First and foremost are the authors themselves, whose constant dedication to the project was inspiring.

This book was conceived at the Modern Language Association annual convention in San Francisco, December 1998. To the members of the dinner party at the Fog City Diner, Chuck, Byron, Debbie, and Ray, thank you for the wonderful conversation about literature and writing. An influence on this book, although she will be surprised to find her name here, is Carol Avery, whose inspired teaching of teachers led me to realize that there is magic in reading aloud to groups of adults. Kathleen McCormick deserves special praise for allowing me to talk shop with her under an umbrella at the beach during the NCTE (National Council of Teachers of English) summer conference at Myrtle Beach in 1999.

Karen Odden deserves my deepest gratitude for providing me with copious references. Her encouragement led me to join a seminar at St. John's College-Santa Fe in the summer of 2000, when I was feeling starved for words. For their inspiring conversation, thanks go to James Carey and David Starr for their ability to lead a diverse group of readers through terrain that was difficult and unfamiliar for many.

To Naomi Silverman, my editor at Lawrence Erlbaum, thank you for your keen advice and your encouragement. Thanks to Eileen Engel at Lawrence Erlbaum Associates and Robie Grant for production and editorial assistance. William Becker at the American Photography Museum suggested that I use the daguerreotype by James Adams Whipple that appears as the frontispiece to the Classroom section. Deborah DeWit Marchant, in addition to creating inspiring images, also provided words of encouragement during the production of the book. Tracy Walker helped me to secure the painting by Albert Joseph Moore from the Manchester City Art Galleries. Eve Cotton at the American Library Association was of great assistance is providing me with the photo of Oprah Winfrey for the opening section of this book. Donald Bowden at AP/Wide World Photos enabled us to use the famous photograph of the Marines raising the flag at Iwo Jima that is featured in Charles Hill's chapter.

Many friends and family members appear in the photographs throughout the book. They are Todd Levy, Patti Niemi, Jennifer McLernon, Richard Niemi, Jane Barnewitz, Kim Edwards, Pamela Gemin, Michael R. Vogt, Antoinette Souffrant, Marcel Souffrant, Julian Souffrant, William Helmers, Emily Helmers, and Caitlin Helmers. Todd Levy took the photographs that appear in chapters 1, 4, 6, 7, and 9. He also helped prepare the photographs for the publisher, going above and beyond in his attention to detail. His kindness in helping me during a busy summer at the Santa Fe Opera is deeply appreciated. In Santa Fe, thanks go to the Lensic Theater, Collected Works Bookstore, and Zele coffee shop for allowing us to photograph in July 2001.

Praise and thanks also go to my department of English. It was the discussions in that department, started by Aaron Dunckel, Pam Gemin, Julie Shaffer, Cary Henson, and Diane Crotty that planted the seed for this idea of teaching reading in college. As we worked together through the first-year student orientation program known as Odyssey, we talked about what students should read and why they should read. Attempting to name the people who have inspired me with their pedagogy in the past ten years will only lead to leaving someone out: thank you all. Mary Cappellari, Amanda Espinosa-Aguilar, and Cary Henson also deserve special credit for being the first to comment on the chapters and the book as a whole. Paul Klemp and Estella Lauter I thank gratefully for their enduring support.

I dedicate the book to my husband William, who is patient with my long stretches at the computer and in the library. Our daughters Emily and Caitlin, the Pony Pals, never cease to amaze me with their insightful textual commentary. They have contributed substantive information to the book as well, by answering my questions about their reading experiences. If we seek interactive reading models, perhaps we should look no further than my living room floor, covered with homemade paper dolls of Harry Potter and his band of merry wizards and Sadako's paper cranes.

CULTURE

READ

Oprah Winfrey
for America's
Libraries

1

Introduction:
Representing Reading

Marguerite Helmers

Writing is the act of creative reading.

—Mina Shaughnessy

My day begins with the newspaper. I open it on the dining table and read the metro section front to back. On the drive to work, I listen to a book on tape. At the university, I check my mailbox, read the memos, answer the surveys, then switch on the computer to check my electronic mail. Later, in class with my undergraduates, I discuss a poem by Siegfried Sassoon. After school, at home, I make a few phone calls to organize the PTA Dr. Seuss Read-In for my daughters' elementary school. At 7:00, I read a chapter of *The Wind in the Door* to the girls. By the time the moon turns the corner to shine in my bedroom window, I am tired and I relax with a novel or an article from the *New York Review of Books*. I turn off the light at 10:00, closing a day fully circumscribed by reading. Roland Barthes calls an intertext, "the impossibility of living outside the infinite text" (36). Intertext neatly describes my day.

This book addresses what it means to live in the intertext, to teach in the intertext, and to teach texts that range from textbooks to web sites. What does it mean to teach reading? The question may seem surprising when it is raised in the context of the first-year college writing course. For many years, the issue of reading in composition has been framed in terms of an argument for or against assigning literary fiction to students enrolled in college writing classes. This argument has as much to do with battles over the proper subject of the discipline of composition as the best reading selections for students. Furthermore, the issue of reading as a practice to be studied and nurtured seems moot, for, by the time the students arrive in college, they are assumed to "know how to read." It is true that these are two distinct issues. One is institutional and the other cognitive. Yet what an instructor believes about reading is an essential precondition to organizing and teaching in a writing classroom.

If we examine our practices as composition instructors, we will realize that teachers of writing daily bring reading into their instruction and make assumptions about the value of reading. We teach reading to establish processes and practices; we select readings to develop habits of selection; we encourage students to reread and revise their written work; and we read their journals and essays. Beyond the classroom, scores indicating reading ability are used for placement into courses. PhDs in English study models of reading as part of graduate work in English. Despite this, despite being surrounded by reading and things to read, assignments given and assignments read, the act of reading is not part of the common professional discourse in composition studies. Reading as praxis, in other words, as a process that lies along the boundary between practice and theory, is the least studied of the present areas of research and emphasis in the field of rhetoric and composition; most of the work on reading as praxis has been conducted in colleges of education. Reading research, largely empirical in nature, has taken place under the auspices of the International Reading Association (IRA), an organization to which most college professors in English do not belong. Furthermore, the publishers who address the teaching of reading as a process tend to focus on the market for Grades K–12, and primarily the elementary grades, thereby giving discussions of reading in college its "remedial" connotation. Much of this literature is based on developmental skills and emphasizes mapping, schemata, and cognition. As David Bartholomae pointed out over fifteen years ago, though,

> The concern for getting the right meaning, for memory, a concern at the center of most reading labs and study skills centers, puts students in an impossible position. . . . Their obsessive concern over the fact that they don't remember everything they read, their concern to dig out the right answers, their despair over passages that seem difficult or ambiguous, all of these are symptoms of a misunderstanding of the nature of texts and the nature of reading that must be overcome if students are to begin to take charge of the roles they might play in a university classroom. (96)

As the essays in this book demonstrate, traditional and institutional notions of reading as "belonging" to courses in literature, teacher education, or even remedial programs are academic constructions that have been naturalized in professional discourse and must be revisited and revised. The concerns of the writers contributing to *Intertexts* is with cultures, discourses, and practices, the material conditions that determine how reading is conceived by readers and taught in the first-year composition classroom. David Bleich identifies such partitioning of fields of interest as the effort to privilege thought over action in the academy; hence teachers of reading (those who predominantly teach literature) and teachers of writing (those involved in the undergraduate composition program) are often at odds, despite being joined in the department of English. As Bleich puts it: "Our style of education, with its emphasis on literate psychology and culture, relies on the separation of reading and writing, teaches them separately, and in the academy, has established different professional institutions to study reading and writing" (61).

Several paradoxes emerge when "reading" becomes the focus of critical and pedagogical attention in composition. For one, in the traditionally structured department of English Studies, formal theories of reading that derive from literary criticism and theory are located within the literary studies area of the department. In the field of literary criticism, "reading" seems somewhat overdetermined and perhaps pedestrian as a concept for "new" examination: *jouissance* (pleasure), *différance* (playful deconstruction), dialogy (the conversational aspects of give and take described by the Russian literary and language critic Mikhail Bakhtin), narratology, and semiotics (symbolic "coding") have, for decades, broadened the literary critic's notion of "reading" in productive ways. However, with the exception of a few critical works in the early 1980s directed at teachers of English (most notably Sharon Crowley's *Teacher's Introduction to Deconstruction*), the insights of critical theory have not filtered into the everyday world of the composition classroom. On the other hand, outside the academy, the subject of reading is never far from the public eye. Recent publications have indicated that histories and practices of reading are of interest to the general reader, albeit an "intellectual readership." Among the books are Alberto Manguel's *A History of Reading*, Lynn Sharon Schwartz's *Ruined by Reading*, and Harold Bloom's *How to Read and Why*. Reading is neither undertheorized or underhistoricized. It is not an invisible practice, but has come to be a *fetishized* practice: equated almost exclusively with literary fiction, misunderstood by teachers and students alike, and not fully actualized as a subject of pedagogical discussions. Yet, as David Bleich points out, despite efforts to separate them, reading and writing are practices that both construct and denote membership in communities. It was James Kinneavy's vision that a department of English might emerge where "rhetoric, poetic (and logic also) are respected and maintained *in fruitful balance*, fruitful for faculty and especially for the student" (cited in Newkirk 5, emphasis added).

This theme of balance and integration recurs throughout the literature of composition. In *A Teaching Subject*, Joseph Harris attributes the disciplinary shift from reading model texts to an emphasis on students' own language and their own expression to the Dartmouth Conference of 1966. In the ensuing thirty years, the predominance of expressivism in writing classrooms led to the demise of "content-driven" courses, courses that were structured around political and literary discourse analysis. The perspective of the 1983 anthology of essays edited by Winifred Bryan Horner, *Composition and Literature: Bridging the Gap*, was that the two disciplines that subsequently emerged within English studies—literature and composition—needed to recuperate their common interests and cease to deny that they shared common intellectual ground as well as office space. At a distance of 20 years, the book has taken on new meaning. We can understand it now as an instance of disciplinary formation in composition studies in which composition, the nonprestigious, general-education, "service" member of the department, was arguing for its own inclusion in the presumably rigorous and publicly-valued discussions of "English" in general. In fact, this issue of disciplinarity has not been resolved. Since Horner's publication, scores of books on the discipline of English studies have been published, each employing a form of utopian disciplinary discourse that idealizes the potential for union between various factions of English studies.[1] Ross Winterowd calls the relationship of composition to literature "yin and yang" (x), but it is a synthesis that is currently out of balance (205). His vision for departments of English is to restore balance by erasing divisive oppositions, "imaginative" texts versus "other literature," "creative writing and composition" (228). He settles on reading theory as the "juncture at which rhetoric and literary theory have met and are becoming one" (227). The complex processes of how readers make sense of texts are inextricably linked to the decisions that writers make about audience, purpose, style, and display.

From another perspective, Art Young and Toby Fulwiler's *When Writing Teachers Teach Literature* argues for an end to disciplinarity in the discipline of English. The introduction to their collection of essays raises a number of practical, reflective questions about language, literature, and learning in general education that sensitively stress the process-centered practices of collaborating, freewriting, rereading, and conferencing. The authors articulate the need to shift pedagogical discussions of reading away from the objects of discourse to the processes of making knowledge:

> In the college literature classroom, should the language of the learner be privileged, or the language of the academy, or some in-between language? What are the consequences for the study of literature when a teacher privileges academic discourse? or personal response? or multiplicity of response? or consensus? What should be the role of the literature teacher in the classroom and what are the consequences? expert authority? mentor? facilitator? (4)

Unfortunately, as so often happens, the dual nature of the term *reading* as noun and verb—object and process—cannot be dismissed easily. "Reading" becomes an elliptical form of "reading literature." Young and Fulwiler argue that reading/literature entails a "focus on the text, not the learner: here is the text, read it, learn about it, tell back what you learned" (2). At its best, such a focus can be described as *telic*, reading to satisfy a requirement (Calinescu 92). As Young and Fulwiler would agree, telic readings take place frequently, whenever readers must meet certain goals in their reading; however, reductionary constructions of the practice of reading as a mechanical process of regurgitation serve neither the individual teacher, nor the students. Young and Fulwiler suggest that the sensitive insights of composition theory—in particular, its attention to the cultural conditions of literate practices—make it the ideal vehicle for reconstructing the languages of reading within English. Gary Lindberg expressed it best when he recast the noun to include the verb:

> Despite the elaborate systems of analysis that characterize academic reading, literary works are not repositories of hidden meanings but human gestures. They record someone's attempt to come to words. And to read them is not to be given an interpretation of experience but *to witness one in the making*. (144, emphasis added)

Yet "bridging the gap" is something of a conceptual struggle for the members of the composition profession. A handful of articles on reading pedagogy appeared in the major journals of composition studies between 1980 and 1999. For many teachers of composition, the most emblematic debate over the relationship of reading to writing in the first-year composition was Erika Lindemann's and Gary Tate's argument in the pages of *College English* in 1993. Lindemann argued that there was "no place for literature" in first-year composition and Tate took the other side. Lindemann offers several reasons for keeping literature out of the first-year composition classroom. The strongest is that "students' attention to writing" will be limited because of the focus on discussion, placing the "focus on consuming texts, not producing them" (313). Tate, on the other hand, argues that students seeking to improve their writing are denied "the benefits of reading an entire body of excellent writing" (317) when literature is removed from the classroom. To Lindemann's assertion that students should focus on joining the community of academic discourse, Tate responds that there is a greater community, that outside the academy, where students will "struggle to figure out how to live their lives—that is, how to vote and love and survive, how to respond to change and diversity and death and oppression and freedom" (320).

The iconic nature of this discussion on curriculum planning obscured the real issue, that teachers of writing daily teach from readings (noun: student essays, textbook articles) and engage in process of reading (verb: scanning and responding to student texts). Furthermore, the debate defined the terms that were to endure: literature and writing, not reading and writing. It also introduced (somewhat indirectly) the divisions that the humanities had set in place between performing writing and reading tasks inside the academy and engaging in similar practices outside the academy (as Tate puts it, voting, loving, and surviving). Gradually, these materialist concerns with community, literacy, and popular culture have broadened the nature of the discussion. It was clear from the Tate and Lindemann discussion that there was a place for "reading," but the essential questions of value—what was being read and how reading was being taught—were omitted from the discussion, as Mariolina Salvatori was quick to note in her published response to Tate and Lindemann. Salvatori brought the discussion back to the essential convictions of composition: what type of processes and practices must students engage in?

> [. . .] "the question of reading in the teaching of composition" is not merely the question of whether reading should or should not be used in the composition classroom. The issue is what kind of reading gets to be theorized and practiced. (Salvatori, "Conversations" 443)

Despite their apparent differences, however, both Tate and Lindemann can be found to agree on the relationship of reading to critical *thinking*, which returns the reading process to the development of rhetorical consciousness: decision making, responding well, understanding the context for written and spoken utterances. Lindemann argues that students should be aware of the processes of making knowledge, including "reading critically, interpreting evidence, [and] solving problems" (313). Tate's arguments that a greater community exists outside the class echo some of the assumptions of the work of Paulo Freire, whose Marxist-based project of "education for critical consciousness" among Brazilian farm workers argued that to read the *word* was to read the *world*. (This concept surfaces again in Mary Ann Cain and George Kalmaras's contribution to this book.) To "read the word" is not a mere phonetic decoding, but a way of investigating the ideological assumptions that construct the word itself. These ideological constructions abound in the world, and so words reveal layerings of ideas, thoughts, behavioral codes, and assumptions about race, class, and gender. Literacy is thus a powerful tool for decoding, interacting with, and prospering in the world. And thus both Lindemann and Tate are agreed that reading, writing, and entering critical conversations are the important consequences of a first-year writing course. What teachers of college English must accomplish, then, is to move readers from a level of reading in which they act upon texts in limited, personal ways to a more sophisticated level of reading in which they are able to distinguish between and articulate varying purposes for reading.[2]

Freire directly addressed the significance that reading has for the developing consciousness in his article "The Importance of the Act of Reading" (1983) and the book (with Macedo) *Literacy: Reading the Word and the World* (1987). Reading, Freire points out, is "a certain form of writing" in which the reader alters, rewrites, or transforms the signs of the world in order to make the world meaningful (10). Freire's description of reading entails a purposeful modification of the material world, as Peter Roberts points out:

> Freire's conceptualization of the sequence of experiences—reading the world first and the word second—has an anthropological and historical basis. Human beings first learned to act on their environment, using and modifying the products of nature, altering the material world. Freire conceives of this transformation of the objective world as a form of "writing reality." As humans began to change the natural world, the reality they had created through conscious practical activity "acted back" on them, modifying their ideas, conceptions and attitudes. From this process of continual reciprocal transformation, human beings emerged as "writers" and "readers" of the world—long before they became writers and readers of the word. (Roberts)

Reading the word and the world is a dialogic process: the world and word alter the consciousness of the reader, while the reader, in retelling, in acting, alters the perception of reality. Using different terms and a different theoretical framework, Nancy Nelson Spivey has articulated a similar philosophy of the interaction of reader upon situation. Her focus is limited to the ways that various readers write by drawing on source material. As the writers read and synthesize the previously published material, they are also composing their own text, Spivey contends. Writing thus has a significant influence on the reading process:

> The writer, when reading, makes inferences, elaborations, perhaps thinking of examples or counterexamples, arguing with a particular point. This generative process can be thought of as inferential and elaborative processing for reading, but it can also be considered an invention process for writing. (259)

Spivey draws attention to what should be obvious to teachers: astute readers read in order to do something with the knowledge that they have gained from what they have read (260). Where Freire argues that a reader must be curious, restless, searching (Roberts), Spivey cites research that demonstrates a similar conclusion: "Writers typically approach texts with intentions to create their own new texts, to make their own contributions" (265).

A good reading is "full of feelings, of emotions, of tastes," writes Freire (qtd. in Roberts). What would such a reading look like? How would it progress? This complex reading that ranges from emotional to physical— but with the intent to craft a new text—is embodied in the memoir *The Year of Reading Proust*. The leisurely chapters written by Phyllis Rose move inward and outward, toward the text of *Swann's Way* or *In Search of Lost Time*, and outward to the dinner parties she attends or the talks with her editor. For Rose, the *recherche* of Proust's title, *A la recherche du temps perdu*, embodies "research as well as searching" (21). Early in the book, when Rose concentrates on her engagement with, as she puts it delicately, "Proust's demands," she outlines a complex process of feeling, writing, reflection, analysis, summary, reaction, and imitation. She traces the life of Marcel in *Swann's Way* and his unforgivable revelation of his Uncle Adolphe's congress with courtesans and pauses to agonize deliciously over Marcel's inability to acknowledge his uncle in public:

> I savored the moment so much that I could not continue. [. . .] I was reenacting the perverse logic of Marcel's snub of his uncle: I felt too much to make the simple gesture of continuing to read. If I moved on, I would leave behind the section I so much enjoyed. Yet if I didn't abandon the beloved part, how would I ever come to know the whole of the novel? (Rose 17)

In twenty printed lines, Rose falters and reflects. As readers, we are aware that she is stalled. Nonetheless, we are moving along physically through the point where she has stopped reading. Eventually, she returns to "real time," the time in which *we* read her memoir, to analyze her own engagement with Proustian style. As she notes, Proust favored the movement "from a solitary mental event (reading) to a physical activity" and she has taken us on the same "spiral" of narrative (17). Ironically, it is only as we read further ahead in her narrative (ahead in time and ahead in the physical presence of the book) that we realize Rose could only have written the reflection on Marcel's encounter with Uncle Adolphe after a long period of study and reflection. She records that in her initial reading of Proust's works, she turned down corners of pages to mark important passages, but then quickly started to write notes at the back of the book:

> By volume 5, my notes were so extensive that I ran out of blank pages at the back of the book and then at the front of it, too. I was copying out whole passages. Passage after passage. I responded so thoroughly to Proust by this point that there was almost nothing I didn't think worth coming back to. I had to start reading at the computer, so I could transcribe the beloved passages quickly enough to move on. (19)

Rose's complete engagement with the text results in her moving away from artificial separations between world and text. Eventually, her world becomes her text; her world becomes Proust's text; Proust's text becomes the commentary on her world. Anthony Petrosky has noted that "our comprehension of texts . . . is more an act of composition" (19). Certainly Rose's reading of Proust's *oeuvre* proves to be a year of reading creatively, composing her own life story with the voice of Proust as her teacher.

COMPREHENSION:
"MAKING PUBLIC WHAT IS PRIVATE"

With the increasing emphasis of colleges and universities on first-year orientation reading programs, the integration of literary theory into the undergraduate curriculum, and the proliferation of reading collections as textbooks for first-year composition, instructors of writing and literature are faced with new questions about the abilities of their own apprentices to read. There are five immediate concerns that departments of English

must now address: the training of graduate students in literature and composition; the development of student orientation reading programs; the initiation of small introductory seminars; the proliferation of reading textbooks in the composition spectrum; and the need to articulate a curriculum for composition studies in the new century.

Clear divisions between those who teach reading and those who teach writing are disappearing rapidly, with PhDs in medieval literature finding themselves as adjunct professors in a classroom of first-year composition students, armed with a contemporary culture reader. Writing specialists, PhDs in rhetoric and composition, have incorporated teaching literary criticism and theory into their repertoire and frequently bring poetry and fiction into the (formerly) expository writing classroom. Writing Across the Curriculum has been shaded further by the demands that all members of the university be responsible for the learning community developed by a first-year reading program typically housed in the English department's composition program.

In order for composition to refigure itself to properly engage the subject of reading, composition and literature must free themselves from a disciplinary gestalt that entails almost the entire history of composition as a separatist discipline within English. As I noted earlier, this argument is not new. In 1982, David Bartholomae and Anthony Petrosky argued for a fully integrated conception of textual construction and reception that sounds similar to Kinneavy's desire for "fruitful balance." In *College Composition and Communication*, Petrosky warned that:

> Reading, responding, and composing are aspects of understanding, and theories that attempt to account for them outside of their interactions with each other run the serious risk of building reductive models of human understanding. Yet we continually focus our attention on them as if they exist in isolation from one another. (20)

Against "isolation" is "the social," what David Bleich and Bruce Horner call "materiality," and Marilyn Sternglass has discussed as "literacy events." Citing previous research, Sternglass maintains that "all human action occurs in a social context" (47). Horner points out in *Terms of Work for Composition*, that materiality takes plural forms from technology, to socioeconomic conditions, social relationships, personal dispositions, and physical working space such as the classroom (xviii–xix). Like writing, then, reading takes place "in relation to other places, activities, and social forces, responding to and conditioned by them, and shaping them in return" (B. Horner xvii). Susan Lehr points out that early reading experiences are communal, taking place in a familiar physical setting for the child and involving sitting close to the reader, who is usually a parent or babysitter (Lehr 93). As children move ahead in school, however, the print setting becomes more disengaged from context. Readers are expected to read "on their own," what is called at my daughter's school "silent student reading" or SSR. Illustrations are assumed to distract from the reading process. Citing the work of Huck, Hepler, and Hickman in *Children's Literature in the Elementary School*, Lehr points out, "children in the upper grades not only choose books based on how many pictures are in them but also prefer a high ratio of pictures to text" (97). As we know, with the exception of a few new "cultural studies" readers in composition studies and the visual rhetoric textbook *Seeing & Writing* (McQuade and McQuade), the visual dimension of literate culture is formally absent in the college writing classroom.

Increasingly writers argue for studying the complete ecology of the reading and writing situations from socio-physical contexts for reading experience to the study of type design and illustration. Deborah Brandt demonstrated that the setting in which literacy events occurred and the attitude of the participants shaped reading development (461). In addition, reading is "not just books anymore," as Dan Melzer comments. He lists some of the types of reading that students undertake in college:

Websites are quickly becoming primary reading material for college classes
[. . .]. In college classes you might be required to "read" films, advertisements, and works of art [. . .]. A communications professor has his students
analyze cartoons [. . .]. A classics professor at Trinity University requires
students to visit the local art museum and compare and contrast artwork
from the exhibits and the information in the textbook [. . .]. (15)

Melzer goes on to list plays, architecture, and religious ceremonies as
artifacts and practices that people read. But, before any of this nonprint-
centered reading can become incorporated into common understandings
of what it means to read, academic attitudes toward images and nonprint
culture need to be revised. The most commonly encountered nonprint
items to appear regularly in traditional composition courses are images
and text design; at the least, these should be reclaimed from their contemporary position as supplementary and dispensable illustration to a position of prominence as a semiotic tool of analysis, as Susan Lehr argues:
"If readers can be impeded from accessing meaning because of poorly
written text, they can also fail to learn from aimless illustrations, such as
those found in many primers. Meaning getting will not occur in a vac-
uum" (97).

Coexisting with the demands of the classroom, images of reading and
readers abound in mass culture, potentially influencing the attitudes of
"real," common readers. Popular reading practices often resist academic
notions of textuality and evidence, Evan Watkins argues, and thus work
in English must "forge connections to popular cultures" (273), the repertoire of texts that readers draw on to construct arguments in daily life.
One of the most obvious signals of the general cultural consciousness is
the ubiquitous reconstruction of the 18th-century salon, the Borders or
Starbucks coffee shop, replete with magazines and newspapers for "readers." To echo the words of the early 20th-century publisher Margaret Anderson, there is a sense in which our culture is demanding "inspired conversation" on literary topics.[3]

Writing about composition studies since 1960, T. R. Johnson points
out that what is most lacking in pedagogical studies is a conception of
"pleasure." To take pleasure in reading and writing is considered "soft,"
he argues. It is neither rigorous nor insightful. Since composition studies
has worked to maintain a professional difference from literary criticism,
while at the same time desiring to be seen as professionally equal with literary studies, the emphasis of expository writing courses has moved away
from expressive writing to Marxist-based cultural criticism. Yet Johnson
points the finger at the continuing predominance—if not invocation—of

classical rhetoric in composition education: "Indeed, ever since Plato banished the poets from his ideal republic and blasted the sophists for trafficking in a similar brand of ecstatic make-believe, the academy has frowned upon pleasure an 'unprofessional' consideration" (3). The value of "magic" in reading is lost. Consider, for example, the work of Ellen Handler Spitz, who argues that there is a connection "between what people experience in literature and the arts as children and their later feelings about culture" (Ruark A18). Spitz's work on children's picture books connects the power of text with the power of images, "experiences with color, with shape, with line," all of which underscore the emotional content of a work and provide necessary cues for reading, rather than serving as "mere decoration." Institutional requirements and attitudes gradually wean the reader from pleasure. Yet broader cultural forces carefully cultivate color, design, and image to associate reading with pleasure.

CULTURE AND THE READER

The textual equivalents of the dark wood shelves of the Borders or Barnes and Noble bookstores are direct-mail book catalogues. Within their pages, the book is inscribed as a fetish, an object of obsession and worship. As a reader and a consumer, I am drawn to the evocative covers of the *Bas Bleu* catalogue, which feature reproductions of the work of Atlanta artist Deborah DeWit Marchant. Her paintings associate reading with freedom, escape, and private life. Initially working as a photographer, she became frustrated by the inability of photography to capture the nuances of the world she was reading. When she began painting, she turned to books as a subject, as she relates in this note:

> I had traveled much to take my photographs and so much of my time was spent reading or writing letters on those trips. Books and letters held possibilities and dreams and adventures as well as an atmosphere of focus and peace. They represented the moments when things made sense to me. The spaces of my images are from different sources. sometimes they are real places, but most of the time they are not, and are idealized or someplace I vaguely remember, and try to reconstruct. Often they involve windows so as to give a direction for the thoughts that are inspired by the writing or reading to go.

In a catalogue for an exhibition of her work, she described books as "rooms of knowledge," thus synthesizing the spatial qualities of her work with the predominant emphasis on the physical objects of books. Symbolically, then, the books in her paintings extend outward from the pages to connect us "with all the preceding readers, all the past thinkers, all those who have sought knowledge and wished to communicate it."

FIG. 1.1. "Rainy Day Consolations," Original pastel by Deborah DeWit Marchant, 1999.

An open book rests on an empty arm chair by a frosted window. A seaside table holds an open book. The reader has just left for a moment, we are invited to imagine. She will return after gathering pinecones or fixing a glass of lemonade. Fresh flowers sit on the table. Aside from the commodity of the book and the chair, the world of the image is a world noticeably free from "culture," that constructed, technological, and ideological nexus that engages our waking hours. The painted environments are empty of humans, inviting us, the spectators, to insert ourselves into the picture. The catalogue and the painting, then, provide readers with the opportunity to escape into a world free of telephones and fax machines. Reading, even reading this catalogue, allows us all the freedom, perchance, to dream. Yet, as Calinescu points out, such socio-physiological considerations as setting are often ignored by critics. While "sensibility to historical context of both literary production and reception has long been a widely accepted requirement of critical-reflective reading," critics since mid-century have preferred "achronic" and "atopic readings of literary works" (101). He continues:

> [. . .] this has rarely involved taking into consideration such blatantly extratextual concerns as the age or place of personal situation of real readers. There is little double that the bracketing of these complicating factors is justified if not necessary in discussing a literary work. (101)

Calinescu proposes adopting the ideas of French critic Georges Perec, who proposed criteria for conducting a socio-physiological investigation of reading that involved studying time slots (such as the time one reads, as in at the dentist's or in bed), corporeal postures (such as slouching in an armchair), social space (at a library or on public transportation), context (such as reading for a class or while on vacation). While Calinescu does not offer collaboration as a defining characteristic of reading, who one reads with and for what purpose is certainly one of the important features of studying any text.

One of the remarkable additions to the Winter 2000 *Bas Bleu* catalogue was the "Lit Class" syllabus, taking up two pages at the beginning of the catalogue. The course indicates a cultural disposition for literate engagement with ideas, intimately tied to pleasure, discovery, and leisure. Something like a commercial correspondence course, the catalogue urged readers to study with Vivian Gornick's *The End of the Novel of Love*. Behind the desire to continue educating the self, the syllabus seemed to speak to a desire for connection and collaborative enterprise. After reading Gornick's short work, students were recommended to purchase *Wide Sargasso Sea* by Jean Rhys, *The Song of the Lark* by Willa Cather, *The Awakening* by Kate Chopin, and *Adultery and Other Choices* by Andre Dubus. There are "no papers, no grades, no exams," promised the catalogue (4). "Just read, think, learn, and enjoy. And, for many of you, remember why you loved being an English major!" (4). The "Lit Class" syllabus could be dismissed as mere advertising, linking consumerism and reading through false-consciousness and transforming self-edification into the realm of materialism. Yet I prefer to read the syllabus through Calinescu's eyes, seeing it as evidence of the need to connect through some sort of physical space. One can hold Gornick's book; one can transport it into a variety of social spaces; one can build a book club around it; or one can seek out the armchair by the window and join a virtual community of readers.

Harold Bloom, known as a literary critic, has also published his own syllabus and lecture notes as *How to Read and Why*. The book is designed to be inspirational. Bloom is an exemplary reader, both through his history of publication and teaching, and through the ethos that he adopts in his work. One of the five rules for reading that he announces in the introduction is the reminder that "A scholar is a candle by which the love and desire of all men will light" (24), which he draws from Emerson. Like Gornick in the pages of *Bas Bleu*, Bloom is that beacon of knowledge in his book, pointing out in proof that he receives letters from strangers that move him deeply: "their pathos, for me, is that all too often they testify to a yearning for canonical literary study that universities disdain to fulfill" (24). Arguments about issues of canonical reading aside, Bloom seems to be echoing the sentiments of the *Bas Bleu* catalogue: people desire to read and search out experiences when they can. At the same time, reading as a practice is holistically divided in our culture between "study" and "pleasure."

Deborah Brandt's important studies of readers and literacy confirm that reading carries with it powerful affective associations. In interviews conducted with nonacademics of all ages in the early 1990s, Brandt discovered that reading—as an isolated, reflective engagement with literary fiction—occupies an elevated position in people's consciousness: "there was a reverence expressed for books and their value and sometimes a connection between reading and refinement or good breeding" (464). However, many of those who expressed this reverence for books and learning did not pursue reading themselves.

It is not a far stretch to argue that, for the common reader, books are presumed to carry a kind of magic. *Bas Bleu*, directly targeted at a construction of the woman reader by invoking the bluestockings of the nineteenth century, goes the furthest in design toward inculcating the sense that reading is something one does for oneself outside of family time or work time, a kind of guilty pleasure. Their reading accouterments include soft pillows, fanciful reader's glasses, and enameled pens. With such powerful commercial images surrounding the students, it is no wonder that the classroom becomes a contact zone of occluded and conflicting expectations. Students bring to the classroom a notion of reading that is solitary, escapist, and pleasurable; instructors expect interrogation and demonstration. Obviously, power imbalances between students and teachers account for differences in responses to texts; not all readers are able to engage in interpretive or analytical discourse in the same ways (Sternglass 49). Yet, the preconditions of instruction also affect the discourse in the classroom. How teachers and students differ in their conceptions of reading, even their naming of reading materials, can result in disjunction. As Lynn Schwartz la-ments, in the world of the classroom, the book becomes a "text" and thus loses some of its magic (108). To avoid the defamiliarization of reading that ultimately takes place in college, Jennifer Ahern encourages students to list favorite books as part of a class discussion. Reflectively, these book lists encourage memory and emotion, while also indicating various students' comfort with styles of discourse. Were the favorite books assigned in English classes? Are they favorites from childhood? What memories are engaged in naming a book a favorite? (Ahern 239).

I am aware that, in this discussion, my use of the designation "the reader" is a construction that ignores differences in race, class, gender, age, and ability; however, this ignorance of the shadings of reading experience is evident within the popular dissemination of images of reading. The direct-mail solicitations that bring *Bas Bleu* and its mail order counterparts to my doorstep are based on numbers: zip-codes, targeting readers with "disposable incomes." My point, however, is not to deny popular attitudes toward reading, but to argue that researchers, teachers, and students should analyze those attitudes to find out how they influence attitudes toward reading that later appear in the classroom. Brandt concluded her 1994 study by calling for ethnographic inquiry, which is useful in this case, as well:

> The actual conditions in which people encounter writing and reading are important to consider because they influence the meanings and feelings that people bring to the two enterprises and can influence the ways people pass on literacy to subsequent generations. (476)

Even the terms "writing" and "reading" need to be clarified by the respondents. Academics such as cultural critic John Fiske may consider television viewing to be an act of "reading," but the popular conception may see it as "escape" or passive consumerism, especially if the television is on during dinner or during the daily activities of the household.[4] The material conditions of reading, such as availability of books to the public in spaces such as pharmacies, grocery stores, and airport convenience stores should be studied as well in order to engage a dialectic between pleasure and study, reading for escape and reading for study, and, ultimately, reading as leisure and reading in school.

In *The Culture of Reading*, Kathleen McCormick identifies three dominant contemporary approaches to teaching reading: the cognitive, the expressivist, and the social-cultural. The cognitive perspective assumed that "comprehension is something that occurs as a result of a reader's purely 'mental' capacities" (17). The expressivist model depends on the "reader's life experience" (13). The social-cultural "privileges the cultural context in which reading occurs" (14). I cite these to note that the contributors to this book do not specifically identify themselves within any of these categories. Yet, six significant models of inquiry can be identified within these chapters. They emerge, as well, as important considerations for teachers of reading at many levels of college instruction and in many departments across the university.

In order of general to specific, the first is the effects of *conditions of production* on readership. Production entails the history of the book, who is allowed by education and status to speak in a given epoch, what is printed, how printing is disseminated, who has the money to afford printed material. Issues of production are social, cultural, political, economic, and rhetorical. Furthermore, they intersect with the assumptions made about public and private reading practices. While that which is public is related to the demonstration of reading in classrooms and written products, that which is private is associated with pleasure or personal edification, something gratuitous and nonessential, despite being culturally ratified. Related closely to issues of production are *conditions of consumption*. These too are determined by social, cultural, and economic forces; however, they also involve technologies of reception, such as solitary reading, oral reading, book club discussions, classroom assignments to write or discuss, author visits, and decoding hypertext. Consumption is often considered as an aspect of literacy, the acquisition of knowledge of how to decode the various texts that comprise the written universe.

A third point of significance in theorizing reading practice is to identify *assumptions of value* at work in our culture. While categories of value are related to production and consumption, they are primarily a consequence of aesthetic and philosophical discussions. Inquiries into production and consumption emphasize the historical through synchronic critique. Aesthetic questions, on the other hand, are diachronic, often pointing back to the eighteenth century. Furthermore, aesthetic questions are often masked as eternal or transhistorical. One of the critiques that Molly Abel Travis makes of *The Gutenberg Elegies*, for example, is that author Sven Birkerts "completely ignores the history of reading": "He makes it sound as if solitary, deep, and intensive reading were the only kind of reading that could be classified as true aesthetic experience" (10).[5] As Travis implies, then, an awareness of the material bases for our pedagogical assumptions and techniques is critical.

The fourth area of inquiry is *cognition*. Through cognitive processes readers decode words and syntax and formulate meanings. By the time students reach college, they are adept at this aspect of cognition; however, not all teachers agree that students comprehend texts. Comprehension is therefore a word whose meaning depends on the acceptance of one of several theories of reading. For some comprehension means telling back, more or less in sequence, the thesis and proofs in the author's text (see Bonnie Meyers). For others, comprehension involves stating with certainty the author's intent. For others still, comprehension involves retention and the more rhetorical process of putting new knowledge to use in speaking and writing. These positivistic theories are mitigated by the theories of reading that relate to interpretation, for interpretative acts involve the intervention of the reader in the text.

Contemplation, a fifth subject, is the reflection on reading that is based on theoretical frameworks. It is most often deployed in institutional contexts, such as classrooms or research. It is, to some extent, maligned by the general intellectual populace as a kind of irrelevant layering—or "reading in"—of "hidden meanings." Yet the insights that have emerged from contemplative practice involve experimentation and speculation. In this book, Marcel Cornis-Pope and Ann Woodlief (chap. 7, this volume) frame contemplation as "athletic reading," and while there is something of a disjuncture in bodily metaphors, the concept is quite similar: both contemplative and athletic readings involve "steady intention of the whole life to the object."

Interpretation is the most often emphasized of the areas of reading, and it seems to take on a particularly important life within departments of English. Interpretation is rhetorical. It involves investigation and articulation of the conditions under which people read and the conditions under which they produce meanings. That social context is broad, however, and can include life experiences, instruction, pleasure, religious teachings, even experiences with purchasing books or visiting libraries and coffee shops. Calinescu uses these types of experiences to describe a kind of "first reading" that people do of texts:

> Even before I decide to read a book, I have not only certain expectations, shaped by my generic acquaintance with the kind of book I have selected from a great many available books, but quite probably some more specific assumptions about the chosen book itself. [. . .] Even when I pick up a new book by an unknown author on a whim, I am better informed about it than I might suspect. This information (which may well turn out to have been misleading) is derived from where the book in question is sold (at a discount bookstore chain, a small specialty bookseller's, or the airport newsstand); from the books that immediately surround it (current best-sellers, mysteries, fiction, science fiction); from the title; from the book jacket; and quite likely from a general impression gained by quickly glancing through the pages. (42)

Eventually, Calinescu argues, when the text is "read" in the traditional sense of cover to cover or beginning to end, that reading is something of a rereading. This rereading confirms or denies expectations. Interpretation, while engaged with contemporary technologies of interpretation such as reader-response, feminist, and cultural studies methods, is also particularly involved with construction of the reader's agency.[6]

Reading, it must be remembered, does not refer to the novel, or the passive consumption of aesthetic literature, but to a process of investigation and articulation. In insightful terms that borrow from the work of Russian language theorist Mikhail Bakhtin, Donna Qualley describes reading as an "essayistic, ethnographic venture . . . a form of hermeneutic inquiry into texts" (61). As reflexive practice, rather than as pure absorption, reading becomes a dialogue with ideas. Developing knowledge about a text proceeds along several trajectories, ranging from reflecting on the readers' preunderstanding of the text, to agreeing with the text's message, to "reading against the grain" (a term she borrows from David Bartholomae and Anthony Petrosky; Qualley 71, 75). Marilyn Sternglass points out that sophisticated readers (and those who write about them) have achieved a level of metacomprehension in which one is able to understand that one has comprehended a text (75). Without schema—cognitive strategies derived from prior experiences—readers are unable to make sense of a text. Metacomprehension refers to the ability of readers to "consciously [reflect] on how the presence or absence of prior knowledge affected their making sense of the readings assigned to them" and how "he or she sets about reading and how closely he or she monitors the purpose of reading" (77). Of the three strategies for reading that Sternglass discusses in *The Presence of Thought*, the one that composition instructors are likely to value most is the third, "making sense." Sternglass's summaries of each are as follows:

> Receiving Sense is a passive activity, requiring the reader only to receive the message already written on the page. Finding Sense requires the reader to search for a meaning hidden just beneath the surface of a text and is most commonly applied to critical readings of literature. Making Sense views reading as *an experience or event that occurs with the participation of the reader* . . . (85, emphasis added)

Sophisticated readers will also be able to comment on the value of particular strategies: retelling, rereading, and reflecting on what it means to be a better reader. In addition, sophisticated readers are able to recognize and conceptually frame the relationships between various iterations of a text. Contemporary publications do not come to readers in a single form, in the way that, say, the 19th century serialized novel reached readers. Texts are excerpted in magazines, or on websites such as BarnesandNoble.com or Amzon.com, or read on National Public Radio. Movies are made from books, and books are made from television programs. Texts are surrounded by different discourses, such as the languages of advertising and criticism. Understanding how these discourses relate to each other and influence the reception of the original text is an important part of reading today.

Reading is a multivoiced and multimedia experience. To teach reading is to teach the relationships between readers and texts and between readers and the spaces where they encounter texts and other readers. In conclusion, teaching reading in college should encompass thoughtful reflection on the culture of teaching and reading. Because teachers of writing are accustomed to considering how writing relates to social experience, we are in an excellent position to influence discussions of teaching reading in college. Let us examine our expectations and experiences with texts, the backgrounds of our students, the popular texts and dominant textual media in our society, and the transference of literate practices from one medium to another.

NOTES

1. I do not mean to suggest that histories of the profession have only appeared since 1983. It is a common impulse for scholars and teachers to share their insights into their life's work. However, the influx of new theories of interpretation into English studies caused something of a crisis in the departments of English, a process documented in two works by Gerald Graff, *Professing Literature* and *Beyond the Culture Wars*. Other publications that detail the often contentious course of the discipline are *The English Department* by W. Ross Winterowd, *What is English?* by Peter Elbow, *The Rise and Fall of English* by Robert Scholes, and *Work Time* by Evan Watkins. Peter Sands has described many of these theories as "utopian" and I borrow the insight, with thanks, from him.
2. Reading researcher J. A. Appleyard posits an ideal reader as an adult who is "pragmatic," reading "for information, for intellectual or aesthetic satisfaction, for relaxation" (Calinescu 92) and significantly selecting between these purposes and identifying texts that will readily enable him or her to accomplish *goals*. Pragmatism is the highest level of reading that may be achieved in Appleyard's scale of levels of reading. The scale ranges from player (preschool), to heroic (ages seven to eleven), to thinker (adolescence), to interpreter (college), to pragmatic. As Matei Calinescu is careful to admonish, however, the highest level of reading allows readers to move between all stages. It is also important to remember that those goals are defined by the reader and the external context in which the reading task is undertaken, whether that is a student reading an assignment in school in order to take a test or a lawyer taking up a copy of *Gourmet* at seven o'clock on a Friday evening to erase the pressures of the work week.

3. Anderson (1886–1973) was the flamboyant Midwestern editor of the *Little Review*, a literary magazine in publication from 1914 to 1916. The magazine recognized the influence of many influential poets and writers of the early twentieth century, including James Joyce and Ezra Pound. The comment about "inspired conversation" appears in her autobiography, *My Thirty Year's War*.

4. Fiske's work on television and other media forms in popular culture has been influential in cultural criticism, but his insights have rarely traveled into composition studies as insights into the cultural situation of our students. Readers interested in Fiske's work should consult the aptly titled *Reading Television*.

5. Birkerts' *Gutenberg Elegies* created a stir when it was released because of its timing. A personal memoir on the loss of the physical book in American society, Birkerts intervened in a culture that was rapidly becoming electronic. As more computers sold, Birkerts rebelled, finding even such electronic devices as Books on Tape to be offensive.

6. Works on typography and book design are especially useful for those studying the affects of texts on readers. In his foundational text *The Elements of Typographic Style*, Robert Bringhurst argues that certain type styles have historical and nationalistic resonances that affect meaning for readers. Similarly, *Illuminating Letters*, the edited collection of essays by Paul Gutjahr and Megan Benton, establishes that type design, the paper and ink used in printing, and even the type of press work to bring ideas into prominence on the page and in our minds. In these works, reading is configured as a tactile experience.

WORKS CITED

Ahern, Jennifer. "Hint Sheet 2 Investigating Why We Read (or Not)." *The Subject Is Reading: Essays by Teachers and Students*. Ed. Wendy Bishop. Portsmouth, NH: Heinemann, 2000. 239–40.

Anderson, Margaret. *My Thirty Year's War*. 1930. Westport, CN: Greenwood, 1971.

Barthes, Roland. *Mythologies*. Trans. Annette Lavers. 1957. New York: Hill, 1972.

Bartholomae, David. "Wandering: Misreadings, Miswritings, Misunderstandings." *Only Connect*. Ed. Thomas Newkirk. Upper Montclair, NJ: Boynton/Cook, 1986. 89–118.

Birkerts, Sven. *The Gutenberg Elegies: The Fate of Reading in an Electronic Age*. Boston: Faber, 1994.

Bishop, Wendy, ed. *The Subject Is Reading: Essays by Teachers and Students*. Portsmouth, NH: Heinemann, 2000.

Bleich, David. *Know and Tell*. Portsmouth, NH: Heinemann, 1999.

Bloom, Harold. *How to Read and Why*. New York: Scribner, 2000.

Brandt, Deborah. "Remembering Writing. Remember Reading." *College Composition and Communication* 45 (December 1994): 459–79.

Bringhurst, Robert. *The Elements of Typographic Style*. Point Roberts, WA: Hartley & Marks, 1996.

Calinescu, Matei. *Rereading*. New Haven: Yale UP, 1993.

Crowley, Sharon. *A Teacher's Introduction to Deconstruction*. Urbana: NCTE, 1989.

Elbow, Peter. *What Is English?* New York: MLA; Urbana, IL: NCTE, 1990.

Fiske, John and John Hartley. *Reading Television*. 1978. New York: Routledge, 1989.

Flynn, Elizabeth A., and Patrocinio P. Schweickart, eds. *Gender and Reading: Essays on Readers, Texts, and Contexts*. Baltimore: Johns Hopkins UP, 1986.

Freire, Paulo. "The Importance of the Act of Reading." *Journal of Education* 165 (1983): 5–11.

Freire, Paulo, and Donaldo Macedo. *Literacy: Reading the Word and the World.* South Hadley, MA: Bergin, 1987.

Graff, Gerald. *Beyond the Culture Wars: How Teaching the Conflicts Can Revitalize American Education.* New York: Norton, 1992.

———. *Professing Literature: An Institutional History.* Chicago: U of Chicago, 1987.

Gutjahr, Paul C. and Megan L. Benton. *Illuminating Letters: Typography and Literary Interpretation.* Amherst, MA: U of Massachusetts, 2001.

Harris, Joseph. *A Teaching Subject: Composition Since 1966.* Upper Saddle River, NJ: Prentice, 1997.

Horner, Bruce. *Terms of Work for Composition: A Materialist Critique.* Albany: State U of New York, 2000.

Horner, Winifred Bryan. *Composition and Literature: Bridging the Gap.* Chicago: U of Chicago, 1983.

Johnson, T. R. *Composing Pleasure.* Unpublished manuscript, 2000.

Lacan, Jacques. *Écrits.* 1944. Trans. Alan Sheridan. New York: Norton, 1977.

Lauter, Estella. *Assuming Aesthetic Authority: Feminist Reconstructions of Aesthetics.* Unpublished manuscript, 2000.

Lehr, Susan S. *The Child's Developing Sense of Theme: Responses to Literature.* New York: Teachers College, 1991.

Lindberg, Gary. "Coming to Words: Writing as Process and the Reading of Literature." *Only Connect.* Ed. Thomas Newkirk. Upper Montclair, NJ: Boynton/Cook, 1986. 143–57.

Lindemann, Erika. "Freshman Composition: No Place for Literature." *College English* 55.3 (March 1993): 311–16.

Manguel, Alberto. *A History of Reading.* London: Harper, 1996.

McCormick, Kathleen. *The Culture of Reading and the Teaching of English.* Manchester, UK: Manchester UP, 1994.

McQuade, Donald, and Susan McQuade. *Seeing Writing.* Boston: Bedford/St. Martin's, 2000.

Melzer, Dan. "Reading . . . It's Not Just Books Anymore." *The Subject Is Reading: Essays by Teachers and Students.* Ed. Wendy Bishop. Portsmouth, NH: Heinemann, 2000. 14–22.

Meyers, Bonnie. "Reading Research and the Composition Teacher: The Importance of Plans." *College Composition and Communication* 33.1 (February 1982): 37–49.

Newkirk, Thomas. *Only Connect.* Upper Montclair, NJ: Boynton/Cook, 1986.

Petrosky, Anthony. "From Story to Essay: Reading and Writing." *College Composition and Communication* 33.1 (February 1982): 19–36.

Qualley, Donna. *Turns of Thought: Teaching Composition as Reflexive Inquiry.* Portsmouth, NH: Heinemann, 1997.

Roberts, Peter. "Critical Literacy, Breadth of Perspective and Universities: Applying Insights from Freire." *Studies in Higher Education* 21.2 (June 1996): 149–64. Available online through EBSCO Host Academic Search Elite, http://www.ebsco.com. Birmingham, AL: EBSCO Publishing. Polk Library, University of Wisconsin Oshkosh, Oshkosh, WI. 13 May 2002.

Rose, Phyllis. *The Year of Reading Proust: A Memoir in Real Time.* Washington, DC: Counterpoint, 2000.

Ruark, Jennifer K. "Scary and Soothing: How Picture Books Shape the Mind of a Child." *Chronicle of Higher Education.* 14 May 1999. A18–19.

Salvatori, Mariolina. "Conversations with Texts: Reading in the Teaching of Composition." *College English* 58.4 (April 1996): 440–53.

Sands, Peter. "Composing Utopias/Utopias of Composing: Teaching Writing in a Cross-Curricular Environment." *Dwelling in Possibility: Essays on Teaching and Learning through Utopian Literature.* Libby Falk Jones, ed. Unpublished manuscript, 2000.

———. "Scenes of Education and Schemes of Utopia in Fiction and Curriculum." Society for Utopian Studies. Vancouver, Canada. 19–21. 2000.

Scholes, Robert E. *The Rise and Fall of English: Reconstructing English as a Discipline.* New Haven: Yale UP, 1998.

Schwartz, Lynn. *Ruined by Reading.* Boston: Beacon, 1996.

Spivey, Nancy Nelson. "Transforming Texts: Constructive Processes in Reading and Writing." *Written Communication* 7.2 (April 1990): 256–87.

Sternglass, Marilyn. *The Presence of Thought: Introspective Accounts of Reading and Writing.* Norwood, NJ: Ablex, 1989.

Tate, Gary. "A Place for Literature in Freshman Composition." *College English* 55.3 (March 1993): 317–21.

Travis, Molly Abel. *Reading Cultures: The Construction of Readers in the Twentieth Century.* Carbondale: Southern Illinois UP, 1998.

Watkins, Evan. *Work Time: English Departments and the Circulation of Cultural Value.* Stanford, CA: Stanford UP, 1989.

Winterowd, W. Ross. *The English Department: A Personal and Institutional History.* Carbondale: Southern Illinois UP, 1998.

Young, Art and Toby Fulwiler. *When Writing Teachers Teach Literature: Bringing Writing to Reading.* Portsmouth, NH: Heinemann, 1995.

2

Closer than Close Reading: Historical Analysis, Cultural Analysis, and Symptomatic Reading in the Undergraduate Classroom

Kathleen McCormick

The overarching question of this chapter is whether it is possible for faculty in a variety of disciplines and at different educational levels to encourage students to read, to provide opportunities for them to take pleasure in their acts of reading, and simultaneously to encourage them to want to read in increasingly complex and critically intensive ways. One possible set of strategies we can use to help students achieve both pleasure and increasingly critical abilities is to enable them to activate some of their street knowledge, which is often checked at the classroom door—including their habituated ways of reading popular culture, for critical ends. I will suggest that teaching students to read written texts "symptomatically" from historical and cultural perspectives can lead to both pleasure and an advance in their critical reading abilities.

MY STUDENTS DON'T READ THE WAY IT SAYS THEY WILL IN THE GUIDE BOOK

Ever since I. A. Richards in *Practical Criticism* first documented his students' "blank bewilderment and helpless inability to comprehend either the sense or the form" of the poems he gave his Cambridge students to read (85), teachers of reading and writing in highly diverse types of English departments and writing programs at all levels of education have been increasingly aware of students' difficulty in reading and thinking carefully about texts of all kinds (Shaughnessy; Hull and Rose; Lu; Erickson; Ogbu; Bartholomae, "Inventing"; Bleich; Rose; McCormick; Fishman and McCarthy; Sternglass; Scholes; Castell and Luke). What we practitioners have long known is supported by empirical research. A colleague of mine at Purchase College in cognitive psychology—the discipline that theorizes the practice of reading most fully and still has the greatest impact on how reading is taught in the schools—has been working on comparing somewhat idealized representations of the reading process in psychology journals with how students he teaches actually read (Needham and Masterson).[1] The results confirm what we have all long known, that there is a gap between concept and practice and, even more important in my view, between practice and the potential for critical reading.

The reasons underlying the difficulties in reading outlined by these teachers and scholars span a full spectrum: cognitive/comprehension problems; socioeconomic inequities in the delivery of education; gender biases and racial caste systems leading to student resistance to learning; inappropriate teacher expectations; and technocractic methods of education and testing. Within these categories, complex social problems become articulated so that no one category eventually explains, for example, the reading successes of children in one school in an Alaskan Athabaskan native village, which shared a common curriculum with other village schools, but whose teachers taught them through subtly different processes (Erickson 223), or the successes or failures of Hispanic and African American boys in Watts who don't want to carry books to school because they don't want to be perceived as "nerds" by their friends (Rose 15). When a particular racial or ethnic group is not rewarded significantly for educational achievements over time, when teachers appear to have low expectations for a particular group of students, how does one account exactly for an individual student's apparent "slowness" in school reading ability (Feiler and Webster; Ogbu 241)? As a teacher from Watts tells other teachers, "Do not think that because a child cannot read a text, he cannot read *you*" (Rose 17).

Such analyses of actual students' difficulties in reading demonstrates that practice is usually harder than theorizing. When one gets into specific classroom settings, many theories, particularly if they have not been tested on a wide cross section of students, simply fall apart. In saying this, I am hardly suggesting that one should not theorize; rather, I'm arguing that theories of reading and writing are more nuanced and comprehensive to the extent that they are grounded in a variety of actual classroom practices. Now, more than ever, in part because of the Reading Excellence Act (REA), passed on October 6, 1998,[2] it is important for teachers conducting work in reading, however they define it—and Ken Goodman, for example, notes that he doesn't think that his own paradigm for studying reading would be included in the REA's interpretation of "scientifically based reading research"—to do whatever they can to ensure that their work gets published and into the national dialogue. Arthur Applebee recently implored researchers in the field of English to enter their "increasingly powerful theories" into dialogue with other researchers and policymakers.

To help us at the college level begin to think about productive interventions we might make into reading research, to explore how our certain types of pedagogies might enable students to develop complex reading skills, we need to think critically about some of the ways in which our students have been situated as reading subjects within our culture—well before we meet them in college. Why are many students entering college today as poor readers? What are these students' histories of reading and how might a fuller understanding of them potentially inflect the way we teach them, the kinds of reading processes we might advocate, and the kinds of research we might engage in?[3]

READING IN THE POPULAR CULTURE

Many well-intentioned people, in both popular and academic sources, have a tendency to blame the media and pop culture—as it is experienced by students inside and outside the classroom—at least in part for a number of students' reading problems today. A decade and a half ago, Allan Bloom argued that rock music was almost singularly responsible for students' inability to read and think (68–81). Margery Sabin, in discussing the "erosion" of the Amherst College English Department, but in the context of a more general discussion of trends in the humanities, complains that courses with such new curricular content as "film, television, [and] advertising" begin with a "conception of reading itself as a suspect social act" (88), missing the point that because students come to college already having performed critical readings of media texts, these popular culture reading experiences can provide a particularly rich starting point for bringing critical reading strategies into the classroom.

The media is an easy target for almost all ills. Of course, there are many distractions today—with video games, the Internet, infinite TV channels, etc.—to keep children (and adults) from reading, to encourage instant gratification, dichotomous thinking, and low attention spans, but there have always been distractions or impediments to reading and literacy development in general. As Harvey Graff points out, industrialization, which is often linked with a rise in literacy and reading abilities, did not, at least initially, increase levels of literacy among the general populace; in fact industrialization "often reduced opportunities for schooling and, consequently, rates of literacy fell as it took its toll on the 'human capital' on which it fed" (88). And Carl Kaestle makes the point that there is not even always a link between schooling and a rise of literacy (102).

Rather than simplifying what is a legitimate but complex matter of concern and just blaming the popular culture as a source of distractions from reading, I think that it is of more interest to explore the kinds of reading practices the media most frequently encourage as well as those that can emerge when media texts are read against the grain. While texts of the popular culture, for the most part, encourage simplistic reading strategies, in particular instances of reception, the consumers of these texts can develop strategies for resistance and critique, even if they are unable to name these strategies or to readily transfer them to school situations. When we have a deeper understanding of the strength of reinforcement of the culture's dominant reading practices as well as the most likely sites of resistance to that dominance, we can begin to think productively about developing in students a sense of the complexities and multiple options they have in reading a text of any kind.

Reading practices are one aspect of a culture's ideology, in the sense—derived from Althusser and Macherey—of representations "of common-sense propositions about the world, which are assumed to be self-evident" (Tickner 357). As an arrangement of social practices and systems of representations, ideology is materially operative through specific institutions. Gary Waller writes that "ideology is a complex of distinctive practices and social relations which are characteristic of any society and which are inscribed in the language of that society." It includes "all the largely unconscious assumptions and acts by which men and women relate to their world; it is the system of images, attitudes, feelings, myths, and gestures which are peculiar to a society, which the members who make up that society habitually take for granted" (9). In any society, one of the functions of ideology is, as far as possible, to define and limit the linguistic and cultural practices, including reading, by which members of that society function. "Reading" in this context is a set of practices that seem natural, common-sensical, and that are reinforced by both "experience" and discourse—ways in which it seems natural to explain those experiences.

One important strand of the dominant reading models that we absorb from much of our culture is to oversimplify, usually by dichotomous judgments and decisions. Thus, our culture surrounds us with popular representations of reading situations that are often oversimplified and tend to extremes: students have seen, both in popular culture and within schooling practices, differences discussed in terms of hierarchies, in terms of inferior and superior, of absolute right and wrong, black and white. Whether watching presidential debates, the world news in a minute, TV sitcoms, most popular films, while listening to pop songs, while playing most video games, the world is simplistically divided into dichotomies of good and bad: the force, as in Star Wars or the much touted Harry Potter series, is either with you or against you. The very binary 1/0 basis of technology reinforces a dichotomized approach to experiences that may well be open to more complex modes of processing.

Yet while the media doesn't usually either represent complex ways of reading or encourage them, in their moments of reception, media texts can become sites of complex, critical reading. For while most texts of the popular culture are produced to encourage simplistic reading strategies, many consumers of these texts, in the process of reception, have in fact adopted somewhat more critical approaches to reading them, even if their attitudes may remain conflicted about them.

One of the reasons that teaching students to critique TV shows or advertisements, or movies, or song lyrics has turned out to be so easy to do in the classroom is that students have already had a lot of experience doing this outside of class. Although they do not have the language to describe their resistant readings to texts, most students have analyzed some media texts quite critically, exploring their biases against certain groups of people—usually based on race, ethnicity, or gender, their contradictory messages, their frequent depiction of spending money as the cure for any problem. Students have usually at some point actively distinguished representations from reality, even if on other occasions they "believe as real anything they see." Further they have often—though again usually without critical vocabulary—recognized that they themselves are divided and contradictory subjects, caught between embracing a particular position advocated by the popular culture and critique or disdain for it.

Most college students, for example, have little trouble critiquing the "All-American" myth surrounding ads for the perfume, Tommy Girl. Students of all colors notice that these ads not only usually have only white people in them, but that most of the people are blond. They also notice the settings of such ads, aware that these settings—often a beach and beach house—convey a sense of leisure and relaxation that only a lot of money can buy. Furthermore, they are aware that the perfume is named "girl," and they can usually speak quite eloquently about the multiple significations of girl. At its most literal, it explains that this is a Tommy H product for females: unlike Calvin Klein, which markets a number of unisex fragrances, Tommy Hilfiger is following the more conventional route of having different fragrances for males and females. "Girl" also implies girlfriend, but definitely with only heterosexual connotations and also with further possible marketing potential: "Tommy Girl" can easily translate to "Tommy's girl" or, from a more specifically consumer orientation, the girlfriend of a man who wears Tommy H products. "Girl" as well is recognized by most students as a diminutive form of woman. Finally, most students see that such ads play on the American myth of independence, suggesting that people who wear this perfume are independent types, and they notice the contradiction that to be independent, you have to conform and buy the perfume and that to do so, you have to have enough money to afford it. So independence is achieved with money, conformity, and heterosexuality, usually by blondes. In the midst of all of this critique, however, many students may also own the perfume. They live in the contradictions, to some extent, knowingly.

Students can also critique pop music quite readily. They may, for example, discuss the pop star Britney Spears as having little talent, as exploiting a sense of innocence, especially in her hit song, "Oops! I Did It Again." On some level, students see the ways in which Spears occupies multiple subject positions—as innocent girl, as experienced lover, as money-making maven—and they regard her with some disdain because they feel she is so transparent. This does not mean, however, that they don't buy her CDs. Again, more contradictions, more examples of multiple subjectivity.

Students show a similar facility to critique television shows and to distinguish representations from reality. While a large majority of students watch and enjoy the TV show *Friends*, few expect that their life after college will be like the characters' on the show, and over the last couple of years, I have observed that fewer and fewer students *want* their life to be like Chandler's or Phoebe's or Rachel's or like any of the other characters. Students, particularly seniors, notice what lousy jobs most of the characters have and how the only intellectual job—Ross's job at the museum—is the butt of many jokes.

So while the popular media by and large does not encourage its consumers to develop critical reading skills, the more closely the media representation comes to the individual, the more likely he or she is to find points of resistance to it and therefore to critique it in various ways. It is for this reason that courses that aim to introduce students to critical reading methods often find using the media to be so successful.

CRITICALLY READING ONE'S PERSONAL EXPERIENCE

Another frequently successful method of introducing students to critical reading methodologies in the classroom is to ask students to write about their personal experiences. While bourgeois conceptions of individualism can, of course, impede students from being receptive to larger ideological critique (Bartholomae, "Writing," 64–67), it is often in their personal experiences with others, as well as in their personal involvement with media texts, that students have been the most analytical: it is these areas of their experience that matter to them most and that are often the most necessary for their survival (Elbow 77–82). In such work, which I discuss elsewhere (McCormick et al. 13–48), students do not simply tell stories about their life, but are asked to become analytical about their narratives, to explore the larger historical and cultural influences on each person involved in their narratives and to analyze why different people in their stories hold different positions (or why particular individuals themselves may have taken up more than one stance).

Such analysis of personal experience is a good starting point for analytical inquiry, but a poor stopping point. I recognize, as bell hooks argues, that we must enable students to "explore ways individuals acquire knowledge about an experience they have not lived" (88) even while we also listen to and help them develop their personal narratives. When students increase their consciousness of how they acquire knowledge and become analytical about experiences they have had—giving names to different aspects of it, sharpening and developing it—they then have the potential to transfer this consciousness and these analytical abilities to other more public texts and contexts.

In addition, when people feel themselves to be positioned outside the dominant in any respect (in terms of race, religion, physical attributes, socioeconomic background, primary areas of interest, popularity, gender, sexuality, etc.), they usually gain experience at reading larger aspects of our culture critically. Students who have felt themselves to be at the margins of the culture in any way usually have clearly worked out not only an understanding of what the culture's dominant position is in that area, but also of the various sign systems associated with it. If the classroom is established as a place of trust and mutual respect, students who have felt marginalized—and eventually, with changing areas of study, this can encompass almost a whole class—can adopt a central role in educating students who occupy more culturally dominant positions in those areas.

So, for example, after reading a piece by Marjorie Garber extolling the cross-sexual freedoms we enjoy today (102–104), a well-intentioned heterosexual woman announced in class that she fully agreed with Garber that our society accepts all forms of dress and sexuality. Other women agreed with her, citing examples of everyone's wearing unisex jeans in the class and a number of males and females wearing plaid shirts with T-shirts under them. A gay man argued in contrast that the celebratory tone of Garber's text—and its primary focus on clothing and accessories—was covering over deep tensions about homosexuality that still exist in this country. Among the points he asked the class to think about were: the kinds of restrictions placed on "acceptable" clothing for men within the dominant to wear; the laws in most states preventing gay couples from marrying; laws disallowing gay couples from being included on each other's health insurance policies; and hate crimes committed against gays. As Terry Eagleton would argue, this student's reading of Garber's text began to "put ideology to work," and helped to "illuminate the absences which are the foundation" of ideology's "articulate discourse" (90). This man opened up a discussion that highlighted the tensions lying just below the surface-level acceptance of all sexual orientations that Garber articulates. He was able to do so, at least in part, because his subject position within the culture provides him with a vantage point for reading it that differed from the students who agreed with Garber and indeed, it would appear, from Garber herself.

I am not suggesting that we run our classes based on identity politics or that all people who have been marginalized in a culture would feel comfortable talking to their classmates about their subject position or that they have experienced similar forms of prejudice. But students need to see from each other's interpretations and reactions to texts that ways of reading a culture will vary depending on a person's position in it. Such a recognition moves us out of simplistic right/wrong notions of reading and into more carefully nuanced understandings that there are reasons underlying different perspectives and that in the process of acquire "knowledge about an experience they have not lived" (hooks 88), students need to gain not only the knowledge that people have different perspectives, but to explore why a text or an individual hold the positions they do.

Thus, students' personal experiences as well as their reception of media texts can provide rich examples of their own ability to critically read a text and a larger culture. Most students already have some experience reading critically, and we will help students to read much more critically in the classroom if we first access those experiences, validate them, and let them see examples of them from each other. This seems to be a major point that Sabin missed in her critique of the Amherst course on reading. It then becomes the teacher's role to coach students' critical reading development, but not to pretend to be introducing them to it. In this way, we work to bridge students' experiences outside school with those in school and enable students with very different types of subject positions to see that their experiences and their critical thought outside of school is invaluable to their critical work in the classroom.[4]

So when students start to critique Britney Spears, teachers can introduce the concept of gender stereotyping and will discover that students can come up with dozens of examples of it. When students begin to analyze the contradictions in the way independence is displayed in Tommy Girl ads, teachers can introduce symptomatic reading (discussed below) and students will again be able to give many examples of having read symptomatically in their own personal life. When students say that they both enjoy the characters on a particular television show, but simultaneously find them ridiculous, teachers can explain to the students that they are providing examples of how each of us occupies contradictory subject positions: we critique the ad, but we still buy the perfume; we don't like the singer, but find ourselves humming her songs while walking to class; we say the characters are silly, but we keep coming back to the show every week.

ENGAGING STUDENTS IN HISTORICAL
ANALYSIS, CULTURAL ANALYSIS,
AND SYMPTOMATIC READING

The students in so many of our classes, especially if we are getting a good cross section of students, and we are not just teaching English majors, have a vast variety of reading experiences and competencies. This diversity of students forces us to address three challenges: Can we find ways to turn students on to reading in college if they don't come already with a love of reading? Is it possible to create processes of reading such that allegedly weaker students can become actively engaged in and succeed at and may in fact excel over conventionally "good" students? Is it possible to make reading more exciting if we relate it to students' own experiences of media and interpersonal analysis—which is closer to critical literacy—rather than to conventional school reading for mere comprehension—which is closer to functional literacy?

Critical reading, writing, and thinking is not only the ability to comprehend the texts one reads and link them with one's own personal worlds. Rather, it is the capacity to analyze and evaluate texts of all kinds for their antecedents—the values, beliefs, and expectations of the culture from which they came—and their implications—the effects they have had on their past readers who lived in particular cultural contexts and the effect they may have on present readers who live in varied cultural contexts (Knoblauch; McCormick; McCormick et al.).

From literacy studies, we have learned that reading does not just happen in school, and many students are more likely to succeed academically in reading if they can identify, develop, and transfer complex models of reading nonacademic texts to school situations (Heath, "Functions"; Heath, "Ways"; Cushman; Erickson; Scribner and Cole). One of our goals in teaching reading on the college level should be to help our students draw on their varied reading abilities, limiting the passive reading strategies they have learned both in school and absorbed from the popular culture, and extending the critical reading they have done of the media, personal experiences, and some school texts.[5]

One process of teaching reading that involves three interrelated types of analysis—historical analysis, cultural analysis, and symptomatic reading—can encourage close, active, and critically engaged reading and can draw on students' past analytical experiences. I will discuss each of these types of analysis in turn.

Historical analysis is the comparison and contrast of beliefs, practices, and assumptions from *different moments in time*. It is more than pretend-

ing that one is "back in time"; rather, it is the active dialectical movement back and forth from the present to the past. Historical analysis functions in two ways to develop students' critical skills. When students see *differences* between past perspectives and their own contemporary perspectives, they see that those past perspectives are rooted in very different assumptions from those they take for granted today. This recognition, in turn, can enable students to begin to see the situatedness—the cultural embeddedness—of their own perspectives.

Let us take as an example students reading seventeenth-century arguments about Galileo's findings using his telescope, that the Earth was not the center of the universe. The notion that Galileo could not both explain truthfully what he had seen with his telescope and be in good standing with the Catholic church seems ridiculously "backward" to many students I teach (Langford 472–84; Santillana 486–90). They focus on their difference from the past and are dismissive of the past, as they often are of differences in the present. Many, somewhat understandably, do find it quite amazing that Galileo wasn't officially pardoned by the Pope until Halloween of 1992 (Reston 491–94). The very moving statement by Little Monk in Brecht's play *Galileo* often does not move my students—at least at first:

> Too often these day when I am trying to concentrate on tracking down the moons of Jupiter, I see my parents [. . .]. They scrape a living, and underlying their poverty there is a sort of order [. . .]. How could they take it, were I

to tell them that they are on a lump of stone ceaselessly spinning in empty space, circling around a second rate star? What then, would be the use of their patience, their acceptance of misery? (Brecht 83)

Historical analysis, as I am conceptualizing it, has to allow students these initial (if frustrating to the teacher) moments of feeling a knee-jerk sense of superiority to those from the past, of feeling enlightened, and having benefited from progress. But of course it cannot stop there.

When students can see *similarities* between past perspectives and their own contemporary perspectives—particularly after they have focused on differences—they can then see that contemporary perspectives are rooted in historical antecedents and that this history may be influencing our points of view without our being fully aware of it. I emphasize differences first because then the discovery of similarities is much more shocking, interesting, and real. It can also have larger ramifications for dealing with difference in the present.

So to return to Galileo. After seeing how different we are from seventeenth-century notions of the earth's being the center of the universe, someone invariably brings up the topic of contemporary technology, artificial intelligence, or cloning. Many students are vehemently opposed to a number of these scientific advances, having a kind of combination of a *2001 A Space Odyssey* and *Brave New World* reaction to technology, fearing that Hal or Big Brother will take over the world, that our humanity is being lessened by scientific advances and that we need to slow down. It is a myth that all eighteen-year-olds come to college in America embracing advances in technology. Such discussions can gradually lead to a recognition of the connection of students' contemporary fear with the fear of scientific advancement of almost 300 years ago. This recognition of possible connection, particularly after having initially felt only a sense of difference, can be startling to students, and can begin to open them up to analyzing the bases of their own beliefs as well as those of the past.

What we've done, then, is open up the notion of historical change, historical difference and continuity, and enable students to want to examine their own historical positioning. This recognition doesn't necessarily dispel students' fear of scientific advancement, but it problematizes it. It suggests to students that their own points of view may be radically biased in ways that were previously not imaginable to them. Rigid boundaries can begin to blur. Discovering historical continuities can challenge students to take seriously perspectives they had previously dismissed simply because they were different. Once students begin to become aware of their own historical situatedness, they can begin to move from taking their own positions for granted as natural and normal to asking *why* they hold them.

Cultural analysis is the linking of a belief or practice to other beliefs, practices, and assumptions that are occurring *at the same point in time.* The goal of the dominant ideology of any society is to encourage its members to accept certain differences and hierarchies within that culture as "natural" and "normal" rather than to see them as the product of complex power and ideological relations. This naturalizing of a dominant viewpoint encourages judgmental stances and can close off people's minds to perspectives other than their own. Cultural analysis can help to avoid simplistic "right/wrong" arguments and move students away from dismissive, judgmental positions toward more reflective and analytical positions by asking them and giving them a way to understand *why* different perspectives exist. In answering why, the perspective is connected to other beliefs and assumptions at the same moment.

Cultural analysis also works in two ways to develop students' critical skills. First, discovering connections, especially unexpected connections, among a perspective, an issue, or a text and other aspects of its cultural moment gives students a sense of the complex interconnections among various attitudes and beliefs. For a number of years at the University of Hartford, I taught a writing class for education majors. We read essays by Ted Sizer, Jonathan Kozol, Myra and David Sadker, among others, and students explored the ways in which social class, gender, and race—which initially to them seem as if they should have nothing to do with education—are inextricably linked to it. These students also had field placements in inner-city Hartford schools where they witnessed discipline problems, often horrible physical conditions—such as a high school built with no windows—and they began to make connections between poverty, race, location (urban vs. rural), and the quality of education one receives in America. Recognizing these complex interconnections prevents students from making overly simplistic cause-and-effect analyses—or from simply dismissing the students they work with as unteachable or unskilled.

When I asked my students to write about their field placement in the context of our readings, they were quite successful at building connections among race, poverty, property taxes, etc.—areas they hadn't seen linked before—but they were terribly fearful about how to even discuss differences, the second aspect of cultural analysis. Discovering differences between a perspective, an issue, or a text and other aspects of its cultural moment requires students to see that a given cultural moment is not static and unified, but rather that there are always tensions among *dominant, re-*

sidual, and *emergent perspectives,* that what someone can say and how they can say it at any given point is significantly influenced by their relation to the dominant. This area of their analysis of their fieldwork dramatically increased my students' awareness of their cultural subject position in large part because it linked the personal and the ideological. And in discussions, students readily admitted that their field placements not only forced them to apply the knowledge gained from our readings, but also worked to call into question representations of African Americans and inner-city schools that they had learned about largely through the media and prejudices that they had often passively absorbed both through family and neighborhood patterns of social interaction and through larger cultural meta-messages. Realizing that although most of them had never been in an inner-city school before, they nonetheless had vivid representations of it—which they now needed to test against the realities of their experiences and those of others described in the class readings. This recognition empowered my students. They had media experiences, if nothing else, to analyze; they were not blank slates. They had some knowledge and it was up to them to explore and question it.

Most of the students I was teaching were white and middle to upper middle class and had never thought about their subject position in society. Unconsciously, they had always just assumed they were "normal." But the theory they had learned and applied to issues in the past had applications to the present as well. And they discovered in themselves a strong desire to move outside their personal reactions and to use the concepts of the course to try to explain their experiences. One student, for example, wrote to me in an e-mail:

> How am I going to explain the fear I felt as a white Jewish girl when I first went into an all African American school? I've always felt like a minority before being Jewish but it was never like this.
>
> Even though I haven't really thought of myself as part of the "dominant culture" growing up because of being Jewish, I now really feel like I share a whole lot with the dominant culture and not very much—culture wise— with the students I'm teaching.
>
> I don't want to write a paper that sounds racist because I don't think I am, and we are all getting along great now, but it was really hard in the beginning and I want to be able to explain it.

The papers students wrote were, for the most part, strongly analytical. The combination of lived experience and analytical concepts other than dichotomous right/wrong ones enabled students to develop sensitive analyses of the difficulties in America of crossing the lines of parallel cultures and the challenges that they would face as teachers. They varied in their degrees of optimism, but what is crucial is that they were able to read, think, and write in complex ways about the problem of difference and parallel cultures in America. And they were able to see themselves as imbedded in, not above conflicts among dominant, residual, and emergent perspectives in America.

The third and interrelated concept I ask my students to use is symptomatic reading, derived from Pierre Macherey who adapted it from Freud. Students are asked to read texts not only for what they are literally saying, but for symptoms of larger cultural tensions, to read the text for "what it does not say" and "what it did not want to say," but which is nonetheless an essential part of its ideological underpinning (Macherey 87, 95). While in some ways, symptomatic reading requires the most critical work, it is also something students are familiar with from their daily life and from critically reading texts of the media. I explain to students that whenever one does not take words—from a person, a written text, an advertisement—for what they are literally saying, but rather interprets them as having a different meaning, a below-the-surface one and one often not even linguistically related to the surface meaning, one is reading symptomatically.

For example, I ask students what they might think if one of their siblings offered to clean their room. Immediately they respond, "He wants something." We discuss how the suspicion they read into the sibling's offer to clean the room has nothing to do with what was literally said, but has to do with larger contextual knowledge—that, say, the sibling has never offered to do this before, that he hates to clean, that he never cleans his own room voluntarily, etc.

A more serious example of symptomatic reading came from a discussion that occurred at a meeting of the Connecticut Writing Project (June 1999). Teachers were trying to come up with real-life, convincing examples of their students' engaging in symptomatic reading which they would then try to help them transfer to a text being read in class. A teacher from the city of Hartford suddenly became quite excited because she had come up with an example of symptomatic reading that students who were conventionally poor-achievers could be demonstrated to have excelled at. There are a number of plainclothes police officers in many Hartford schools, and students and teachers vary significantly in their abilities to spot them, with teachers, for a variety of reasons, usually being the last to notice them. Students in the city of Hartford who have been arrested must check into school with "jail bracelets," and the students wearing these

were observed by teachers to be the best and most rapid spotters of plainclothes police officers in the school. These students are reading symptomatically, more than literally, reading for hidden meanings that appear to
elude teachers. She later reported that this example was quite effective in
class and that students were able to list a whole series of signs in the dress
and demeanor of the plainclothes police officers that enabled them to be
recognized as something other than what they literally were dressed as.
Eagleton remarks in a statement about literary texts that can be general-
ized to texts of the culture at large that "the presence of the real is a presence constituted by its absences" (69), and it is, in some ways, the absence
of the uniform combined with the students' refusal to read the civilian
clothes literally—and the contradictory significations that these plainclothes detectives are sending out—that enables students to recognize the
presence of the police in their school.

    Students can also readily relate a symptomatic reading strategy to their
analyses of popular culture texts. Recall, for example, the critique of
Tommy Girl ads students made, contending that while literally saying a
person would show independence by wearing this perfume, the ad actually suggested that its viewers had to conform, not be independent, and
that to do so, one needed money to afford the perfume, good looks, and
ideally blond hair. This is a symptomatic reading: it demonstrates that
while the text is saying one thing, it is also more subtly saying something
else, something that actually contradicts its literal message.

    This method of reading is empowering for students; many say that it is
the first time they read for a "hidden" meaning and actually understood it
and enjoyed the process. That is, of course, because the initial texts on
which they do symptomatic readings are not difficult and because of the
significance given to this method of reading. We are not looking for
deeper meaning for their own sake: we engage in symptomatic reading to
develop agency in the world, so that we can look beyond the literal message of any kind of text and analyze the ways in which it might be attempting to put forth dominant ideological views as natural and normal,
to reinforce our beliefs in them without consciously articulating them.
Again, to quote Eagleton: "What is in question here, indeed, is a double
relation—not only the objectively determinable relation between text and
ideology, but also (and simultaneously) that relation as 'subjectively'
flaunted, concealed, imitated or mystified by the text itself" (80–81).

    We also engage in symptomatic readings of texts to explore the ten-
sions of a culture that particular texts might be working to cover over.
The Tommy Girl ad suggests that anyone can run around on an ocean
beach barefoot, but this is not true. Many inner-city students or people

who cannot afford to travel throughout middle America, have never seen the ocean. A number of the Hartford city students my class was tutoring, for example, had never been to the beach. The Tommy Girl ad covers this over. Symptomatic reading, therefore, is a process of reading that encourages students to analyze the contradictory assumptions underlying a text, to investigate some of the larger cultural underpinnings that can support those contradictory assumptions, and to therefore gain some insight into the conscious and unconscious workings of the culture's ideology.

For example, before the education majors I discussed above began to read contemporary texts on education, I asked them to read a 1918 U.S. report on Reorganizing Secondary Education to develop a symptomatic reading of the gender roles inscribed by the report, reminding them that this report was written right after World War I had ended (Commission on Reorganization). While there are "7 Cardinal Principals" in this report, I'll focus only on one: "Worthy Home Membership" (home, meaning the hearth and home, not the country). We are told:

> In the education of every high school girl, the household arts should have a prominent place. [. . .] The attention now devoted to this phase of education is inadequate, and especially so for girls preparing for occupations not related to the household arts and for girls planning for higher institutions [. . .]. The majority of girls who enter wage-earning occupations directly from the high school remain in them for only a few years, after which home making becomes their lifelong occupation. (Commission 294)

Students had previously read an essay from 1893 by Charles Eliot and a committee of ten in which the federal government had advocated a "classical education" for all who went to high school (Eliot et al. 279–87). They wanted all students to be taught Latin, Greek, English, other modern languages, math, sciences, history, and geography, and argued that "every subject which is taught at all in a secondary school should be taught in the same way and to the same extent to every pupil so long as he pursues it, not matter what the probably destination of the pupil may be, or at what point his education is to cease" (Eliot et al. 284–88). Students see that the 1918 report, written only twenty-five years later, constitutes a dramatic change in defining the goals of a high school education, moving from a focus on the classics for all to a focus on civic responsibilities with clear gender distinctions spelled out and a near abandonment of the conventional subjects put forth in 1893. I ask students to first read the text literally: for the most part, they can follow the line of argument and if this were all they were asked to do, they would be bored to death—this is, after all, an old government document.

But I also ask them to explore the text symptomatically in two different ways: to analyze the tone of the piece for symptoms of larger cultural
tensions it may be trying to cover over, and to explore some of the possible social factors that may have influenced the authors—consciously or
unconsciously—to develop such a change in curriculum, especially for
girls, from only twenty-five years before. The students are shocked that
the American myth of progress appears not to be true—educationally,
things clearly got worse for all, and particularly for girls, at this time.
Further, the tone of the report is somewhat overly patriotic and is vio-
lently anti-intellectual: learning to "keep the household budgets" and
learning "worthy use of leisure" are tasks that are said to help "preserve
democracy." The students can't help themselves from moving out of the
literal and into the symptomatic. There is clearly tension underlying this
document about the preservation of democracy, about how the new
generation will settle in—as moral married people—and as good workers. But the war and capitalism are never explicitly named. They are, as
Macherey says, what the text definitely does not want to say, but they
are the key material realities underlying it. Most students who reported
hating to "read for hidden meanings" were quite taken by this new form
of close reading.

In doing small amounts of research, students learned that women were
working in factories during the war—and succeeding—and they interpret
this new educational initiative as an attempt to get women out of the
workforce and back into the home. A few idealistic conventionally
"good" students planning to become teachers ask if this means that educational initiatives are not always for the good of the students involved,
but rather may be about something else completely. The conventionally
"weaker" students smile—these are the students who have rarely felt that
school initiatives were in their best interest anyway. A discussion ensues
about who education is for in America that gets to just about every issue I
planned on addressing when we would read Jonathan Kozol later in the
term. And for the first time, the "weaker" students are leading the discussion because it turns out that they are quite skilled at symptomatic reading, but have just never used it actively in the classroom.

Reading symptomatically has made this text come alive for students
and they are reading so closely—finding and linking quotations in order
to read them for more than they are literally saying. This text may not be
Shakespeare or Joyce, but it is an important American document, and
students, with varying degrees of preparedness, are reading it with deep
attention and some relish. Perhaps what these students experienced is
akin to what happened to Gerry Graff when he realized in college that lit-

erature can be about the conflicts of reception rather than about universal truths (66-71).

Of course not every student performed well in class, but the introduction of historical analysis, cultural analysis, and symptomatic reading has had a variety of positive effects on students' reading. It turned reading from a functional literacy task to a critical literacy task and this made it more interesting to students because it gave them some agency. It leveled the playing field to some extent because students outside the dominant who have tended to be less successful in school actually have more highly developed symptomatic reading skills than those inside because these are necessary life survival skills. It helped students to bridge school and world knowledge—bringing to the classroom more complex reading skills that all of us use to some extent in everyday life. The recognition of a tension, a contradiction—something that most of the students thought was to be avoided at all costs when they entered the classroom because it was an "error"—became a stimulus for thought and analysis.

The students in the freshman writing program I directed at Hartford offer various forms of anecdotal evidence suggesting that they can generalize these reading skills beyond the courses in which they learn it. Some say that symptomatic reading has ruined Disney for them. Others report that watching TV in general is much harder because they keep seeing gender, class, or racial issues that the programs are trying to cover over. Still others have found gender biases among fellow students (and even teachers) and have reported that they went on to talk with the students or teachers and had productive discussions about a "hidden curriculum."

Discovering differences across time. Recognizing conflicts and contradictions within the same time period. Connecting a particular issue to other issues. Tracing how it is woven into the larger cultural and social fabric. Making different connections at different points. This is where genuine critical reading begins. Historical analysis, cultural analysis, and symptomatic reading are methods that can be used to revitalize reading in our schools and colleges.

NOTES

1. Needham and Masterson suggest that part of the problem with many scientific experiments is that they are often carried out on students at major research institutions in which the percentage of "skilled readers" is higher than average. Furthermore, while these theories often underpin reading instruction in textbooks, particularly in the schools, they are often not examined extensively for their effectiveness in classroom settings beyond the experimental context in which they occurred, in settings in which there

are fewer controls and where there is frequently a more diverse population than in an experiment. Timothy Shanahan of the National Reading Panel, which is strongly weighted in favor of empirical studies of reading, recognizes that "even 'research proven' methods have not been studied under all conditions or circumstances."

2. The Reading Excellence Act, passed on October 6, 1998, is helping to define how reading gets taught across the United States. While ostensibly focused on the better training of reading teachers, the Act has the potential to establish control over state and local methods of teaching reading by the establishment of a review panel who will determine what research is and is not "scientifically based reading research." Although anyone is obviously still free to do whatever types of reading studies she or he wants, much of the funding for that research and the subsequent status and dissemination of such research is now potentially in the hands of the government. If research is not deemed to be "scientifically based," it will not be approved for use in any training of teachers that is funded by the government. Many researchers fear that this Act and the various government agencies it spawns will decrease rather than increase both the models of teaching reading that are currently available to teachers and the representations of ways of reading that exist within the cultural dominant. (See further discussions by Timothy Shanahan, "The National Reading Panel: Using Research to Create More Literate Students" www.readingonline.org; posted August 1999 © 1998–2000 International Reading Association, Inc., and Alan Berger, "Literacy and Politics: A Conversation with Myself" www.readingonline.org; posted January 1999 © 1998–2000 International Reading Association, Inc.)

3. In what follows, I focus only on students' reading experiences outside of their school experiences. I address the issue of schooling in a companion essay to this one, entitled "Common Critical Reading Problems That Cross Class Boundaries," which is currently in progress.

4. We have to acknowledge that for the majority of students in the schools, this is not the case: in a conventional school setting, students do not regard school as a place where knowledge will be gained that is applicable to life (Willinsky 16–24). This alienation from school and the resistance to seeing school learning as relevant is one of the major impediments to teaching students to foreground analytic work both in school and outside of school (Kozol; Anyon; Shor; Giroux and McLaren; Willinsky).

5. Despite many teachers' attempts at using whole books and bringing in children's literature into the classroom that require deeper engagement with actual books, technocratic models of literacy in the schools prevail (Castell and Luke; Fletcher and Lyons; Snow et al.; Jehlen). Reading tests in the schools, requiring memorization or rapid recall of facts—the very kinds of tests that are on the rise nationally, and are being used to read the success of teaching and whole school systems—are clearly one of the major forces in teaching and reinforcing such a self-defeating method of reading as memorization (Needham and Masterson). In these tests remembering events that occur in proximity, whether or not they are conceptually connected, has meaning. Every time students are encouraged to use superficial reading and writing strategies requiring little active thinking and no synthesis of ideas, reading becomes a less engaging and interesting process.

WORKS CITED

Althusser, Louis. *Lenin and Philosophy.* London: New Left Books, 1971.

Anyon, Jean. *Ghetto Schooling: A Political Economy of Urban Educational Reform.* New York: Teachers College P, 1997.

Applebee, Arthur. "Building a Foundation for Effective Teaching and Learning of English: A Personal Perspective on Thirty Years of Research." *Research in the Teaching of English* 33.4 (1999): 352–66.

Bartholomae, David. "Inventing the University." Kintgen et al. 273–85.

———. "Writing with Teachers." *College Composition and Communication* 46.1 (1995): 62–71.

Berger, Alan. "Literacy and Politics: A Conversation with Myself." *Reading Online*, www.readingonline.org. Posted August 1999; links updated June 2000. © 1999–2000 International Reading Association, Inc.

Bleich, David. *Know and Tell: A Writing Pedagogy of Disclosure, Genre, and Membership.* Portsmouth, NH: Heinemann, 1998.

Bloom, Allan. *The Closing of the American Mind.* New York: Simon, 1985.

Brecht, Bertoldt. *Galileo.* Trans. Charles Laughton. Ed. Eric Bentley. New York: Grove, 1966.

Castell, Suzanne de and Allan Luke. "Defining 'Literacy' in North American Schools: Social and Historical Conditions and Consequences." Kintgen et al. 159–74.

Commission on the Reorganization of Secondary Education. "The Magnificent Seven Cardinal Principles of Secondary Education: 1918." McCormick et al. 289–96.

Cushman, Ellen. *The Struggle and the Tools: Oral and Literate Strategies in an Inner City Community.* Albany, State U of New York P, 1998.

Eagleton, Terry. *Criticism and Ideology: A Study in Marxist Literary Theory.* London: Verso, 1976.

Elbow, Peter. "Being a Writer vs. Being an Academic: A Conflict in Goals." *College Composition and Communication* 46.1 (1995): 72–83.

Eliot, Charles, et al. "In the Beginning . . . The 1893 Report of the Committee of Ten." McCormick et al. 279–87.

Erickson, Frederick. "Literacy, Reasoning, and Civility." Kintgen et al. 205–26.

Feiler, Anthony, and Alec Webster. "Predictions of Young Children's Literacy Success or Failure." *Assessment in Education: Principles, Policy & Practice* 6.3 (1999): 341–56.

Fishman, Stephen M., and Lucile McCarthy. *John Dewey and the Challenge of Classroom Practice.* New York: Teachers College P, 1998.

Fletcher, J.M. and G.R. Lyons. "Reading: A Research-Based Approach." *What's Gone Wrong in America's Classrooms.* Ed. W.M. Evers. Stanford, CA: Hoover Institution P. 49–90.

Garber, Marjorie. "Pushing Borderlines: Gender Crossover." McCormick et al. 102–104.

Giroux, Henry and P. McLaren. *Critical Pedagogy, the State, and Cultural Struggle.* Albany: State U of New York P, 1989.

Goodman, Ken. "Comments on the Reading Excellence Act." *Reading Online*, www.readingonline.org. Posted December 1998. © 1998–2000 International Reading Association, Inc.

Graff, Gerald. *Beyond the Culture Wars: How Teaching the Conflicts Can Revitalize American Education.* New York: Norton, 1992.

Graff, Harvey J. "The Legacies of Literacy." Kintgen 82–91.

Heath, Shirley Brice. "The Functions and Uses of Literacy." *Journal of Communication* 30 (1980): 123–33.

———. *Ways with Words: Language, Life, and Work in Communities and Classrooms.* Cambridge: Cambridge UP, 1984.

hooks, bell. *Teaching to Transgress: Education as the Practice of Freedom.* New York: Routledge, 1994.

Hull, Glynda, and Mike Rose. "Toward a Social-Cognitive Understanding of Problematic Reading and Writing." Lunsford and Slevin, 235–44.

Jehlen, Alain. "Interview: Lorrie Shepard—How to Fight a 'Death Star.' " *NEA Today* 19.4 (2001): 19.

Kaestle, Carl F. "History of Literacy and Readers." Kintgen 95–126.

Kernan, Alvin, ed. *What's Happened to the Humanities?* Princeton: Princeton UP, 1997.

Kintgen, Eugene R., Barry M. Kroll, and Mike Rose, eds. *Perspectives on Literacy.* Carbondale: Southern Illinois UP, 1988.

Knoblauch, Cy. "Literacy and Politics of Education." Lunsford 74–80.

Kozol, Jonathan. *Savage Inequalities: Children in America's Schools.* New York: Crown, 1991.

Langford, Jerome J. "The Trial of Galileo." McCormick et al. 472–84.

Lu, Min-Zhan. "Reading and Writing Differences: The Problematic of Experience." *Feminism and Composition Studies: In Other Words.* Ed. Lynn Worsham. New York: MLA, 1998. 239–51.

Lunsford, Andrea Helene Moglen, and James Slevin, eds. *The Right to Literacy.* New York: MLA, 1990.

Macherey, Pierre. *A Theory of Literary Production.* Trans. Geoffrey Wall. New York: Routledge, 1978.

McCormick, Kathleen. *The Culture of Reading and the Teaching of English.* Manchester: Manchester UP; Urbana: NCTE, 1994.

McCormick, Kathleen, et al. *Reading Our Histories, Understanding Our Cultures.* Boston: Allyn, 1999.

Needham, William P., and Erika Masterson. "Representations and Processing of Text in Skilled and Less Skilled Readers." Unpublished manuscript.

Ogbu, John U. "Literacy and Schooling in Subordinate Cultures: The Case of Black Americans." Kintgen et al. 227–42.

Reston, James B. "Galileo Reconsidered." McCormick et al. 491–94.

Richards, I. A. *Practical Criticism.* London: Kegan Paul, Trench, Trubner, 1935.

Rose, Mike. *Possible Lives: The Promise of Public Education in America.* Boston: Houghton, 1995.

Sabin, Margery. "Evolution and Revolution." Kernan 84–103.

Sadker, Myra, and Sadker, David. "Missing in Interaction." McCormick et al. 314–23.

Santillana, Giorgio de. "Galileo's Crime." McCormick et al. 486–90.

Scholes, Robert. *The Rise and Fall of English.* New Haven: Yale UP, 1998.

Scribner, Sylvia, and Michael Cole. "Unpacking Literacy." Kintgen 57–70.

Shanahan, Timothy. "The National Reading Panel: Using Research to Create More Literate Students." *Reading Online,* www.readingonline.org. Posted August 1999; links updated June 2000. © 1999–2000 International Reading Association, Inc.

Shaughnessy, Mina. *Errors and Expectations.* New York: Oxford UP, 1977.

Shor, Ira. *Culture Wars: Schools and Society in the Conservative Restoration.* New York: Routledge, 1986.

Sizer, Theodore R.. "What High School Is." McCormick et al. 269–78.

Snow, Catherine E., Susan Burns, and Peg Griffin, eds. *Preventing Reading Difficulties in Young Children.* Washington, DC: National Academy, 1998.

Sternglass, Marilyn. *Time to Know Them: A Longitudinal Study of Writing and Learning at the College Level.* Mahwah, NJ: Erlbaum, 1997.

Tickner, Lisa. "Sexuality and/in Representation: Five British Artists." *The Art of Art History*. Ed. Donald Preziosi. New York: Oxford UP, 1998.

Waller, Gary. *English Poetry in the Sixteenth Century*. 2e. London: Longman, 1993.

Willinsky, John. *The New Literacy: Redefining Reading and Writing in the Schools*. New York: Routledge, 1990.

3

Reading as a Site
of Spiritual Struggle

Lizabeth Rand

Since there is no innocent vision, our eyes should be as sinful as possible—seeing all the licit and illicit pleasures so that we know from what possible worlds we choose the one we live in.
—Stephen Olsen, "Reading as Believing"

If I could, I would have shutters over my eyes and a gatekeeper deciding what was appropriate for me to see. Of course I can close my own eyes, but sin is sometimes so intriguing that it's hard to look away.
—Jennifer Mae Barizo, Seventh-day Adventist Christian,
"Truth Is on the March"

Having attended public schools all my life and worshiping at a local Methodist church only on occasion, I was most decidedly raised in a secular environment. I suppose I thought of myself as a Christian, however, this designation seemed more polite convention than a genuine statement about the kind of worldview that actually shaped my thinking. Of course I did believe in God but I was not accustomed to calling upon the presence of anything "spiritual" very often. Grace before meals was the only public moment for prayer in my family: if you prayed at other times it was clearly a private affair. In the classroom, the only mention of God that I recall was during the reciting of the Pledge of Allegiance. Essentially, the religious identity of students themselves was an "unknown" except perhaps for those people with whom you established more intimate friendships outside of school boundaries. It is clear to me now that the culture of my middle-class, secular upbringing—the attitudes, behaviors, and beliefs that I acquired during the years of my childhood and young adulthood—gave only the slightest nod to religion as a component of the social development that ultimately leads one to claim particular kinds of identities or selfhood. Religious sources of meaning had little influence upon what or how I learned or the way that I made sense of my life.

A few years ago I taught first-year writing part time at a Seventh-day Adventist Christian school I'll refer to as James College. It was this experience of stepping out of my comfort zone that caused me to notice how completely I embraced a secular approach to thinking about the world and how much I took that kind of approach for granted. Suddenly I was teaching at a school clearly guided by a Christian philosophy and by a discourse often unfamiliar to me. Especially during the first several months, I felt slightly uneasy there, although the students and faculty were very friendly and no one tried to actively convert me to Seventh-day Adventism. Being surrounded by Christian people in an outwardly spiritual environment revealed my insecurities about such open expression of faith and left me perhaps somewhat vulnerable; it also, however, gave me a greater appreciation of religion as a sociocultural force that shapes people's lives and learning in quite profound ways. From almost my first day on campus, I discovered that the Adventist subculture has a rich and detailed history that clearly sanctions particular kinds of textual and interpretive approaches—often different than my own—for understanding the ways that human beings come to make meaning of the world around them.

The Seventh-day Adventist church was founded in the mid-nineteenth century in Battle Creek, Michigan.[1] One of the cofounders was Ellen White, who in 1844 at the age of seventeen received her first vision of the Advent people and the path that God desired them to follow. One week later, White received a second vision, which called her to be God's messenger. Advent believers soon began to revere her prophetic ministry. Before her death in 1915, Ellen White wrote over forty volumes on such topics as history, religion, health, family, and education—her literary efforts the result of the more than 2,000 visions she experienced during her lifetime. The church's primary source of knowledge continues to be the Bible (Adventists, in fact, refer to themselves as "people of the Book"); nevertheless, it is not only biblical text that shapes followers' identities or their encounters with public discourse. It is also the interpretive sensibilities detailed at length by their founding mother.

Early in my first semester of teaching at James College, one of my students submitted an essay about "honor" in which she quoted from an Ellen White testimony and referred to White as her "favorite author." Others used biblical support for their argumentative positions about issues such as vegetarianism, preservation of the environment, and proper marriage relationships. During previous years of writing instruction, I had almost never dealt with students who called upon evidence from religious sources. I'm sure there must have been people with deep spiritual convictions in my secular classrooms; however, probably because I did not invite discussion of faith-related systems of meaning, few of them cited scripture or religious identity in general as the authority for the ways they made sense of text or for the claims they constructed. I had been warned before I started teaching at James College that some students would probably not be comfortable reading or writing about certain issues connected to sexuality and also what the church referred to as "spiritualism."[2] I recall being anxious that semester about almost every decision I made, from the readings I selected to my response to student writing. It was during this time that I committed to a more formal investigation of evangelical Christian identity (Adventism in particular) in the hope of gaining a better understanding of the decidedly real influence of religion on human personality and the life of the mind. In the words of legal scholar Stephen L. Carter, whose 1993 book *The Culture of Disbelief: How American Law and Politics Trivialize Religious Devotion* received widespread critical attention, "faith may be so intertwined with personality that it is impossible to tell when one is acting, or not acting, from religious motive" (111). I embarked on a three-year ethnographic study of the James College community in order to examine the ways that evangelical faith shapes people's social identities and impacts their learning. Of particular interest to me were the reading and writing practices of Adventist Christian believers.

In gathering the data necessary for my study, I employed qualitative research methods. These methods, with their origin in anthropological and sociological fieldwork, have become increasingly popular within the discipline of composition studies.[3] Data collection began in the fall of 1997 and was completed in the spring of 2000. Research was gathered through extensive participant-observation in the James College community. During 1997–1998, I attended four semester-length undergraduate courses (offered by the English, psychology, and religion departments). I also began to participate in worship functions such as Sabbath School and Sabbath services at the neighboring James College church (Adventists worship on the Jewish Sabbath from sundown Friday to sundown Saturday). In addition, I went to chapel services held each Tuesday morning. Students must earn a certain number of "worship credits" during the school year, and attendance at chapel is one way to acquire them. All of these sessions were either tape recorded or detailed fieldnotes were written during and after each event. Participation in worship activities continued until the end of 1999.

Besides participant-observation within a variety of the school's educational and community-related activities, I also interviewed over forty Seventh-day Adventists connected to James College (and collected many of their writings). These interviews have been primarily with students and teachers but have also included the college chaplain and the pastor of the college church. All of these interviews were taped and I cycled back transcripts and many of my own reflective writings in order to gain participants' interpretations and comments. During the first year of data collection, especially, the questions that I asked of participants were often quite broad in scope:

- How long have you been a Seventh-day Adventist and is religious faith important in your life? Can you describe the ways that it is important?
- Tell me about your education before coming to James College. Did you go to Adventist schools or public schools? How did you use reading and writing in your studies?
- As a student at James College, what were your reasons for coming here? How would you like to use the college education that you're receiving once you've graduated?
- What do you see as the goal of your education? Do you think that James College is helping you to achieve this goal?
- As a teacher at James College, what were your reasons for coming here? What are the goals and objectives that you have in mind when you teach [course title] and how do you try and accomplish these goals? What do you want your students to learn most from this class? How do you use reading and writing in your classroom?
- Does being a Christian involve rejecting "worldly" kinds of attitudes or behaviors? Explain. Does being a Christian affect the choices that you make about reading and writing?

The first year that I was an ethnographer at James College, I spent the majority of my time simply trying to find out more about the lives of students and teachers within this community and about the ways that the Adventist faith shaped the kind of education that young people received. It was during this time that I discovered that the evangelical response to reading and writing is much more complex than I had ever understood, or, frequently read about in essays published within the field of composi-

tion studies.[4] As readers, Seventh-day Adventist Christians often struggle
not only with *what* to read but *how to approach* "worldly" texts.

One of my first interviews at James College was with a member of the
community who told me about his conversion as a young adult to Seventh-day Adventism. During the time that we talked, he spoke at some
length about his experiences as a "new Christian" and the changes that
conversion brought to his life. I still remember the feeling of disbelief that
came over me when he explained that his religious identity, especially at
that time when he first joined the Adventist church, required him to be so
vigilant about worldly reading practices:

> When I committed my life and my love [. . .] to God, I didn't know if the
> devil, Satan, existed really and that wasn't a huge part of my belief system.
> But I would on occasion wake up after I'd made my decision [. . .] and I
> would be scared of an unknown presence—chilling, whatever—that I had
> not experienced before. And I uh, I would pray. I'd pray for [my family]
> and for myself. And there was just a kind of nameless dread. And I remem-
> ber one night, I got out of bed. [. . .] I went over to my bookcase and I
> looked in it. I just felt like something wasn't right. I pulled down three
> books—I don't even remember what they were. I opened up each book and
> the first word that my eyes hit on in each book had to do with Satan—the
> devil or that kind of thing. And that was jarring to me as you might imag-
> ine. It was freaky, strange. I don't know—I tossed them. I tossed those
> books. [. . .] I ended up tossing out a lot of books and I can remember going
> into the dump with a boxload of books and heaving them out into the
> dump and just saying "there goes my old life." I'm not talking Harlequin
> Romances now. In fact what I'm talking is some books I wish I had back.
> But at the time I felt I had to do it. I had to make a break.

When I was around Adventist believers, I noticed how frequently and
with what conviction they expressed concern about the influence that evil
has in the world over sinful human beings. Facing temptation from the
devil, in fact, would seem to have caused this believer to get rid of particular books. The ability of the self to choose between good or evil, then, appears to be at the center of his struggle. His words bring to mind the opening testimony of Jennifer Mae Barizo—"Of course I can close my own
eyes, but sin is sometimes so intriguing that it's hard to look away."

Many Adventist readers seem to face a spiritual battleground. Also
during the early stages of my research, a James College teacher who I
knew had been born into the church, passed along to me a small, delicate
book, the pages slightly yellowed, titled *Give Attendance to Reading*
(1966) that he had discovered tucked away inside the drawer of his desk at
school. This book, by L. W. Cobb, is a collection of quotations drawn

primarily from Ellen White but also from the Bible, along with Cobb's advice and counsel on proper reading strategies for the Seventh-day Adventist Christian. When I opened the book, its sentiments still quite influential in the church I gathered from its owner, I came upon the following words of introduction from Cobb. I took note almost immediately of the military metaphor, the function of which seemed to be to compare Adventist readers to soldiers preparing themselves for combat:

> How eager we are to read! Yet before we set out, let us think of a bombing mission. Though expertly trained and equipped, the crew, before taking off, are carefully briefed about their objective and the plans of the enemy to be thwarted. So with reading. When we learn of the snares and pitfalls in improper reading first, then the positive instructions stand out clear and meaningful. The wealth of counsel from Heaven centers in one great guiding principle: read what will strengthen and perfect character; avoid the opposite. (13)

Wrong reading for Seventh-day Adventist Christians clearly has the ability to put religious identity at risk. A meaningful reading experience, according to Cobb, should ideally strengthen what he refers to as an individual's "character" and weaken the effects of sin. Cobb, too, describes an enemy that Christians must be mindful of if they want to remain free from bondage and enslavement. This enemy must be "thwarted" by a carefully trained reader, thoroughly equipped with the proper critical and interpretive weapons. The "carefully trained Christian reader" will next be the focus of my attention. I will argue that this kind of individual, who may very well defer to religious sources of knowledge and authority in the textual choices that he or she makes, has often been socialized into a subject position that by its very nature encourages a critical and resistant stance. I believe that, as compositionists, we need to know more about the source of this resistance and about the boundaries of religious selfhood. We should not assume that those students who identify as evangelical read or write from a "naive" or "anti-intellectual" stance. Teachers of writing would benefit from a more rich understanding of the subject position behind much of the evangelical worldview.

READING AND THE STRUGGLE AGAINST SATAN: READING AND THE STRUGGLE AGAINST SELF

In her essay "Textual Interpretation as Collective Action," Elizabeth Long points out that similar to the modernist image of the writer as "solitary scribbler" (180), representations of the reader, too, have often shown this figure as located most appropriately within the realm of private life. The solitary reader has a "complex iconographic history" (181) and images abound of the isolated, erudite scholar or philosopher who has withdrawn from worldly pursuits, or, as women gained access to literacy, of the female reader encompassed by the interior and domestic space of the home and the family circle. Long contends that these images "not only oppose reading to sociability" (181), they also tie specific kinds of literacy to gender (i.e., woman as frivolous and passive consumer; man as serious and contemplative creator of culture). The central claim of this essay, which informs my own argument, is that reading viewed as a fundamentally solitary practice suppresses the collective nature of making meaning from text. Long reminds us that a "social infrastructure" is needed to support and sustain reading practice within literate communities: first, that reading must be taught; and second, that "socialization into reading always takes place within specific social relationships" (191). Reading, then, although intensely private in many ways, is socially framed: "[C]ollective and institutional processes shape reading practices by [. . .] defining what is worth reading and how to read it. In turn, this authoritative framing [. . .] [legitimates], as well, certain kinds of literary values" (192). For Seventh-day Adventists (and, I would argue, for many Christians in other denominations), reading practice is socially framed by the collective and institutional processes of the corporate church. Adventism, from its inception, has sought to define appropriate responses to and attitudes about text. Many of the students at James College have therefore been encouraged to be readers and writers in ways that support the kind of Christian identity that the church views as necessary not only for their well-being but for their very salvation. This identity is meant to empower them to resist the temptations of living a too worldly and potentially sinful life without God.

The Adventist Church Manual, the official statement of the values, beliefs, policies, and procedures of the world church, states quite clearly that Christian identity should be nurtured and sustained, first, through the reading of specific texts. Of primary importance is the study of the Bible:

> Spiritual life is maintained by spiritual food. The habit of devotional Bible study and prayer must be maintained if we are to perfect holiness. In a time when a great flood of reading matter pours forth from printing presses everywhere [. . .] it is incumbent upon us to close our eyes and our ears to much of that which is seeking entrance to our minds, and devote ourselves to God's book—the Book of all books, the Book of life. If we cease to be the people of the Book, we are lost, and our mission has failed. ("Fifteenth" 70)

Adventists who are born into and/or raised in the church typically begin to read "God's book" at an early age. Family devotional time is common; children are read Bible stories until old enough to decipher text on their own. In church Sabbath school, they recite "memory texts" assigned on a regular basis. They also attend Sabbath services where bringing a Bible is expected and encouraged. When young Adventist Christians reach their teenage years, the opportunity to read and to learn scripture often increases not only because they approach baptism but because many begin attending one of the Adventist boarding academies located across the country. These schools provide private Christian education: included in the curriculum are required Bible classes as well as mandatory attendance at chapel services and other worship-related activities. By the time students enter college, a social infrastructure is firmly in place that encourages them not only to read and study the Bible, in private as well as public settings, but to be unafraid to call upon its wisdom and authority. Ideally, biblical doctrines become integrated into every part of life.

In my role as a participant-observer within the James College community, I noticed that students were presented with many opportunities to participate in a collective process of reading and interpreting scripture. These always aimed to strengthen their ties to the church, though in varying degrees also allowed them a measure of freedom to think critically about their own belief systems. Students were required to take courses such as "Christian Beliefs" that provided a detailed review of the funda-

mental tenets of Seventh-day Adventism and asked them to learn the biblical principles upon which these are based. Many attended college Sabbath School classes every Saturday morning. These worship experiences, frequently organized and run by students themselves, often included small-group study of particular Bible passages followed by a collective sharing of ideas and opinions. Finally, students participated in weekly Chapel with time devoted to scripture readings and offerings of personal testimony. Such an extensive process of socialization seeks to ensure that as Adventist Christians, they continue to call upon the word of God in order to strengthen and maintain not only their own spiritual identities but also that of the global church.

The Bible is clearly presented as the primary form of sustenance for Adventist readers: they are told of the spiritual and intellectual nourishment that it provides—empowering them to shut out worldly influences including various sorts of texts that might be destructive to faith. The church, however, socializes its members to supplement the "spiritual food" of the Bible with that of their founding mother, Ellen White. By the time students reach James College, they have often heard parents, pastors, or teachers appeal to and cite her work. Many of them have read at least one of White's books and are familiar with much of the history surrounding her life and the role she has played as a spiritual leader of the Advent movement. White did not intend for her own authority to replace that of the Bible; nevertheless, her words are quoted so frequently that on occasion, someone in the church speaks up to remind fellow believers that their first loyalty should always be to the scriptures. A magnificent stained-glass window in the James College church seems to suggest the appropriate relationship between these two sources of authority: "Mrs. White," as she's often called, is pictured in a center frame but holds up an opened Bible in one hand. Accordingly, as one student explained to me, she is best thought of as "a prophet from God. God spoke through her [. . .] and we should definitely hold that in high regard. But she's not above [the Bible]." White's literary efforts generally return to a central . theme: Christians should know Jesus on an intimate and personal level and the best way to build this kind of relationship is through Bible study and prayer. Her attitudes about other kinds of texts, though, are probably what intrigued me the most as I learned more about Seventh-day Adventism. White condemned a substantial number of secular reading choices—including and with a particular vengeance the reading of novels and fiction. She admonishes her readers: "[If children's] minds are filled with stories, be they true or fictitious, there is no room for the useful information. [. . .] [Light reading] has destroyed the principles of sincerity

and true godliness, which lie at the foundation of a symmetrical character" (qtd. in Cobb 17).

From talking with several teachers in the English department at James
College, I know that White's counsel is still taken quite seriously by more
than a few Adventist parents and students. Alternatives must sometimes
be found for assigned classroom reading; complaints are still issued on
occasion. Ellen White's voice in quite powerful ways often speaks
through the officially expressed positions of the modern-day church and
thus through its members. Her words have helped to legitimate certain
collective attitudes about reading that seem to remain a persuasive force
within the Adventist educational system.[5]

The social infrastructure that Adventism relies on to guide readers in
the appropriate choice of texts encourages them to make selections that
will strengthen and build Godly character. Adventists are not limited to
the Bible and Ellen White's writings; however, the church clearly presents
these as the most edifying and worthwhile. The institutional church is also
aware that right reading habits are best learned as one studies these
knowledge sources directly: both call for Christians to adopt specific textual sensibilities because these build the proper kind of selfhood. The Bible and Ellen White explain that believers must be willing to "put on"
Christ and to be saved by the profession of a new or "born again" identity: only then will they become convicted to think, speak, and act in ways
that reflect the gospel message and the sacrifice that Jesus made on the
cross for all sinners. I want to point out that a significant number of
Christians, though individual beliefs and practices vary across denomi-
national lines, claim a selfhood that is similar at this most fundamental
level. From such a position, many of them, not only Seventh-day Adventists, form decisions about public discourse. Teachers in both secular
and Christian schools almost inevitably encounter students whose world-
views are derived from this kind of identity. They are the readers and
writers that we often struggle to respond to and make a place for within
our classrooms.

The Bible calls upon all believers to serve as witnesses for Jesus Christ.
This is the subject position at the center of the Christian worldview and
the one from which right reading takes place. In the New Testament, Acts
1:8 explains that after Jesus's death and resurrection, he called his disci-
ples to share their faith with others: " '[Y]ou shall receive power when the
Holy Spirit has come upon you; and you shall be my witnesses [. . .] to the
end of the earth.' " To be a witness involves an act of self-emptying. Paul
instructs in his letter to the Philippians:

> Do nothing from selfishness or conceit, but in humility count others better
> than yourselves. Let each of you look not only to his own interests, but also
> to the interests of others. Have this mind among yourselves, which you
> have in Christ Jesus, who, though he was in the form of God, did not count
> equality with God a thing to be grasped, but emptied himself, taking the
> form of a servant, being born in the likeness of men. (2:3–7)

Paul says that Jesus humbled himself in obedience to God; therefore, God
has "highly exalted him and bestowed on him the name which is above
every name" (2:9). He tells the Christians of Philippi that every knee
should bow at the name of Christ; that "every tongue [should] confess
that Jesus Christ is Lord" (2:10–11). I became familiar with the term "witness" during that first semester I spent at James College. I remember a
teacher's comment that Adventist students were encouraged to be "good
witnesses." This subject position calls believers to testify that without the
unconditional love and forgiveness offered to them through Christ—they
would be nothing. In other words, in giving glory to God their goal is to
"renounce the clandestine imperialism of [the] self-enclosed self" (Volf
44). A witness makes a radical move when she openly acknowledges Jesus
as her personal savior; this assertion works against a fundamentally limited (and profoundly alienating) construction of the self as somehow in
control of human destiny. The primary way for such an individual to realize a selfhood is through a profound act of surrender. It thus becomes impossible to "be" or to make meaning from language except in and
through Christ.

Pride is, according to Christian teachings, the overwhelming cause of
alienation from God. It is the reason that witnesses must "die" on a daily
basis—emptying themselves of the desire for sinful indulgence. In the Seventh-day Adventist church, Ellen White cautions that entertainment (including reading) can be dangerous for anyone who professes such a belief
system: "[E]very gathering for pleasure where pride is fostered or appetite
indulged, where one is led to forget God and lose sight of eternal interests,
there Satan is binding his chains upon the soul" (*Patriarchs* 460). Adventist doctrine teaches that only the love and mercy of Christ saves human-
kind from alliance with Satan and the bondage of sin. Because human beings are the objects of God's grace, the devil despises them and seeks to
corrupt the plan of redemption in order to cause grief and bring dishonor
upon the Creator. Both the Bible and Ellen White describe Satan as a
fallen angel of God whose presence in the world is palpable and star-
tlingly real. He is at once both an external being and an innermost force

that operates deep within the self. The devil takes pleasure in spreading the belief that he does not exist and that only foolish people readily acknowledge his influence. He is an insidious master of deception—a skilled rhetorician who works to infiltrate people's thoughts and shape their words and actions (though finally, not without their consent). Satan is well aware that language shapes thought; he uses words to tempt people away from the cross. Early Adventist writing frequently employed metaphors of combat in order to show that the most effective means Christians had to defend themselves against his arsenal of cunning and sophisticated rhetorical "weapons" were reading and interpretive skills built upon a powerfully resistant critical stance. Ellen White warns all who seek Christ to remember that the devil is best thought of as a "mighty general" whose aim is to wage war against the truth of God's message: "He seeks to draw away the soldiers of the cross from their strong fortification, while he lies in ambush with his forces, ready to destroy all who venture upon his ground" (*Great* 506, 530). Witnesses must become "soldiers," then, prepared to protect their claim from the threat of a stealthy and persuasive enemy. They must not wander onto his territory or risk "capture" and permanent enslavement to sin.

THE EVANGELICAL READER AND THE CLASSROOM

Many Seventh-day Adventist Christians experience reading as a spiritual struggle because it has the potential to lead to self-indulgent thoughts, feelings, and actions. These, it is believed, give rise to the ego and cause human beings to forget their dependence upon God. It is important to note that the self-emptied approach to meaning making that Adventists and other evangelical Christians rely on to strengthen themselves against sin may come into conflict with the kind of "surrender" that some scholars encourage student readers to practice. In "Reading as Believing," for instance, Stephen Olsen, citing philosopher Michael Polanyi, explains that a "passionate pouring of oneself" (17) into the text is what he imagines taking place within his classroom. Making reference to Peter Elbow's notion of "methodological belief," he argues that for students to get the most out of reading, they should be encouraged to enter into or surrender themselves to unfamiliar ideas and experiences: "Our sympathies can be enlarged when we read wholeheartedly enough to identify with characters. Our minds are expanded when we let the fiction hold sway" (17). In his book *Textual Power*, Robert Scholes, too, states that belief welcomes a kind of pleasurable "submission" to the intentions of another (40). It seems apparent that neither Scholes nor Olsen conceives of "submission" or "surrender" in the same ways that an evangelical reader might. Olsen, in fact, makes it clear that by "belief," he does not mean "faith"—"with its religious implications of loyalty, purity, and unswaying devotion to the sovereignty of Logos" (17). Instead, he calls upon the heathen roots of the word, the Old English "lefan" ("to allow"): "We allow the text to work its magic—we make believe—but do not grant it final authority" (17). The metaphor that Olsen uses throughout his essay to describe the process by which he teaches reading is that of "promiscuity." Reading as believing involves "a willingness to try on an experience wholeheartedly but without promises—like passionate sex before marriage" (17). Olsen's choice of metaphor, again, mirrors the language that Peter Elbow uses to describe his vision of teaching reading as methodological belief. In *Embracing Contraries*, Elbow says:

> [T]he believing game asks us, as it were, to sleep with any idea that comes down the pike. [. . .] Being "promiscuous" and sleeping with the widest range of ideas (in the safety of provisionality) gives us the best chance of *finding out* what's actually in our mind and *deciding* what to keep and what to throw out. We gain some measure of control only by immersing in the dangerous element. (283–84)

The problem, of course, is that for many students who identify as evangelical, a promiscuous reading experience is decidedly forbidden. "Sleeping with" a wide range of ideas may put their identity in Christ at risk.

In their essay "Whatever Happened to Reader Response Criticism" (included in this collection), Patricia Harkin and James J. Sosnoski argue that in many composition textbooks, reception-oriented inquiry (represented by theorists such as David Bleich, Stanley Fish, and Wolfgang Iser) has been "reduced and recontextualized" into "instructions for 'finding' authorial intention as the stable meaning of texts" (104). Looking at Ramage and Bean's *Writing Arguments*, for instance, they point to the ways that students are invited to take an "unproblematized reader-response orientation" toward essays that they might be assigned. Invoking Peter Elbow's doubting and believing game, *Writing Arguments* invites students to read as believers, as doubters, or as "analysts." Harkin and Sosnoski note that reading as believing, practiced by summarizing and restating a given argument, is not seen as "in any way problematic. Instead, instructions [. . .] are given as if students who held beliefs contrary to the one argued could suspend them at will, clearing the ground for a detached engagement of opposing beliefs" (118). Interestingly, in *Embracing Con-*

traries, Peter Elbow explains that theorist Stanley Fish responded to a draft of his essay on methodological doubting and believing, and that his reaction was one of skepticism. Fish, reiterating Harkin and Sosnoski's position, argued that it did not make sense to talk about "choosing" or "rejecting" a viewpoint "because to do so implies a self that stands outside its own beliefs" (268). Elbow's reaction to Fish's claim is that doubting and believing must be deployed as a method; thus, even though human beings cannot really stand outside of their own positions, they can at least "artificially" do so in an act of playing an imaginative game. While I appreciate the desire that Elbow has to move his students, at times, out of their own comfort zones and to engage with ideas unfamiliar to them (an objective that I think most writing instructors share), I'm not entirely convinced that the metaphor of "promiscuous game" serves his argument, or teachers in the classroom, best. I do believe that students for whom reading is a spiritual struggle will be more likely to engage critically with texts if "free will" or the power of choice is emphasized to them (as mentioned previously, the Bible makes it clear that the devil does not, finally, control people's thoughts or ideas without their consent). With evangelical students, however, this approach would be untenable if devised in the form of a dangerous or risky "make believe" game.

When a student who identifies as Christian refuses to read an assigned text, he or she is most likely responding to a fear that submitting to it may lead to sinfulness. Teachers of writing who encounter religious readers in the classroom would serve these students best by resisting the urge to immediately label their response "close minded" or lacking in readerly sophistication. The Adventist reader whom I quoted much earlier in this essay, for example, explained to me that several years after purging his bookshelves of certain texts, he was asked to read *The Turn of the Screw* for an English class. He almost had to drop out of the class because of his refusal to do so:

> I got into it and I said, no [. . .] I just felt like it was taking me where I didn't want to go. And if it weren't for one professor who stepped in and said "Well, let's find an alternate book" [. . .] you know, I was reading *Tom Jones* at the time, I was reading *Light in August*, I was reading a number of different things, so I mean we're not talking about just reading Christian, per se, books. [. . .] However, this one, James, you know, the spirit, kind of creepy—it just seemed to be of the enemy. And I just didn't want it. It just didn't work for me.

Although he opted not to finish James's novel, this reader expressed the conviction that he had tried to act from integrity: "I was willing to read a number of other things [but] I did not want to glorify the dark side." He also suggested that for some Christians, the "implied author" can be a powerful force working within a text:

> I'm not of the belief that, you know, a "letter" is evil or a word is evil. But symbols communicate. Symbols have power to our minds and different symbols can act in different ways. For me, the symbols that I was confronting in James were leading me to a place that I didn't want to go. I just didn't feel like I could be faithful doing this. I felt uncomfortable with it and, you know [. . .] I acknowledge it's a classic. And I acknowledge that there are a lot of good things about it. In good conscience, I couldn't go there. And I would say that there are feminists who feel the same way in certain areas, you know. There are Muslims who are going to feel the same way in certain areas. There are just certain places where you say I'm not going to do that because of who I am and [what guides] my life.

Every reader makes meaning of language from a particular social and cultural stance; thus, our own ideological convictions, even if these are not primarily religious, shape our attitudes about text and the comfort level that we feel when we confront ideas that may be different or disturbing to us. In "good faith," sometimes, we decide that—as this reader states—certain ideas may lead us to places where we simply do not want to go (though I am sure that we ourselves would not want to be labeled "naive" or narrow-minded). For some evangelical students who decline to read a book that we have assigned, then, the best possible solution may be to negotiate and to choose an alternative selection. Other students may be willing to read if we prepare them, in advance, for what they are likely to encounter.

Several years ago at James College, two English teachers in separate classes assigned the same novel for their students to read. In one class, complaints about the book and its depiction of spiritualism eventually reached the dean. In the other class, however, few problems occurred. I spoke with the instructor who used the book without controversy and he explained to me that before students ever begin reading an assigned text, he discusses its content with them. "In most cases, I can get a feel for [students who might be tentative about reading] even before we begin a text, and prepare them for what's there. I try to be quite straightforward about what the student will encounter." This instructor often uses analogy to help students become more comfortable with content that might be disturbing to them. For example, when teaching a play such as *Macbeth*, he spends time describing the opening scene (in which three witches are conjuring spirits) and compares it to the story of Saul, in the Bible, who visits a medium in order to conjure the spirit of Samuel (1 Samuel 28). Thus, by drawing upon a text that is familiar to students, he is able to ease their fears about the spiritual elements of the play and creates a more safe reading environment: "So we're pushing, we're questioning, but we're also doing it within an environment that is safe to do that." Students can also be warned in advance about sexual content or language that they may consider to be offensive. Teachers then have the opportunity to ask readers to think about why a text has been constructed in such a way and what effect those choices have upon an audience.

Evangelical students will be more likely to "soldier on" if their apprehensions are treated seriously and addressed. To quote, again, L. W. Cobb, they will feel "better trained and equipped," learning of the "snares and pitfalls" first—"then the positive instructions [will] stand out clear and meaningful" (13). Teachers in the composition classroom can help them by emphasizing that, in the spirit of Peter Elbow's argument, readers do have some measure of "free will" to reject or to accept the ideas that they encounter. Doubting or believing is not done in promiscuous fashion, however; for Christians, certainly, the power of choice is a central part of biblical theology:

> To be able to understand that you can encounter an idea, try it on, accept or reject as you are moved to do, that is a very powerful concept. I think that one avenue in making that move with students [who identify as Christian], is to look at the idea of the power of choice. That informs Adventist theology throughout. [Our theology] is a matter of decisions and choices. And to emphasize that's something that we're doing. [. . .] Otherwise, we would be paralyzed in this life because, you know, we're obviously exposed to a great deal—whether it be language or sexual content in advertising or whatever. We can't completely insulate ourselves. We have that power to choose.

This Adventist teacher, the same individual quoted earlier, explained to me that in building a theology of the devil, writers most often imagined and described Satan as nefarious, ubiquitous, and overwhelmingly compelling. The objective, of course, was to create a worthy adversary. The result, however, is that the devil is thought of as something more powerful than human beings and their abilities to choose. God is, in fact, the master of the devil and each individual has the ability to reject Satan's influence in his or her daily life.

In conclusion, I want to argue that perhaps all of our students, not only those who read from a religious perspective, benefit from the work that we do in advance to prepare them for what they are going to encounter in a text. Especially in the first-year classroom, they may be more receptive to thinking critically about reading if teachers have initially taken the time to build a culture that emphasizes the safe exploration of new or perhaps uncomfortable ideas. Rather than asking students to "play games" of believing and doubting, teachers should be up front about the very real ways that our culturally constructed identities shape our attitudes about text and the uncertainties that we feel when confronting beliefs different than our own. Our classrooms should be spaces that, in good faith, promote conversation about the complexities of readerly responses.

NOTES

1. The Adventist church was cofounded by Ellen White and her husband James along with Joseph Bates, a former sea captain, in Battle Creek, Michigan. Its origins, however, can be traced to the 1830s when a Baptist preacher from New York, William Miller, became convinced of the imminent return of Jesus Christ ("Adventist," in fact, comes from the word *advent*, which means the coming of something). Miller and his followers believed that Christ would return in 1843–44. Many believers eventually sold their homes, farms, and other worldly possessions in the faith that Miller's prediction would be correct. The "Great Disappointment," however, occurred on October 22, 1844, and it was a month later that Ellen White, a convert from Methodism to the Advent movement, received her first vision from God at a Portland, Maine, prayer meeting.
2. "Spiritualism," in the words of one Adventist, can be defined as "the first great deception. In Genesis when the serpent was in the garden and Eve was offered the fruit, he told her 'ye shall surely not die.' So throughout the ages, [Satan] has been scheming through all these spiritual ways to get people to think that they won't die when they die. So he is the one who will show up as people's relatives. And if somebody tells me, you know, it kind of puts a fear through my heart when they say 'Oh, you know, my mom came and visited me.' " Seventh-day Adventists believe that when human beings die, their souls sleep until the time of the Second Coming. The spirit of a person who has been "saved" does not immediately go to heaven. Thus, some believers are troubled by reading books, novels, etc. that include elements of spiritualism, i.e., communicating with people from beyond, new age theory, hypnosis or altered states, ghosts or other spirits, etc. They believe supernatural occurrences, because they lead people to believe that they will live forever (regardless of the consequences of their sinful actions) are of the devil.
3. For more information about current research methodologies in the field of composition studies, see such texts as *Methods and Methodology in Composition Research*, eds. Gesa Kirsch and Patricia Sullivan (Carbondale: Southern Illinois UP, 1992). Also *Into the Field: Sites of Composition Studies*, ed. Anne Ruggles Gere (New York: MLA, 1993) and *Ethics and Representation in Qualitative Studies of Literacy*, eds. Peter Mortensen and Gesa E. Kirsch (Urbana: NCTE, 1996).
4. In composition studies, some essays have appeared that challenge writing instructors to consider more fully the powerful role of religion in students' lives. These include Amy Goodburn's "It's a Question of Faith: Discourses of Fundamentalism and Critical Ped-

agogy in the Writing Classroom" (*Journal of Advanced Composition* 18 [1998]: 333–52) and Janice Neuleib's "Spilt Religion: Student Motivation and Values-Based Writing" (*Writing on the Edge* 4 [1992]: 41–50). See also my essay "Enacting Faith: Evangelical Discourse and the Discipline of Composition Studies" (*College Composition and Communication* 52 [2001]: 349–67). Nevertheless, I would argue that conversation about religious identity and faith-related response to reading and writing remains lacking. Issues of race, class, and gender have been foregrounded most often in the field's analyses of the ways that identity influences response to reading and writing. Discussions about religion have, in the past, often taken the form of complaints about students' "dogmatic" habits of mind or embarrassing testimonials that they have written.

5. Matei Calinescu, in *Rereading*, points out that as far back as the sixteenth and seventeenth centuries, reading for pleasure was associated with "escape and irresponsibility" (89). He contends that sacred texts (particularly the Bible) create a "habit of awed attention," but "this habit can only be misapplied to what should normally be the quick linear reading of lighter entertaining texts" (79). Calinescu's argument points to a central tension about reading within the Seventh-day Adventist church. "Lighter entertaining texts" are so vilified in historical Adventist writings that it may be difficult for some devout believers to treat them as anything but potentially dangerous and destructive.

WORKS CITED

Barizo, Jennifer Mae. "Truth Is on the March." *Adventist Review* 20 April 2000: 22.

Calinescu, Matei. *Rereading*. New Haven: Yale UP, 1993.

Carter, Stephen L. *The Culture of Disbelief: How American Law and Politics Trivialize Religious Devotion*. New York: Anchor, 1993.

Cobb, L. W. *Give Attendance to Reading*. Portland, 1966.

Elbow, Peter. *Embracing Contraries: Explorations in Learning and Teaching*. New York: Oxford UP, 1986.

"Fifteenth Business Meeting Actions." *Adventist Review* 20–27 July 2000: 67–76.

Long, Elizabeth. "Textual Interpretation as Collective Action." *The Ethnography of Reading*. Ed. Jonathan Boyarin. Berkeley: U of California P, 1993. 180–211.

Olsen, Stephen. "Reading as Believing." *ADE Bulletin* 102 (1992): 17–19.

Scholes, Robert. *Textual Power: Literary Theory and the Teaching of English*. New Haven: Yale UP, 1985.

Volf, Miroslav. "Truth, Freedom, and Violence." *Christianity and Culture in the Crossfire*. Eds. David A. Hoekema and Bobby Fong. Grand Rapids: Eerdmans, 1997. 28–50.

White, Ellen G. *The Great Controversy*. Nampa, ID: Pacific, 1950.

———. *Patriarchs and Prophets*. Boise, ID: Pacific, 1952.

THEORY

Albert Joseph Moore, *A Reader*, © Manchester City Art Galleries.

4

The Master Double Frame and Other Lessons from Classical Education

Nancy L. Christiansen

"Classical education" is "Hellenistic education," H. I. Marrou reminds us in his renowned *Education in Antiquity* (95). In the generation after Aristotle and Alexander the Great, when education became standardized throughout the Greek world, rhetoric held center place in the curriculum. Founded not on Plato's, but on Isocrates's educational program,[1] primary and secondary schools prepared scholars in civilized practices through literary and language-arts-based instruction. Marrou says of this curriculum, "The primary fact is that ever since the time of Isocrates and the Sophists, and in spite of all the political and social revolutions that had taken place, eloquence had been the main cultural objective, the crown and completion of any liberal education worthy of the name" (196). This curriculum remained in place in those parts of the world influenced by Greek civilization until well into the Middle Ages. Roman educators merely adopted and added onto the Hellenistic curriculum, making it suitable for Roman circumstances. This Greco-Roman tradition is best described by Quintilian, the great Roman schoolmaster, who in the four-volume *Institutio Oratoria* details what had been for almost two centuries the education of a youth from birth to manhood. Donald A. Russell has explained why we can look to Quintilian for an account of this system:

> The conservatism of rhetorical teaching over such a long period makes it possible to give an account of it as a system, based on the late textbooks

which survive, without feeling that one's conclusions are likely to be fundamentally wrong for the earlier period. Quintilian is undoubtedly the best
guide. (25)

It was then the rediscovery of the complete text of Quintilitan that significantly influenced the curricular reform of the humanists, whose rein-
stantiation of this system helped to usher in the Renaissance throughout
Western Europe and preserved Greco-Roman foundations for Western
education until the mid-eighteenth century.

Any discussion of what it means to read, what relations inhere between reading and writing, literature and composition, "the word and
the world,"[2] and how reading and writing should be taught must consider how these questions can be answered from this tradition that not
only invented the language arts, but also influenced the literary achievements of Western civilization for at least two millenia. The longevity of
the tradition—the fact that numerous educators from diverse cultures
and time periods found value in its precepts and methods—also invites
a consideration of whether those precepts and methods continue to
hold value today.

THE CLASSICAL LANGUAGE-ARTS CURRICULUM

Reading—the analysis and criticism of texts—held a central place, alongside writing and speaking, in this curriculum. The goal of this curriculum
was *facilitas,* or eloquence, which included the ability to speak extemporaneously and appropriately on any subject to any audience on any occasion and the ability to hit upon the right solution when making decisions
in the complexity of human affairs. In a world where human knowledge,
because a construct, remains less than certain, but where decisions still
must be made, *facilitas* was the mark of the genuinely cultivated human.
In order to develop this ability in both fluency and judgment, pupils engaged in reading, writing, and speaking activities, which together taught
both reason and speech. Quintilian explains not only the natural reciprocity among these activities, but also their utter inseparability:

[Writing, reading and speaking] are so intimately and inseparably connected, that if one of them be neglected, we shall but waste the labour which
we have devoted to the others. For eloquence will never attain to its full development or robust health, unless it acquires strength by frequent practice
in writing, while such practice without the models supplied by reading will

be like a ship drifting aimlessly without a steersman. Again, he who knows what he ought to say and how he should say it, will be like a miser brooding over his hoarded treasure, unless he has the weapons of his eloquence ready for battle and prepared to deal with every emergency. (X.i.1–3)

Activities in these three skills were integrated into a uniform method of study known as Imitation. The steps of Imitation, applicable to both elementary and advanced exercises, were as follows for the pupils once they knew the rudiments of reading and writing.

Reading Aloud

The chosen text is introduced to the students through an oral performance. Either the schoolmaster or a more advanced student gives this reading. The focus here is on not only enunciation, but also pronunciation (delivery)—that is, the proper use of voice and gesture. Quintilian advises:

> In this connexion there is much that can only be taught in actual practice, as for instance when the boy should take breath, at what point he should introduce a pause into a line, where the sense ends or begins, when the voice should be raised or lowered, what modulation should be given to each phrase, and when he should increase or slacken speed, or speak with greater or less energy. In this portion of my work I will give but one golden rule: to do all these things, he must understand what he reads. (I.viii.1–2)

The understanding required in order to decide on the proper voice and gesture involves an interpretation not only of subject matter, but also of the author's motives, attitudes, passions, strategies, and judgment—in short, "the character of the speaker" (XI.iii.62, 66, 150–81). Gaining this understanding requires locating texts not in print, but in performance, and seeing texts as purposeful "acts" before hearers in a certain place, time, and social situation. It also assumes these acts have meaning and that text is fundamentally behavior, mental and social. A complete reading requires interpreting not only the main ideas expressed in the words or signs, but also all the meanings expressed by the performance. It requires returning the text to life—seeing, hearing, and enacting the words or signs as the expression of a character in a drama.

The texts chosen came from all the genres: poetry, drama, myth, history, philosophy, epistle, oratory. Quintilian asserts, "[E]very kind of writer must be carefully studied" (I.iv.4).[3] The implication that follows is that all texts, no matter the genre, are authorial performances reflecting character. The texts were chosen to suit the student's age, theme assignment, and precepts being taught.

Analysis of Text

Either the *grammaticus* (teacher of literature, elementary level) or the *rhetor* (teacher of oratory, advanced level) takes students through a close analysis of the chosen passage, pointing out not only the main ideas, but also the authorial decisions, both macro and micro, pertaining to the principles the students are to learn and apply. In this step, the teaching of precept is combined with the modeling of precept. These precepts derive from the practice of the experts and describe "nature." These meta-cognitive principles have been identified in order to teach the processes and bring them under conscious control. Under the *grammaticus,* the focus remains on grammar, style, usage, etymology, orthography, meter, rhythm, and narrative. Under the *rhetor,* logic and rhetoric receive greatest attention.[4] In pointing out authorial decisions, the master also evaluates their effectiveness, and though being thorough, shows good judgment himself by not becoming "encumbered with superfluous detail" (I.viii.18). When the students are ready, the teacher is to help increase their judgment by presenting them with faulty examples alongside the good (II.v.10) and by leading the students through the critical process by means of questions until they can proceed independently: "For what else is our object in teaching, save that our pupils should not always require to be taught?" (II.v.13–14).

James J. Murphy has observed that this reading method "is the beginning of the application of judgment. [. . .] The immediate intent is to show the students how the author made good or bad choices in wording, in organization, in the use of figures, and the like: the long-range objective is to accustom the student to what today we could call a 'close reading' of texts" (46). Indeed, students learned that reading involved both comprehension and evaluation and that both required an attention to detail, to the whole, and to the context. In focusing the reader's attention on the decisions the text's author made and on the meaning and quality of those decisions, this analytical approach focuses the reader's attention on the author's judgment or artistry with the purpose of developing the reader's judgment or artistry, a judgment that will show up in the writing and speaking of the reader.

Memorization of the Good Models

Since the objective is to have not only words, expressions, and quotations, but thought patterns, subjects, and procedures ready for extemporaneous use, memorization is a necessary component of language learning. In addition, memorization provides, according to Quintilian, "an intimate acquaintance with the best writings" and will enable students to "carry their models with them and unconsciously reproduce the style of the speech which has been impressed upon the memory" (II.vii.3–4).

Transformation of Models

After analysis, the students move to writing activities that require various manipulations of the model text. These writing exercises involve translation, paraphrase, metaphrase, and imitation proper and are practiced in conjunction with the *progymnasmata* (preliminary exercises), the *gymnasmata* (exercises), and real-life declamations. These rewritings of models depend upon textual interpretation and reveal revisions to be interpretations. These activities teach the kind of "athletic reading" Marcel Cornis-Pope and Ann Woodlief also argue for (chap. 7, this volume), the metaphor itself coming from the Greek.[5]

The *progymnasmata* were a graded sequence of fourteen themes providing practice in reading/writing both narrative and expository genres and the various parts of a declamation. In the elementary years, the student usually practices writing the first four themes: the *fable,* the *tale,* the *chreia* (elaboration of a famous person's speech or action), and the *proverb* (elaboration of a maxim), although not necessarily in this order. As the student advances, he progresses through the remaining exercises: the *confirmation, refutation, commonplace* (denunciation for punishment), *encomium* (praise), *vituperation, comparison, impersonation* (speech-in-character), *description, thesis* (defense of general question), and *legislation* (praise or denunciation of a law).[6] He also repeats all these exercises in varying order, transforming them in more complex ways.[7] When ready, the student advances to the *gymnasmata* or mock-declamations, of which there were two: the *suasoria* (advice to a specific person for a particular course of action) and the *controversia* (a plea either in defense or prosecution of a person or idea). Although based on possible-life scenarios, these expository speeches were fictional.[8] Finally, the budding orator witnesses and judges declamations actually delivered in law courts (judicial), in advisory situations (deliberative), or on ceremonial occasions (epideictic), and then prepares his own. The master provides the model texts for the younger students; the more advanced choose their own.

Translation. The Roman system, because founded on both Greek and Latin literature, of necessity required bilingual training. Hence, one method for learning involved translating a Greek passage into Latin or vice versa. Students must recapture as closely as possible the explicit and implicit meanings of the original. Besides requiring close reading, translation awakens students to the transferability of general artistic principles and meanings, but the nontransferability of particular signs, structures, and nuances.

Paraphrase. In this exercise, the pupil must rephrase the original, capturing the same ideas but expressing them in either fewer or more words. The pupil may work with a sentence, a passage, or an entire work. The pupil's purpose, however, as Quintilian explains, is always "to rival and vie with the original in the expression of the same thoughts" (X.v.5). This exercise teaches the reader to find the main idea, but also to appreciate the changing nuances expressed as she recasts the idea. In addition, Quintilian explains that "there is no better way of acquiring a thorough understanding of the greatest authors. For, instead of hurriedly running a careless eye over their writings, we handle each separate phrase and are forced to give it close examination" (X.v.8). This exercise also teaches the writer that there are many ways to express a thought, but that "brevity and copiousness each have their own peculiar grace, the merits of metaphor are one thing and of literalness another, and, while direct expression is most effective in one case, in another the best result is gained by a use of figures" (X.v.8). Furthermore, this exercise develops *copia*, as Erasmus so aptly demonstrates by turning one sentence into one hundred and forty-five restatements in his Renaissance school textbook, *De Copia* (348–54).

Metaphrase. This variation, so named by the Renaissance schoolmaster Roger Ascham in *The Scholemaster* (243), requires the student to turn prose into verse or verse into prose, or to shift from one meter to another. This exercise Quintilian treats as a kind of paraphrase (X.v.4) and John Brinsley, another Renaissance schoolmaster, treats as a kind of translation (193), suggesting its close affiliation with the exercises preceding. This exercise certainly blurs the boundaries between prose and poetic genres, suggesting that meter and rhythm become one of the most significant distinguishing features between the two, a conclusion Cicero explicitly expresses in *De Oratore:*

The truth is that the poet is a very near kinsman of the orator, rather more heavily fettered as regards rhythm, but with ampler freedom in his choice of words, while in the use of many sorts of ornament he is his ally and almost his counterpart; in one respect at all events something like identity exists, since he sets no boundaries or limits to his claims, such as would prevent him from ranging whither he will with the same freedom and license as the other. (I.xvi.70–1)

Students would not only have to interpret the poem or prose in order to recast it, but also consider the new constraints of occasion for the new genre. The student would also practice a variety of styles and would come to understand the different meanings of those styles.

Imitation Proper.   The student produces a full-length text of his own by adding to, subtracting from, substituting, or altering the model's content or form or both. Guidelines for such transformations of *fables* or *tales,* for example, include adding or subtracting descriptions, speeches for the characters, other narrative illustrations from history or myth, an explication, or praise of the author; moving the moral from the end to the beginning or retelling the tale by starting in the middle or at the end; or changing place, character, time, thing done, the manner of doing, or the cause. The pupil also may confirm or refute the tale. To rewrite a *chreia* or a *thesis,* a pupil would add or subtract new proofs, analogies, testimonies, precedents, praise or criticism of the first author, figures of speech, *exempla,* and so forth; choose a new subject and invent proofs that matched the kinds given in the model; or rearrange the order, change the style, or possibly transform the expository form into a literary form—one that enacts the argument as a debate between characters.

Such practice makes students aware of the many features of discourse and provides them a rich repertoire of discursive choices. Stored in their mental cornucopia would be ready-made elements that could be imported whole into new discourses, but also heuristics for finding proofs, methods for developing the parts of any speech (exordium, narration, proposition/ division, confirmations, refutations, peroration), and stylistic strategies for phonetic, lexical, syntactic, generic, and pragmatic fashioning of discourse. (This classical tradition provided a detailed list of textual features.) Besides elements, though, students would also acquire knowledge of the elements' functions/effects and, by extension, the principles guiding their use. Since rewriting requires producing a better text, students must do more than simply find textual elements; they must see how and how well those elements in the model function. Since functions mirror motives, students see that purposes guide the construction of texts and that the processes of construction can be brought under conscious control. By looking for the elements in application, students also benefit from precept without mistaking precept for formula.

Self-Correction

The process of choosing the best words, patterns, strategies, order, subject, and style—of exercising good judgment—entails frequent revision. Quintilian does not recommend that revision be postponed until the composition is drafted; rather, we should "exercise care from the very beginning, and [. . .] form the work from the outset in such a manner that it merely requires to be chiselled into shape, not fashioned anew" (X.iii.18). "Correction," Quintilian tells us, "takes the form of addition, excision and alteration" (X.iv.1). Making these changes entails the same reading procedures as those used in transforming one's models.

Recitation and Public Correction[9]

With schoolmaster and peers as audience, the student now either performs from memory or reads aloud his own finished composition. The advanced pupil may invent the declamation extemporaneously before the live audience. The pupil's text (performance) is then analyzed, evaluated, and corrected by peers and master. Quintilian defends this practice because it creates incentive to win commendation, it allows the more advanced pupils to set examples for the younger students, and it makes it possible for all students to benefit from the praise and corrections given to all every day (I.ii.21–26). Although Quintilian does not say so, this practice connects the word to the world, since texts only fully exist in performance, behavior.

   A frequent criticism levied against this system is that it prevented students from learning to think for themselves and fostered adherence to traditional ideas, rather than discovery of new. Such a charge, however, overlooks four significant details. First, even though the pupils imitate models, the resulting compositions are not copies, but transformations of the originals. Second, the pupils acquired from this practice not only memorized quotations, patterns, and typical lines of argument, but also the principles by which to create new discourse-chunks and to make judgments about their use. The precepts of grammar, logic, and rhetoric (meta-cognition) name the experts' principles of judgment. These principles, it is true, functioned as models—standards—to be imitated; however, principle had to be considered for its appropriateness to context. It was then the judgment of the good author the pupils were to imitate primarily, not necessarily the particular words, patterns, strategies, opinions, or rules. Third, because the pupils were always to "rival and vie" with the models and because the new text, having its own new purpose, author, and audience, could never match the achievement of the original if it remained a copy, the new text could never be a mere imitation. If the practitioner imitated the good judgment of the model author, the new text would naturally differ from the original. This effort to vie with the original made the imitator's own compositions arguments with their models, even if confirmations of them. Fourth, with imitation focusing primarily on judgment (critical thinking), not specific content, and the rules general enough to transfer from context to context, the tradition passed on not formulaic conventions and unexamined beliefs, but heuristics and decision-making strategies. Imitation produced not copy, but *copia*—a synonym for *facilitas*,[10] which results from a large storehouse of materials and heuristics and good judgment to govern their use.

Quintilian defends imitation along these lines. It is impossible to learn without imitation, he says: "In fact, we may note that the elementary study of every branch of learning is directed by reference to some definite standard that is placed before the learner. We must, in fact, either be like or unlike those who have proved their excellence. It is rare for nature to produce such resemblance, which is more often the result of imitation" (X.ii.3). But, he then cautions, we cannot merely imitate, for then we would never discover anything new (X.ii.5), add to our knowledge (X.ii.9), nor achieve the excellence of our models, for mere imitation "is artificial and moulded to a purpose which was not that of the original orator" (X.ii.11). Furthermore, "it is quite impossible to teach everything that can be accomplished by art" (VII.x.9). The pupil must keep his eye on nature (VII.x.9). In addition, not all models are equally good nor appropriate for one's purposes, and even great authors "have their blemishes" (X.ii.15). "Consequently the nicest judgment is required in the examination of everything connected with this department of study" (X.ii.14). Stressing the importance of competing with the model, Quintilian asserts, "But the man who to these good qualities adds his own, that is to say, who makes good deficiencies and cuts down whatever is redundant, will be the perfect orator of our search" (X.ii.28).

Further justification for such a pedagogical method comes from contemporary research in the cognitive psychology of education. Ruth Garner in *Metacognition and Reading Comprehension,* for example, defends a method very similar to this classical one. She explains that teachers must render overt the processes involved in reading while modeling the processes (131) in order to create readers—"interactive learners who direct their own cognitive resources to learn from text" (15). In modeling, the teacher needs to show in many examples how and why the strategy is applied and how appropriately it has been applied (110). The teacher must also use contrastive examples, so the students can distinguish the sophisticated from the immature (132). The teacher must show the strategies to be applicable to texts in different disciplines and genres (134), and finally, "teachers must teach strategies over an entire year, not in just a single lesson or unit" (135). Enough practice is requisite for these strategies to become habit and students should gradually be given responsibility for self-evaluation and self-direction (136). Evidence suggests that these pedagogical practices are necessary in order to teach judgment and transfer. Without explicit focus on processes, the strategic activity will be largely unobservable, she claims (131). Without the proper modeling, "learners [. . .] are likely to apply routines in rote fashion in both appropriate and inappropriate instances" (108).

Roland G. Tharp and Ronald Gallimore in *Rousing Minds to Life* also cite evidence to support their claim that "Modeling is a powerful means of assisting performance, one that continues its effectiveness into adult years and into the highest reaches of behavioral complexity" (49). They quote from A. Bandura, who from his research also argues:

> Modeling has been shown to be a highly effective means of establishing abstract or rule-governed behavior. On the basis of observationally derived rules, people learn, among other things, judgmental orientations, linguistic styles, conceptual schemes, information-processing strategies, cognitive operations, and standards of conduct. Evidence that generalizable rules of thought and conduct can be induced through abstract modeling reveals the broad scope of observational learning. (qtd. in Tharp and Gallimore 49)

But, Tharp and Gallimore remind us, modeling needs to be accompanied by "cognitive structuring" (precepts), questioning, feeding-back, and instructing in order to be most effective (63).

Even in this compilation, Cornis-Pope and Woodlief (chap. 7, this volume) and Mariolina Salvatori (chap. 9, this volume) report from their experiences that students need models and that the activities of rereading and rewriting lead to "critical production." So, too, Cain and Kalamaras assert that reading cannot be separated from writing, since "interpretation becomes an integral part of composition via observation of its forms" (chap. 8, this volume). But, I would add, as Garner and Tharp and Gallimore do, that along with models, students need precepts. Leaving students to describe their own analytical processes without introducing to them already known features of text and context asks them to continually rediscover the wheel, a slow and chancy endeavor, when by showing them the wheel, we can then enable them to invent the turbine.

THE CLASSICAL DECLAMATION
AS THE MASTER DOUBLE FRAME

An important implication to emerge from this instructional program, one that enables its efficiency and effectiveness, is that there is a master genre—the declamation—framing all discourse, a genre that is by nature double—both drama and argument. Rhetoric provided the theory of composition and criticism for all discourse. Even though superficial differences between genres were acknowledged, all texts were read fundamentally as declamations. Indeed, as Walter J. Ong and Don Paul Abbott have both commented about the Renaissance curriculum, during this time we find the tyranny of the oration (Ong 53; Abbott 106). Besides the fact that the concluding exercise for which all preliminary study prepared the orator was the full-fledged oration, each preliminary model and theme was itself treated as both a dramatic performance and an argument.

All texts from all the genres were "declaimed"—they were performed. From beginning to end of the imitation process, the written text was treated as if it were a transcript of oral performance. Quintilian quite explicitly indicates that "there is absolutely no difference between writing and speaking well, and that a written speech is merely a record of one that has actually been delivered" (XII.x.51). Not only the declaiming, but also the school exercises themselves highlighted the dramatic nature of texts.

For example, the *impersonation* (speech-in-character) is direct instruction in dramatic monologue. The student must write a speech for a particular mythological or historical person speaking to a particular audience on a particular occasion, and must use a style appropriate to the speaker's character. In its writing, the student would discover that the speech itself creates the character, just as it reveals how the student interprets the character. For models, the student would find an endless supply in epic and dramatic poetry. The *commonplace* too becomes an impersonation. In this exercise, the student must put on the role of advocate and imagine speaking to the courtroom audience. Since the commonplace is the portion of the trial when the condemned's crimes are denounced in order to argue for an appropriate sentence, the student must have also imagined the earlier portions and participants of the trial. Exercises in the mock *declamations* are also role plays, evidenced by the examples themselves being dramatic dialogues.[11] Even though "a false semblance of reality" (X.v.17), these speeches Quintilian considers a valuable learning tool, for "if we speak with a desire for improvement, there will be no difference [between] our declamations and genuine [. . .] oratory" (II.x.9).

The other less obviously dramatic exercises also would have provided similar insights. One of the ways to elaborate a *fable* or *tale* is to give extended speeches to the characters, and once students glimpsed the characters' speeches as *impersonations,* they would inevitably see the fable/tale itself as a dramatic monologue of an author. Because the *confirmation* and *refutation* were both written about the same myth, together they form a dialogue, debate. The *thesis* and *legislation* themes, in incorporating both argument and counterargument, combine the dialogue within one frame. Once every text is seen as a performance of a speaker participating in dialogue or debate, it is a short step to see life itself as a drama. Interestingly, the metaphor "life is a stage" seems to be endemic to societies influenced by this rhetorical tradition, as E. R. Curtius notes in *European Literature and the Latin Middle Ages* (138–44). Kenneth Burke also understands the rhetorical tradition in this way when he claims that "the ultimate metaphor for discussing the universe and man's place in it must be the poetic or dramatic metaphor" (*Permanence and Change* 263).

Not only are texts performances, but they are also arguments. Some genres from the school exercises are obviously so: the *chreia, proverb, refutation, confirmation, encomium, vituperation, comparison, commonplace, thesis, legislation,* and *declamation.* But even the remaining types—the *fable, tale, description,* and *impersonation*—are treated as arguments. Both *fables* and *tales* have didactic intent. The *fable* comes with a moral that can be stated as a maxim. The maxim was understood as a proposition, argument, and the story as illustration, proof. *Tales* too could function as proofs within a larger speech. Furthermore, one way to transform the fable or tale is to refute or confirm it, using such criteria as consideration of possibility, consistency, clarity, propriety, and rationality.[12] Indeed, the exercises called *refutation* and *confirmation* required not a pro and contra treatment of an issue, but instead a favorable or unfavorable judgment passed upon the verisimilitude and morality of myths/tales. Also, it is only a short step from refuting/confirming a narrative through the genre of criticism to refuting/confirming it through a narrative retelling, especially since a common transformation of the narrative was an adding, deleting, or changing of detail and/or moral in order to vie with the original. The pupil would be asserting that the revised tale was a better rendition than the original—more true to life. Once again, a confirmation would not entail an exact duplication of the original, but a recasting that made the same argument. Since narratives function as proofs in arguments and narratives are "speech acts" of authors, narratives standing alone would also naturally function as arguments. Renaissance educators saw them so. Erasmus says the fable was invented to persuade (*De Copia* 631–32). Richard Rainolde, who wrote a textbook of the *progymnasmata* in the Renaissance, comments that the fable's purpose is to move an audience to virtuous action (sig. A.ii.v–iii.r).

The *description* is also argument. Its purpose is to develop the orator's capacity to present vividly to view the place, object, person, event, or thing being set forth. Yet, the purpose for such vividness is to "penetrate to the emotions of the hearer[s]" (Quintilian VIII.iii.68), moving them to action. Furthermore, when the description stands on its own as a theme, it functions to illustrate the theme's central point, usually a judgment about the quality of the thing described (Aphthonius 280; Rainolde sig. N.iv.r–O.i.r). Description, by nature, implies judgment, it seems.

The *impersonation* readily reveals all speeches to be arguments. Scenarios commonly used for this exercise included how Niobe might have spoken after her children were murdered, Achilles over the body of Patroclus, Medea about to slay her children, Ajax when deprived of the arms of Achilles, Medea on Jason's marriage to Creusa, Juno when unable to deflect the Trojan King from Italy, or Zeus when upraiding Helios for lending his sun-chariot to Phaethon.[13] These speeches moved from a focus on the present circumstances, to a recollection of the past, and then to a consideration of the future. Whether a soliloquy or an address, the speech-in-character expressed praise or blame and was ultimately concerned with future action. These speeches became, then, both *controversia* and *suasoria* at once, even if not organized as formal arguments. Indeed, Quintilian recognized the close affinity between this exercise and both deliberative and judicial oratory (III.viii.49–54). In searching for literary and historical occasions that would provide settings for the impersonation, students would come to see that any occasion would do, since all speeches are consciously designed "acts" performed before audiences in order to produce an effect upon and elicit a reaction from them. Hence, all texts are *suasoria.* Since no decision about action takes place without praise or blame (defense or accusation), all texts are also *controversia.* The same insights come when students write speeches for the characters in tales and when advanced students write declamations for historical or fictional persons.

Once the inseparable relationship between the *controversia* and *suasoria* is recognized, all the theme exercises are seen both to imply judgment and elicit action. The *description* entails both, as explained above. In the epilogues to the *chreia* and the *proverb,* students are advised to urge or eschew emulation.[14] The *encomium* or *vituperation* implicitly encourages or discourages emulation. When defending or attacking a law, the student must consider what actions would follow from its instantiation, that is, whether the law can be enforced, what degrees of punishment should be affixed, and whether the law has universal applicability. Both judgment and decision about a future course of action are also combined in the *commonplace,* for this speech before a judge blames a person or thing and then argues for a sentence based upon that judgment. The *thesis* deliberates about an action based upon its quality. The *fable* or *tale* commends advantageous behaviors. Every text, then, argues for a course of action and for a system of values upon which to judge. The principles a speaker bases his judgments upon become models for those persuaded to act as he or she has wished.

Even though classical oratory divides arguments into three general types—the epideictic, deliberative, and judicial—the three naturally entail one another, then. Grounds for accusing and defending (judicial oratory) encompass the grounds for praising and blaming (epideictic oratory), so that the *controversia* models the process of making judgments about the likelihood and quality of acts, ideas, choices, and characters. Decisions about action (deliberative oratory, *suasoria*) naturally follow from and are implicit in judgments about the proper and improper. With the declamation the fundamental genre and that genre inclusive of both judgments about action and calls for action, every text places the audience in the role of judge and the speaker in the role of an advocate who has already judged. The teaching of judgment to both reader and writer is indeed central to this curriculum.

The fact of a master frame receives further reinforcement from the generic inclusiveness of these exercises and their capacity to generate either a nonfictional or fictional product. The *tale* produces both fictional and historical narratives; the *refutation/confirmation* of the tale produces either literary or historical criticism in either an expository or narrative form. The *thesis,* which argues for an answer to a question not tied to any particular person or historical moment, produces a philosophical discourse, either political or scientific, in either an expository or dramatic form. The *fable* is a literary defense of a philosophical maxim; the *chreia* and *proverb* are expository defenses. Inasmuch as the first topic for the development of the *chreia,* the encomium of the speaker, can turn into a character description and the second topic, the occasion for the saying, can turn into an extended narrative, the *chreia* can generate a story just as easily as an exposition. The *encomium/vituperation,* the *commonplace,* the *comparison,* and the *description* generate praise or blame for not only literary or historical persons, but also places, times, deeds, ideas, laws, things, character types, and virtues/vices. Because these exercises suggest that the topics used for praising/blaming persons be applied to these other subjects as well, these subjects can be personified and the resulting themes be allegories. Inasmuch as praise or blame of a particular thing can become a description of an ideal, even exposition can easily turn into allegory. Transformations of models produce parodic or serious revisions. Since any of these can be written in prose or verse or can serve not only as the outward frame for a declamation, but also as an inner frame—a piece of—a longer declamation, the lines between genres are very blurry indeed. That these exercises did produce a variety of literary genres, both public and private, we have the literary output of the classical, Renaissance, and early Enlightenment periods as examples.[15]

Reciprocally, this generic mutability draws attention to frames as frames. The students become extremely self-conscious about "perspective" (contingency), "scope" (genre, difference, sizing), "intertextuality" (generic multiplicity), and "generalization" (cross-boundary repetitions). They also become extremely self-conscious about the designing of discourse and adept at transfer—an act of invention that is possible only because there is a master frame that connects all domains of discourse.[16] The textual double frame becomes an extremely powerful heuristic.

IMPLICATIONS FOR READING:
THEORY AND PRACTICE

Based upon the practices of this classical curriculum, a reader/writer, then, seeks to understand and then evaluate all texts as arguments and dramatic performances in order to decide on an appropriate response. The double master frame that guides such interpretation could be diagramed as follows:

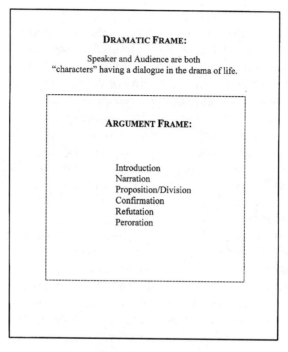

FIG. 4.1.   Framework of argument.

According to this frame, action, that which is motivated, is differentiated from motion, that which is unmotivated. The "text" is motivated behavior, composed of signs (verbal only one kind) that point to the speaker's decisions and their meanings in the larger social context. The meanings include the speaker's explicit and implicit interpretations of reality, both that which is the subject and that which is the context of the discourse, and the speaker's character, both the persona (image) that he or she intentionally adopts and the person (identity) that unintentionally emerges from the text's totality. The text's subject is the socio-physical-psychological world and the context includes both that world and the moral world—the relationships between the speaker and the audiences, as well as the assumptions the speaker makes about the characters of self and audience, the relationships inhering between them, the appropriate way to treat the audiences, and the bases for good judgment.

This definition of "text" assumes its identity and meaning to be dependent upon its inescapable placement within an irreducible context. Signs in use (in context) have meaning, whereas signs not in use have only potential meaning. Inasmuch as this meaning, because designed, is naturally persuasive, Kenneth Burke expresses the implications of the classical

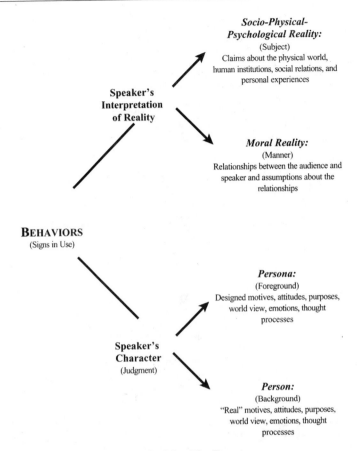

Socio-Physical-
Psychological Reality:
(Subject)
Claims about the physical world,
human institutions, social relations, and
personal experiences

Speaker's
Interpretation
of Reality

Moral Reality:
(Manner)
Relationships between the audience and
speaker and assumptions about the
relationships

BEHAVIORS
(Signs in Use)

Persona:
(Foreground)
Designed motives, attitudes, purposes,
world view, emotions, thought
processes

Speaker's
Character
(Judgment)

Person:
(Background)
"Real" motives, attitudes, purposes,
world view, emotions, thought
processes

FIG. 4.2.   The Text.

model when he claims that "Wherever there is persuasion, there is rhetoric. And wherever there is 'meaning,' there is persuasion" (*Rhetoric of Motives* 172). Rhetoric, then, applies to anything meaningful. Charles A. Hill's suggestion that visual signs should also be included within our reading instruction and Kathleen McCormick's advice that students' quite sophisticated abilities to read their teachers and popular culture should be transferred to the reading of written texts are entirely relevant and necessary (chaps. 6 and 2, respectively, this volume). In the irreducible context, there is always the speaker (who has been shaped by many environmental influences, but who also shapes self and environment) using a medium (signs) to comment on a subject (some aspect of "reality") in a certain manner (behavior) in order to elicit a response from an audience (who has been shaped, but also shapes) with whom the speaker shares physical, historical, cultural, and moral experiences.

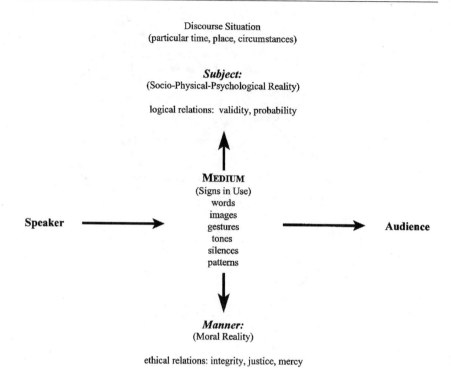

Discourse Situation
(particular time, place, circumstances)

Subject:
(Socio-Physical-Psychological Reality)

logical relations: validity, probability

MEDIUM
(Signs in Use)
words
images
Speaker ——————→ gestures ——————→ **Audience**
tones
silences
patterns

Manner:
(Moral Reality)

ethical relations: integrity, justice, mercy

FIG. 4.3.   The Context.

The audience may be another or the speaker him or herself, but inasmuch as a speaker is, to differing degrees, self-conscious about his or her craftsmanship, the self always remains an audience. In addition, many texts have more than one external audience, intended or not. As a consequence, it is more accurate to assume multiple audiences for each text (each its own frame) and to distinguish those the speaker is aware of and those not. Discourse is always dialogue, as M. M. Bakhtin asserts (72) and Cain and Kalamaras assume (chap. 8, this volume). This fact would explain why electronic chat rooms, hypertextual commentary, and interactive authorship help students become better readers and writers. These pedagogical techniques, espoused by Cornis-Pope and Woodlief (chap. 7, this volume), highlight the text's place in the broadest possible context— the drama of life—and thereby activate the multiple perspectives necessary in constructing the text's most complete interpretation.

Inasmuch as the communication act is behavior with physical, social, and psychological consequences, it is by nature entailed in moral relations and judgments. The speaker is always acting in a particular way toward audiences, while reasoning about courses of action with implications for further actions, in order to elicit actions from the hearers. Because texts exist within an external physical, historical, cultural, and moral world, the perspectives they present about that world must be compared not only to the audiences' perspectives, but also to a standard perspective that is as reliable as possible. The standard a rhetorical critic uses to establish this "grounded" perspective derives from evidence, gathered and evaluated according to the principles of grammatical, logical, and rhetorical decorum—the probable universal rules of art. The view that takes into account as completely as possible the totality of relevant textual and contextual meanings most consistently has the highest degree of reliability. This concern for finding the most rational "reality" on which to ground interpretation is not an objectivist fallacy that valorizes absolutism, but a rhetorical necessity that valorizes probability and credibility. One must win authority by the quality of one's evidence, reasoning, and behavior, but that authority always remains open to question, given that constructs should change as more evidence is gathered.

This model presents a more complete depiction of rhetorical context and hence leads to more complete readings than does the standard "communication triangle" of speaker, audience, and message, or than does the advice Harkin and Sosnoski point out we find in many critical thinking

textbooks (chap. 5, this volume). This view also offers a more complete depiction of text than those who identify either the argument, the narrative, or the drama alone as the master genre.[17] Other advantages of this view are that it is general enough to avoid reductionism—it identifies what all human communication has in common, and it is specific enough to preserve its own distinguishability—it identifies an outside to itself (signs not in use).

Because of its general character, the model of the master double frame incorporates all textual features into the subcategories of argument and drama. When examining the text as an argument, the reader sees it as a response to an issue and looks for the central proposition, stated or implied, that offers a judgment on the issue and identifies the course of action the speaker/author wishes the audience to take. The reader then looks for the proofs given that justify such judgment and action. The proofs come as both confirmations and refutations in any part of the text and include assumptions and implications (i.e., consequences of such judgment and action).

When examining the text as a drama, the reader sees it as an enactment of character and looks at the strategies the author has used in its presentation. The strategies compose the style and point to the text's delivery—the speaker's tones of voice and gestures, which reveal attitudes, passions, mental habits, and motives. The performance also reveals the speaker's interpretation of the audience's character, the relationships they share, and the speaker's values. Together the two frames reveal the speaker's worldview.[18] The following table summarizes the kinds of textual details examined in each frame.

Argument	Drama
proposition	word choice
proofs	syntactical patterns
syllogisms and enthymemes	discourse patterns
assumptions	inclusions/exclusions
conclusions	strategies
data and examples	genre
implications	manner of reasoning

Because the text points to a perspective/character and calls for a response, the reader must decide whether to be persuaded. The criteria for evaluation of each frame are similar:

Argument	Character
1. Evidence	1. Credibility
a. validity	a. rationality
b. truth (degree of probability)	b. honesty
1) sufficiency	c. informed understanding
2) relevance	
3) accuracy	
4) consistency	
2. Course of Action	
a. possibility	2. Practicality
b. expediency	
c. honorability	3. Honorability
1) legality	
2) justice	
3) equity	
4) appropriateness	
5) consistency	

Just because every speech is an act does not mean that every speech is in some measure insincere. The degree of sincerity is measured by the degree of consistency between the persona the speaker intentionally presents and the person the whole speech act creates.

Even though the frames of argument and drama provide two ways of looking at the text, the two are so integrally connected that each contributes to an understanding of the other. The performance provides implicit logical, pathetic, and ethical proofs or disproofs for the judgments made and actions proposed; the actions and judgments argued for in turn point to the kind of character speaking. The type of character speaking implicitly argues for a standard of judgment and a course of action, just as does the argument. An inevitable insight from such reciprocity is that argument and character are two faces of the same phenomenon. People become the characters of the arguments they believe and enact. Inasmuch as people can be persuaded, they can adopt new arguments and new characters. Inasmuch as people construct arguments, they construct their identities, but the relationship between arguments and characters remains essential. Another conclusion that also follows is that no one speech act points to the totality of a speaker's character. Only all of a speaker's behaviors/texts can indicate such a totality.

This identicality of argument and character is further evidenced when we apply the double frame to fiction. Characters reveal themselves by what they say and do. These speeches/performances are arguments for particular philosophies that rationalize the various roles the characters wish for themselves and others to adopt. We can analyze these speeches as we do nonfictional ones—according to the double frame. Yet, in making explicit the narrative context surrounding these speeches, fiction shows how this context, in revealing the relationships among the characters, clarifies their motivations and draws attention to the quality of their judgments. With the context made explicit, the story itself is revealed to be a speech by a storyteller, whose tale interprets and judges the arguments/ characters of the fictional figures and creates an argument/character for its speaker. When this storyteller is the author, the double frame appears twice. When, however, this storyteller is a fictional narrator with a fictional audience, the author's argument/performance forms the third frame standing outside the second.

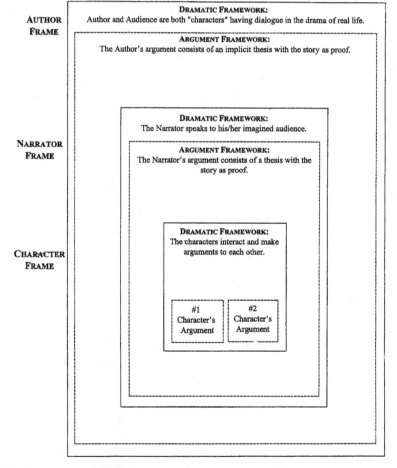

FIG. 4.4.   Framework of drama/narrative.

The formal distinction between nonfiction and fiction, then, is not a difference of kind, but of number. Nonfiction calls into the play the double genre as the master framing device only once. Fiction calls it into play at least twice and most often thrice. Even if the author denies any purposeful or didactic intent for the work, the work functions inevitably as both argument and drama—as declamation. New criticism's attempts to isolate literature from the social context and to castigate as fallacies the search for the text's pathetic and intentional meanings were not only antithetical to this rhetorical tradition, but also semiotically untenable. So too were poststructuralism's proclamations on the death of the author.

In portraying characters' responses to other characters, fiction also reveals the audience's reading of and response to a text as itself a text, and hence, an argument and performance—one subject to analysis according to the same double frame and rhetorical context. The diagram need only reverse the direction of the arrows in order to represent the contextual elements to be considered in an analysis of a reader's response.

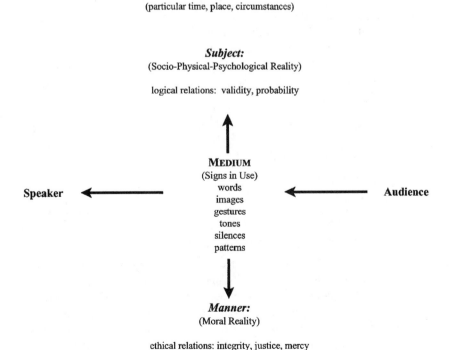

FIG. 4.5. The context.

Readers are writers: the interpretation and judgment a reader constructs is a response to the author and a model of behavior for others to emulate. Because it's an act with social and psychological consequences, a reader's interpretation and judgment of a text/author is by nature a moral act, subject to the principles of decorum. A subjectivist theory of reading ignores and is irresponsible to this larger rhetorical context. If the reader misses the speaker's intentions, the reader misreads, and misreadings cause damage, just as fallacious arguments do. Such awareness produces within readers/writers a sense of responsibility for the readings they write.

Such an awareness also awakens readers to all texts as readings of and responses to prior texts, to writers as readers. With this insight comes a recognition of intertextuality as a fundamental fact of invention. Such is the awareness of the Renaissance humanists who adopted the classical pedagogical program in their schools. Roger Ascham assumes this interdependence of reading and writing as he describes the process of textual analysis involved in imitation:

> *Erasmus,* the ornament of learning, in our tyme, doth wish that som man of learning and diligence, would take the like paines in *Demosthenes* and *Tullie,* that *Macrobius* hath done in *Homer* and *Virgill,* that is, to write out and ioyne together, where the one doth imitate the other. [. . .]
> But if a man would take this paine also, whan he hath layd two places, of *Homer* and *Virgill,* or of *Demosthenes* and *Tullie* togither, to teach plainlie withall, after this sort.
>
> 1. *Tullie* reteyneth thus moch of the matter, thies sentences, thies wordes:
> 2. This and that he leaueth out, which he doth wittelie to this end and purpose.
> 3. This he addeth here.
> 4. This he diminisheth there.
> 5. This he ordereth thus, with placing that here, not there.
> 6. This he altereth and changeth, either, in propertie of wordes, in forme of sentence, in substance of the matter, or in one, or other conuenient circumstance of the authors present purpose. In theis fewe rude English wordes, are wrapt vp all the necessarie tooles and instrumentes, wherewith trewe *Imitation* is rightlie wrought withall in any tonge. (*The Scholemaster* 267–68)

The fictional work is a mirror of dramatic reality: it makes the rhetorical context apparent. The nonfictional work is a mirror of rhetorical reality: it makes the persuasiveness of human performance apparent. We need the fictional in order to make clear the lessons rhetoric has to teach, just as we need rhetoric to make clear the lessons fiction has to teach. Composition, then, benefits not only from the excellent stylistic examples of literature, but from the dramatic perspective literature foregrounds. And literary study benefits not only from rhetorical criticism, but from the persuasive perspective expository writing foregrounds. The master double frame makes obvious that rhetoric applies to nonfiction and fiction alike and that all human discourse, reading and writing, is both fictional and nonfictional at once.

The inseparable connection between literature and composition, reading and writing, the word and the world; the universality of the double frame; and the effectiveness of imitation as a pedagogical method—these are lessons I have learned from the long-standing classical rhetorical tradition. These lessons have been reconfirmed by my classroom experience. Whether teaching composition, literature, rhetorical criticism, or critical reading, I have found that students read and write better and learn more quickly when trained within this expansive, rich, generative paradigm. Consequently, these ideas also undergird the curriculum I have prepared for the BYU Reading Center, a service designed to help students from any discipline learn the kind of critical analysis necessary for success in college reading and writing tasks. While I add my witness that these pedagogical ideas work, I also suggest that we can add to, subtract from, substitute for, and transform them to meet the ever-changing needs of the present.

Reading well, then, means putting all signs back into performance where meaning fully resides. It means reading both "through" and "at" the text—"through" in order to compare the speaker's argument to the world outside the text and "at" in order to compare the speaker's performance to the principles of decorum.[19] It means reading both content and style, both intention and achievement. It means critically resisting texts until persuaded, the kind of response Lizabeth Rand suggests is appropriate (chap. 3, this volume). It means reading as a speaker/writer/artist oneself, examining another speaker's art in order to improve that of one's own and one's audience's. This analytical practice develops metacognitive awareness about the principles of good judgment so that one can learn to exercise control over one's own behavior, turning it into "art"—excellence. Such excellence is by nature ethical, decorum inevitably rhetoric's central concern.

NOTES

1. Isocrates and Plato were contemporary schoolmasters who each set up competing schools in Athens. One of the ironies of history is that even though it was Isocrates's curriculum and rhetorical theory that won that contest and influenced education until well into the eighteenth century, today few remember Isocrates or have any knowledge of the educational and philosophical paradigm before the Cartesian revolution. It is not Plato's, but Isocrates's views that best characterize the classical rhetorical tradition.
2. See Helmers's reference to Freire, chapter 1, this volume.
3. See *Institutio Oratoria,* X.i.46–131, for Quintilian's suggested reading list.
4. That logic is taught along with rhetoric, we have Quintilian's witness: "Such were the subjects on which the ancients as a rule exercised their powers of speaking, though they called in the assistance of the logicians as well to teach them the theory of argument" (II.iv.41).
5. In Greek, *gymnasmata* (mental exercises) derives by metaphorical extension from *gymnazein* (physical exercise, discipline, training).
6. Quintilian briefly mentions all of these exercises (fable, narrative, aphorism, chreia, description of character [I.iv.2–3]; praise, denunciation, comparison, commonplace, refutation, confirmation, thesis, praise or denunciation of laws [II.i.10–33]; speech-in-character [III.viii.49–54]; description of detail [VIII.iii.61–65]), but not in any systematic treatment, showing he expects his audience to have familiarity with them and that they belong to a long tradition: "On such subjects did the ancients, for the most part, exercise the faculty of eloquence" (II.iv.41).

   Stanley Bonner in his *Education in Ancient Rome* suggests that these exercises had become a set several hundred years before Quintilian:

   > It seems likely [. . .] that the formation of the standard set of preliminary exercises, known to us mainly from writers of the imperial period, was a gradual process, which took place during the Hellenistic Age. It must, however, have been fairly complete by the first century B.C., and maybe earlier, for already in the late Republic the set, or a good part of it, was being used by teachers of rhetoric in Latin. (250–51)

   The collections of *progymnasmata* that survive, however, date from the second to fifth centuries A.D.: that of Theon of Alexandria in the early second century, that of Hermogenes of Tarsus in the late second century (whose work was translated into Latin by Prisian around 515 A.D.), that of Aphthonius in the latter fourth century, and that of Nicolaus Sophista of Myra in the latter fifth century. Even though Theon lists only ten exercises, he actually treats of all fourteen. He includes the confirmation and refutation with the chreia, fable, and narrative; the proverb with the chreia; and the vituperation with the encomium. Hermogenes lists thirteen, but groups the encomium and vituperation as one, thereby also treating of all fourteen. Aphthonius lists all fourteen separately. Nicolaus's list is similar to Hermogenes's and Aphthonius's.

   For contemporary studies of the *progymnasmata,* see Bonner's *Education in Ancient Rome,* Donald Lemen Clark's *Rhetoric in Greco-Roman Education* and *John Milton at St. Paul's School,* and James J. Murphy's "Roman Writing Instruction as Described by Quintilian." For contemporary adaptations of the *progymnasmata* in composition teaching, see Frank J. D'Angelo's *Composition in the Classical Tradition* and Sharon Crowley and Debra Hawhee's *Ancient Rhetorics for Contemporary Students*. None of these studies, however, have explored the theory of text and interpretation to emerge from these exercises, as I do in the discussion that follows.

7. Specific evidence for this practice of repeating these exercises in more complex transformations comes from Theon, a schoolmaster of Alexandria and probably a younger contemporary of Quintilian, who in his textbook makes gradations of difficulty within each individual type. The chreia, for example, can be paraphrased, Theon says,

> 1) in the manner of a maxim, 2) in the manner of an explanation, 3) with wit, 4) with a syllogism, 5) with an enthymeme, 6) with an example, 7) with a wish, 8) in a symbolic manner, 9) in a figurative manner, 10) with double entendre, 11) with a change of subject, 12) in a combination of the forms mentioned above. (89)

After paraphrase, Theon lists other transformations: "1) recitation, 2) inflexion [change of number, case, tense], 3) comment, and 4) objection. We can also 5) expand and 6) condense the chreia. In addition, we 7) refute and 8) confirm it" (95). Theon then comments that "more advanced students" who write the chreia should use the topics of the thesis instead of those he has just listed (107). More advanced elaborations of fables and tales, Theon teaches, involve (a) integrating descriptions, speeches-in-character, and other narrative illustrations from history or fable or (b) refuting and confirming them (Bonner, *Education* 255, 263).

Nicolaus, a fifth-century schoolmaster, also indicates that beginning students primarily use the chreia for practice in inflexion, while more advanced students analyze and commend it (254–63). Although not as explicit, Quintilian too indicates that these exercises and steps of imitation were practiced by both the elementary and advanced pupils. He mentions the *progymnasmata* not only in Book II when he outlines the course of study under the *grammaticus* and the *rhetor*, but also again in Book X when he directs the independent study of the budding orator (X.v.1–23).

8. Bonner provides insight on the Roman practice of these mock-orations in *Roman Declamation* and *Education in Ancient Rome*, chapter 19. Clark devotes chapter 7 of *Rhetoric in Greco-Roman Education* to the declamation. The Elder Seneca provides a collection of model scenarios and declamations in his two volumes *Controversiae* and *Suasoriae*. Students would be given a case or dilemma and asked to prepare arguments for and against each side. A sample case from the Elder Seneca's *Controversia* illustrates the exercise:

> A man killed one of his brothers, a tyrant. The other brother he caught in adultery and killed despite the pleas of his father. Captured by pirates, he wrote to his father about a ransom. The father wrote a letter to the pirates, saying that he would give double if they cut off his hands. The pirates let him go. The father is in need; the son is not supporting him. (1.7)

After presenting the bare case, Seneca then presents arguments from various persons who plead in behalf of either the accused or the plaintiff. Afterwards, he provides an analysis and evaluation of the arguments. Students then compose arguments either for or against from the points of view of the various persons involved in the cases or decisions.

9. Clark identifies four of these six steps of imitation: prelection, memorization, translation, and paraphrase (*Rhetoric* 157–76). Murphy divides the steps into seven: reading aloud (lectio), praelectio, memorization, paraphrase, transliteration (prose to verse), recitation, and correction (46–52). I have listed translation, paraphrase, and translitera-

tion (metaphrase) as ways of transforming models and also included imitation proper, which Roger Ascham calls *imitatio*, but that neither Clark nor Murphy discusses. By leaving out this step—the transformation of models—neither Clark nor Murphy integrates the *progymnasmata*, the *gymnasmata*, and genuine oratory into the practice of imitation, where they belong.

10. In their introduction to Erasmus's *On Copia of Words and Ideas*, Donald B. King and H. David Rix point out that *copia's* various meanings include "abundance," "variation," "eloquence," and "the ability to speak appropriately and effectively on any occasion to any audience," this last meaning equivalent to *facilitas* (9).

11. See Seneca's textbooks *Controversia* and *Suasoria*.

12. Aphthonius 270. Theon lists for criteria clarity, possibility, seemliness, consistency, and expediency (Bonner, *Education* 263).

13. Bonner, *Education* 268–69.

14. Hermogenes 27–28.

15. Bonner makes reference to a number of these literary examples as he describes the *progymnasmata* in *Education in Ancient Rome* (250–76) and the influence of declamatory practice on the literature of the early empire in *Roman Declamation* (149–67).

16. According to Ellen D. Gagne in *The Cognitive Psychology of School Learning*, the following are prerequisites for learning "transfer": students are taught why they are learning something, how it will lead to success, and when it will be useful (197); they are given appropriate conditions for generalization with succession of like examples, examples that vary widely on irrelevant attributes, and nonexamples (109); they are given a meaningful framework for interpretation and knowledge accessibility (158); and they are given practice in elaboration (variation and connection making between contexts) and organization (division into parts) (83 & 89). David Perkins in *Smart Schools* gives a similar list (123–26). These conditions are met in the classical curriculum.

17. Walter Fisher and Mark Turner argue that narrative is the master genre of human discourse. Jerome Bruner opposes the genres of argument and narrative as the two basic, but contrasting modes of thought (11). Andrea Lunsford and John J. Ruszkiewicz argue that all texts are arguments. Kenneth Burke comments that the drama is the best genre for envisioning all discourse and looks for the persuasive elements in discourse in his analyses. Even though he does not say so, the master double frame I propose explains his analytical practice and suggests how his practice can be extended to its logical conclusions. James Boyd White's discussion of the court argument as a drama also suggests this master double frame.

18. One's worldview or foundational philosophy includes the answers to these five questions: (a) What is ultimately real and what is its nature? (b) What is human nature? (c) What is knowledge, how do humans know things, and how certainly can humans know things? (d) What is ultimate good and how is it determined? (e) What is the value and meaning of life?

19. The idea that we must read both "through" and "at" a text comes from Richard Lanham's *Analyzing Prose* (1). That this necessity to oscillate between frames leads to an awareness of a master double frame is an extrapolation of not only Lanham's, but also classical rhetoric's principles and methods.

WORKS CITED

Abbott, Don Paul. "Rhetoric and Writing in Renaissance Europe and England." *A Short History of Writing Instruction.* Ed. James J. Murphy. Davis, CA: Hermagoras, 1990. 95–120.

Aphthonius. *The Progymnasmata of Aphthonius.* Trans. Ray Nadeau. *Speech Monographs* 19 (1952): 264–85.

Ascham, Roger. *The Scholemaster.* 1570. *English Works.* Ed. William Aldis Wright. Cambridge: Cambridge UP, 1904.

Bakhtin, M. M. *Speech Genres & Other Late Essays.* Trans. Vern W. McGee. Austin: U of Texas P, 1986.

Bonner, Stanley. *Education in Ancient Rome.* London: Methuen, 1977.

———. *Roman Declamation.* Liverpool: UP of Liverpool, 1949.

Brinsley, John. *Ludus Literarius.* 1612. Ed. R. C. Alston. Scolar Press Facsimile 62. Menston, England: Scolar, 1968.

Bruner, Jerome. *Actual Minds, Possible Worlds.* Cambridge: Harvard UP, 1986.

Burke, Kenneth. *Permanence and Change.* 2nd ed. Indianapolis: Bobbs-Merrill, 1965.

———. *A Rhetoric of Motives.* Berkeley: U of California P, 1950.

Cicero. *De Oratore.* Trans. E. W. Sutton. Loeb Classical Library. Cambridge: Harvard UP, 1942.

Clark, Donald Lemen. *John Milton at St. Paul's School.* New York: Columbia UP, 1948.

———. *Rhetoric in Greco-Roman Education.* New York: Columbia UP, 1957.

Crowley, Sharon, and Debra Hawhee. *Ancient Rhetorics for Contemporary Students.* 2nd ed. Boston: Allyn, 1999.

Curtius, E. R. *European Literature and the Latin Middle Ages.* Trans. Willard R. Trask. New York: Bollingen Foundation, 1948.

D'Angelo, Frank J. *Composition in the Classical Tradition.* Boston: Allyn, 2000.

Erasmus. *De Copia.* Trans. Betty I. Knott. *Collected Works of Erasmus.* 24. Toronto: U of Toronto P, 1978.

———. *On Copia of Words and Ideas.* Trans. Donald B. King and H. David Rix. Milwaukee: Marquette UP, 1963.

Fisher, Walter R. *Human Communication as Narration.* Columbia: U of South Carolina P, 1989.

Gagne, Ellen D. *The Cognitive Psychology of School Learning.* Boston: Little, 1985.

Garner, Ruth. *Metacognition and Reading Comprehension.* Norwood, NJ: Ablex, 1987.

Hermogenes. "The Elementary Exercises of Hermogenes." Trans. Charles Sears Baldwin. *Medieval Rhetoric and Poetic.* Gloucester, MA: Macmillan, 1959. 23–38.

Lanham, Richard A. *Analyzing Prose.* New York: Scribner's, 1983.

Lunsford, Andrea A., and John J. Ruszkiewicz. *Everything's an Argument.* Boston: Bedford/St. Martin's, 1999.

Marrou, H. I. *A History of Education in Antiquity.* Madison: U of Wisconsin P, 1956.

Murphy, James J. "Roman Writing Instruction as Described by Quintilian." *A Short History of Writing Instruction.* Ed. James J. Murphy. Davis, CA: Hermagoras, 1990. 19–76.

Nicolaus. "On the Chreia." Trans. Ronald F. Hock and Edward N. O'Neil. *The Chreia in Ancient Rhetoric.* Atlanta: Scholars, 1986. 253–65.

Ong, Walter J. *Rhetoric, Romance and Technology.* Ithaca: Cornell UP, 1971.

Perkins, David. *Smart Schools.* New York: Free, 1992.

Quintilian. *Institutio Oratoria.* Trans. H. E. Butler. Loeb Classical Library. Cambridge: Harvard UP, 1920–21.

Rainolde, Richard. *The Foundacion of Rhetorike.* 1563. *The English Experience* 91. New York: Da Capo, 1969.

Russell, Donald A. *Criticism in Antiquity.* Berkeley: U of California P, 1981.

Seneca, the Elder. *Controversiae and Suasoriae.* I and II. Trans. Michael Winterbottom. Loeb Classical Library. Cambridge: Harvard UP, 1974.

Tharp, Roland G., and Ronald Gallimore. *Rousing Minds to Life*. Cambridge: Cambridge UP, 1988.

Theon. "On the Chreia." Trans. Ronald F. Hock and Edward N. O'Neil. *The Chreia in Ancient Rhetoric*. Atlanta: Scholars, 1986, 83–107.

Turner, Mark. *The Literary Mind*. New York: Oxford UP, 1996.

White, James Boyd. *Heracles' Bow: Essays on the Rhetoric and Poetry of Law*. Madison: U of Wisconsin P, 1985.

5

Whatever Happened
to Reader-Response Criticism?

Patricia Harkin
James J. Sosnoski

Not long ago, as we met to compose questions for a PhD examination in literary theory, a colleague raised the question that has become our title. He raised it (somewhat) whimsically—as a query about institutional history, prompting the candidate to explain why reader-response criticism[1] is rarely mentioned *by that name* in contemporary conversations. Although the examinee chose to answer one of the other questions on the exam, we found ourselves pondering that one: what, indeed *has* happened to the emphasis on reading that we found so exciting in the seventies and eighties?

From an historical point of view, an obvious—too obvious—answer is that reading theory seems to have been subsumed and/or displaced by more recent, grander and trendier theories. The current emphasis on the constructedness of *every* aspect of communication processes, for example, has entailed a corresponding de-emphasis on the relatively more limited question "what happens when people read?" that Wolfgang Iser raised more than two decades ago. The notion that what Stanley Fish called interpretive communities foster meaning making in relation to indeterminate texts, once associated only with reader-response theory, plays a major role in deconstruction, cultural studies, performance, and queer theories. The emphasis on individual feelings that dominated the work of Norman Holland and David Bleich is crucial to body theory and performance theory; the conception of discourse communities plays a major role in ethnographic studies of the rhetoric of the everyday,[2] and so on. In cultural studies, the notion that readers make meaning has become a commonplace; discussions have turned to the ways in which members of various cultures *use* the texts they read. Analyses of the politics of reading are central to cultural studies, where reception theory has been effectively articulated with theories of ideology, of the psyche, of culture, and of history. Perhaps most important, the notion of "literariness"—of a special class of privileged texts that requires special techniques of reading and specially educated kinds of readers—has been rather thoroughly exploded theoretically and replaced politically by the emphasis on the popular.

But has reader-response criticism therefore become a curious relic of the seventies, to be consigned to the theory junkyard?[3] Would it be more accurate to say that, like bell bottoms and platform shoes, reader response is returning (slightly changed) to fashion? In her introductory essay for this volume, Marguerite Helmers suggests that even as reader-response criticism per se seemed to fade from specifically literary discussions, compositionists continued to raise questions about the place of reading in the writing classroom. Many of these discussions were not merely quarrels about whether first-year students should be writing about "literature," but rather inquiries into intersections between theories of reading and theories of writing. Anthony Petrosky and David Bartholomae, for example, used reading theory to reach the basic writers at the University of Pittsburgh (*Ways of Reading* and Petrosky, "From Story to Essay"). Mariolina Salvatori showed writing teachers how Iser's conceptions of gap and consistency building might help their students *read* their own writing in such a way as to turn writer based into reader-based prose. Kathleen McCormick's course design for "Reading Texts" at Carnegie Mellon, and Patricia Harkin's for "Writing About Reading" at the University of Akron both resulted in textbooks in which syntheses of several theories of reading elucidate and address students' writing processes (*Reading Texts* and *Acts of Reading*). Even Maxine Hairston, certainly no fan of "mandarin" literary theory, recommended Jane Tompkins's *Reader Response Criticism* in her 1985 Chair's Address at the Conference of College Composition and Communication ("Breaking Our Bonds").

Nonetheless, we find that the discussions of reading in many current writing textbooks retains little—if any—of the critical, counter-hegemonic promise that we recall from the early days of reception aesthetics in the United States and Europe. It seems to us, in other words, that reader-response criticism has moved from literary studies through to cultural studies without substantially influencing mainstream composition studies. In the context of this study of *Reading Pedagogy in College Writing Classrooms,* then, we raise our eponymous question in all seriousness. What *has* become of the notion that readers make meaning?

Our answer is that the principles of reception study have been reduced to "theoroids." We use the term "theoroid" by analogy with "factoid." If a fact is a function in a systematic theory, a factoid is an utterance detached from the system that might give it meaning or usefulness. That Roger Clemens's fastball travels at a speed of 98 mph, for example, is a factoid. A factoid doesn't tell us how the fact is systematically related to others; for example, it doesn't tell us how fast the Yankee pitcher's fastball was last year (or last pitch), whom he's pitching against today, whether the stadium is domed, the velocity of the wind, whether the sun is in his eyes, whether he seems to be aiming the fastball at the batter's head, and so forth. By analogy, a theoroid is an *aperçu* ("there is nothing outside the text"; "gender is a performance"; "everything is ideological"; "we're all cyborgs") removed from the theory in which it wields conceptual power, domesticated into the ordinary, and thereby made unthreatening. When theories become "theoroids," they become maxims, conceptual proverbs.

In *Professing Literature,* Gerald Graff observed that threatening theoretical discourse has historically been assimilated by the field coverage principle. Rather than offering a challenge to existing critical procedures, Graff asserted, a movement like feminism would be domesticated into ordinary academic staffing, so that every department would have *a* feminist, and that appointment would allow the rest of the professors to continue their (masculinist) business as usual.

Graff's context was, of course, the staffing of English departments. But the processes he described are even more prevalent—and alarming—in the textbook industry. As they increase market share through consolidation, corporate publishers can no longer afford "niche books" that offer a single focus; they need products that offer all things to all people. Writing program administrators need to provide support for inexperienced TAs and for contingent staff members who have little time to prepare classes. Consequently, the production of "omnibus textbooks," single volumes that combine a general rhetoric, a handbook, an overview of the modes or genres, a style manual, and a primer on reading, has begun to dominate the industry. But the omnibus textbook raises a theoretical problem: in the absence of any widely held "general field theory" of writing/reading, each of these sets of bundled maxims is likely to be derived from different theories—of rhetoric, of genre, of writing, of reading. And multiple theories occasion demands for coherence from copy and development editors. Is the definition of rhetoric compatible with the conception of usage that prevails in the handbook and the genre theory that informs the discussion on the "modes"? For example, does an audience-centered approach to rhetoric coalesce with a sense of usage that marks certain constructions and locutions as "incorrect"? Does the emphasis on the constraints of genre in chapter 1 preclude the "originality" that chapter 7 requires? If, as is often the case, the theories conflict, the incompatibility rarely becomes a topic for inquiry. On the contrary, the resolution too often is merely a "common denominator" definition that reduces the original theorems to platitudes. Simplicity comes at the expense of the intellectual complexity of the issues.

To be sure, the exigencies of textbook production make it impossible for disparate theories to be fully explained and elucidated.[4] Hence, the vast majority of textbooks reduce theories to theoroids—snippets that work like the "samples" in contemporary music—in which one artist appropriates another's work for different aesthetic or commercial purposes. In the process, the theory is stripped of its critical power. With specific respect to reading, we shall argue in this essay that textbooks take key conceptions from the works of Fish, Iser, Holland, Bleich, and Louise Rosenblatt, strip them of their critical power, and combine them to produce a set of instructions for reducing, rather than celebrating or even investigating, the indeterminacy of texts. As such basic conceptions of reception-oriented inquiry as, for example, *interpretive community, efferent and aesthetic readings,* and *identity themes* have been reduced and recontextualized into "theoroids," what has happened to reader-response criticism, at least in argument textbooks, is that it has become a set of instructions for "finding" authorial intention as the stable meaning of texts. The authoritative voice of the teacher/author, as David Bleich has recently demonstrated ("In Case of Fire"), further reduces the emphasis on the play of meanings that early reception aesthetics tended to celebrate.

This essay analyzes the reading theoroids offered by three argument textbooks: John Ramage and John Bean's *Writing Arguments* (Allyn and Bacon); Annette Rottenberg's *Elements of Argument* (St. Martin's); and Timothy W. Crusius and Carolyn Channell's *The Aims of Argument* (Mayfield). Admitting that we are taking the textbook passages out of context, we offer them as evidence that, their superficial adherence to the principles of reception theory notwithstanding, the authors characterize reading as a neutral process of decoding authorial intention. They teach their student-readers that close and careful reading will reveal authorial intention, that finding authorial intention is the purpose of reading, and that the meaning of an argument is readily available to any close reader who is willing to respond.

READER-RESPONSE CRITICISM
AS A CHALLENGE TO NEW CRITICISM

Although we cannot, in the scope of this short essay, offer a comprehensive survey of reading theories, we herewith present a selection of concept names from the heyday of reception aesthetics in an attempt to show *why* so many traditionally schooled academics found them threatening, and *what* had to be removed in order to turn them into theoroids.[5]

The most controversial issues in the debates had to do with the production of meaning. One of the earliest theorists to call attention to the problems associated with deriving meaning from texts was I. A. Richards, whose *Practical Criticism,* first published in 1928, sent a cautionary tremor through the literary world. In an effort to "provide a new technique for those who wish to discover for themselves what they think and feel about poetry (and cognate matters) and why they should like or dislike it," and "to prepare the way for educational methods more efficient than those we use now in developing discrimination and the power to understand what we hear and read" (3), Richards removed the names of the authors from the poems he was expected to teach at Cambridge and asked his students to write about them. As a consequence of his experiment, Richards discovered not only that his students tend to prefer the work of poets whom he regarded as inferior, but also that their "misreadings" (understood here as their divergence from Richards's own interpretation) revealed an astonishing variation. For Richards and his followers, this variation indicated, not diverse interests, but rather poor reading habits. He therefore established a list of "the chief difficulties of criticism," a few of which we reproduce here:

- the difficulty of making out the plain sense of poetry [. . .]
- [. . .] the difficulties of *sensuous apprehension* [. . .]
- [. . .] difficulties that are connected with the place of imagery [. . .] in poetic reading [. . .]
- [. . .] the powerful very pervasive influence of *mnemonic irrelevance.* These are the misleading effects of the reader's being reminded of some personal scene or adventure, erratic associations, the interference of emotional reverberations from a past which may have nothing to do with the poem. [. . .]
- [. . .] the critical traps that surround what may be called *stock responses.* These have their opportunity whenever a poem seems to, or does, involve views and emotions already fully prepared in the reader's mind, so that what happens appears to be more of the reader's doing than the poet's.

- *Sentimentality* [. . .] the question of the due measure of response. This over-facility in certain emotional directions is the Scylla whose Charybdis is

- *Inhibition* [. . .] somewhat masked under the title of Hardness of Heart.

- *Doctrinal Adhesions* present another troublesome problem. [. . .] [W]hat should be the bearing of the reader's conviction, if any upon his estimate of the poetry?

- The effects of *technical presuppositions* have to be noted. When something has once been well done in a certain fashion we tend to expect similar things to be done in the future in the same fashion, and are disappointed or do not recognize them if they are done differently. Conversely, a technique which has shown its ineptitude for one purpose tends to become discredited for all. Both are cases of mistaking means for ends.

- Finally, *general critical preconceptions* (prior demands made upon poetry as a result of theories—conscious or unconscious) about its nature and value, intervene endlessly, as the history of criticism shows only too well, between the reader and the poem. (12–15)

It was widely believed that paying closer attention to the details of the text would be a good corrective to the problems Richards so disturbingly brought to light. In many respects Richards's experiments led to the emphasis on "close reading" that characterized the New Criticism.

Although Louise Rosenblatt, whose *Literature as Exploration* first appeared in 1938, theorized reading during the height of New Criticism, her work went largely unnoticed by members of English departments. Susan Suleiman, for example, writes that she became aware of Rosenblatt's work only as *The Reader in the Text* went to press:

> Rosenblatt's book challenged the objectivist assumptions of the New Criticism as they affected the teaching of literature in high schools and colleges. Rosenblatt first proposed the term *transaction* to designate the relationship between text and reader. [. . .] Although her work was influential among those most concerned with questions of pedagogy, its relevance for literary theory was recognized only recently, when it was rediscovered by Bleich and others. (Crosman and Suleiman 45)

Suleiman's opposition between "pedagogy" and "literary theory" is telling. It was, perhaps, Rosenblatt's interest in teaching, and her acute observations of students' behavior, that led her to propose that reading can usefully be considered as a transactional process in which readers make *both* "efferent readings"—ones that carry away information from the

text—*and* aesthetic ones—in which readers construct an aesthetic object
in transaction with the text. The difference between efferent and aesthetic,
for Rosenblatt, is in the reading, rather than in the text. Whether it was
her interest in pedagogy, her association with English Education at NYU,
her gender, or her insight that meaning is a function of the use to which
readers put their readings, it was difficult for her to be heard in the American academy of the last century.

Even without Louise Rosenblatt's work as a spur, however, it soon became important to develop frameworks for describing how and why readings differ—from person to person, from context to context, from culture
to culture. As a consequence of theoretical developments in linguistics,
anthropology, psychology, philosophy, and anthropology during the
1970s and 1980s, thinkers working within a number of institutional for-
mations raised the question "what happens when human beings read
texts?" Structuralism, as a widespread movement across disciplines, had
focused upon the ways in which the mind structures experience to make it
meaningful. French linguist Ferdinand de Saussure's inquiries into the binary oppositions that structure understanding, coupled with his declara-
tion that the relation between signifier and signified is arbitrary, led to the
perception that reading depends on familiarity with various "codes."
Such structuralists as Roland Barthes (in his early period) then set about
enumerating and describing those codes, most notably in his *S/Z*. Attention to the disciplinary principles of linguistics suggested to Gerald Prince
that readers make meaning by processing instructions that are embedded
in a text. Prince discriminates the "narratee" (the fictive reader whom the
narrator addresses) from the virtual reader (whom the author "bestows
with certain qualities, faculties, and inclinations according to his opinion
of men in general") and the ideal reader ("who would understand perfectly and would approve entirely the least of his words, the most subtle
of his intentions") (Tompkins 9). For example, the narratee of Ernest
Hemingway's "A Clean Well-Lighted Place" needs to know both "The
Lord's Prayer" and that *nada* is a Spanish word for "nothing" if she or he
is to understand "our nada who art in nada, nada be thy name thy king-
dom nada thy will be nada in nada as it is in nada" (383). The virtual
reader would represent Hemingway's (often contemptuous) sense of his
readership, but the ideal reader would be the reader Hemingway would
have wanted.

Umberto Eco sought to describe "the co-operative role of the ad-
dressee in the interpretation of messages" (vii). In his inquiries into the activities of reading, he contributed the notion of the "open work," *opera
aperta,* a text whose meaning is not fixed but rather "open" to the

semiotics of reading. Frank Smith, working within the disciplinary structures of psycholinguistics, drew his audience's attention to "a trade-off
between visual and non-visual information in reading": in addition to recognizing the material signifiers, readers "must know something of the
language in which the material is written, and about its subject matter,
and about reading" (6–7).

But linguistics and semiotics stopped short of providing explanations
for differences in readings. Psychoanalysis prompted Holland, and later
Bleich, to look at the ways in which readers might be said to project their
own "identity themes" onto the texts they read. Holland maintained that
any unity that could be said to exist in literary texts was a fulfillment of
the reader's desire to find unity. It might be said that Holland took precisely the "problems" that troubled Richards and turned them into a psy-
choanalytic account of the inevitable: we impose ourselves on the readings we make. As a consequence, Holland asserted in *Five Readers
Reading*, psychoanalytically describable differences among readers accounted for differences in the "meanings" these readers construct.

Critics everywhere began to take note of how the individual reader's
mind affected the process of interpretation. Making careful use of Roman
Ingarden's monumental *The Cognition of the Literary Work*, Wolfgang
Iser looked to phenomenology in order to describe and account for "the
act of reading" as the coalescence of a group of innate processes of consciousness. Readers encounter "places of indeterminacy," or "gaps," he
noted, when the text seems to provide less information than they require
or desire. Individual readers might experience more, fewer, or different
gaps than others do, but every reader, according to Iser, reads by "closing" gaps. Iser connects the urge to close gaps with a desire for "consistency" that pervades consciousness. The text activates those desires and
readers make meaning. For example, metaphors call on us to find a consistencies between tenor and vehicle; thematizing is a process through
which a reader makes whatever is present to his or her consciousness into
a consistent "theme" in a work; what formalists call "character" is the result of a reader's a process of building a consistent notion of a particular
textual form known as (say) Squire Allworthy. Iser gives the name "repertoire" to "all the extratextual reality to which the text refers." A much
broader conception than setting, "repertoire," he writes in *The Act of
Reading*, "does not consist solely of social and cultural norms; it also incorporates elements and, indeed whole traditions of past literature that
are mixed together with these norms" (79). As an example, Iser offers
Lockean epistemology as a repertoire for Sterne's *Tristram Shandy:* Mrs.
Shandy's inopportune question, "Pray, Mr. Shandy, have you remem-

bered to wind up the clock?" invokes the Lockean doctrine of the association of ideas. Mrs. Shandy associates sexual congress (which occurs in the
Shandy's domestic establishment on Sunday evenings) with another Sunday evening occurrence, the winding of the clock, such that the one
always reminds her of the other. Sterne's fiction, says Iser, calls its
(Lockean) repertoire into question through the (comic) juxtaposition of
sex and clocks.

IS THERE A TEXT IN THE READER
OR A READING IN THE TEXT?

Stanley Fish takes a similar position with respect to interpretive frameworks in "How to Recognize a Poem When You See One." He explains
that, in the summer of 1971, he taught two courses back to back, the first
in stylistics and the second in seventeenth-century poetry. At the end of
the first period he wrote on the board the names of several linguists, with
a question mark to register his uncertainty about the spelling of Richard
Ohmann's name:

Jacobs-Rosenbaum

Levin

Thorne

Hayes

Ohman (?)

When the students in the poetry class entered the room, Fish asked them
to interpret what he had written on the board. Drawing heavily upon the
first name—Jacob and Rosenbaum (rose tree, the means of ascent to
heaven)—Fish's students found a poem "celebrating the love and mercy
shown by a God who gave his only begotten son so that we may live" (and
asking, through the concluding interrogation mark, the extent to which
that mercy was deserved by its beneficiaries). For Fish, and for us, the implications of this anecdote are that the words of the text are made meaningful by the frameworks that readers bring to them.
    In his "Why No One's Afraid of Wolfgang Iser" Fish attempts to dis-
mantle Iser's argument that, although the reader's frameworks structure
the text's meaning, nonetheless the text "guides" the reader's interpre-

tive activity. Fish denies the phenomenological argument that conscious-ness is predisposed to interact with texts. For him, all reading behavior is learned. In the process, he makes what seems to us the prescient point that Iser's thought is so readily adaptable to the tenets of the New Criti-cism that it is susceptible to being co-opted into a kind of "New Criti-cism for Readers."

The Fish/Iser debate underscores a larger issue: what are the condi-tions that inform meaning? Among those conditions are, of course, emo-tions. In *Readings and Feelings,* Bleich focuses upon students' *affective re-sponses* to the texts and regards the meanings they derive from them, no matter how "subjective," as appropriate. Though Bleich's work provoked less controversy than Fish's—perhaps because his position was often re-jected out of hand—we link his emphasis on feeling in the act of reading to a feminist, politically oriented form of reader-response criticism initi-ated by Judith Fetterley in *The Resisting Reader: A Feminist Approach to American Fiction.* Fetterley was among the first reading theorists to point to the ways in which a reader's gender influences her response. Analyzing Hemingway's "Indian Camp," for example, she asserts that a woman must certainly have a different response than a man to the doctor's insis-tence that he does not listen to the Native-American woman's screams in childbirth because they are unimportant. Fetterley retained a conserva-tive notion of authorial intention throughout her first book. That is, she seemed to be asserting that the authors she discussed intended for their

readers to have her feminist responses. It was another conceptual step for Fetterley and others to see that readers could make meanings that authors did not intend and that those readings could be seriously discussed in scholarly situations.

Not surprisingly, these theoretical inquiries engendered anxiety among more traditional literati. At the vortex of the controversy was the extent to which the reader constitutes the meaning of *any* text. Objections to reception-oriented theories of meaning took predictable forms; critics accused Fish, Bleich, and Iser of attacking the integrity of texts, the preeminence of authorial intention, and even the "genius" of authors. Insofar as it holds that the distinction between genres is in the reader rather than in the text, moreover, reception theory problematizes the easy distinction between literary and nonliterary works. And that distinction entails the corollary one: that literary works evoke and sustain emotional responses, while arguments appeal to reason alone.

THE VIEW OF READING IN ARGUMENT TEXTBOOKS

As a consequence, perhaps, of the intense emphasis on reading in literary theories, most argument textbooks now contain a chapter on "reading arguments." But the argument textbooks that we consider do not present reading as constitutive of meaning; rather, they assume and neutralize isolated tenets of the reception theories we've described as part of their instruction in "finding meaning." As a consequence, the books give students a simplistic outlook on their roles in the reasoning process, confine discussions of affect to sections on "appeals to emotion," and suggest throughout that, while logic is unassailable, feelings skew the picture. The authors of the textbooks we are about to examine rarely discuss the politics of reading and seem to view argument as emotion free. It is not our intention in what follows to "blame" textbook authors for "erroneous" views. Rather, we see the tendencies we are about to describe as symptomatic of the reduction of (constructed) knowledge to (commodified) information in what Bill Readings, in *The University in Ruins,* has called "the managed university," really a corporation, in which student/consumers purchase credits rather than achieve understanding. What we hope to do instead is to point to a lacuna in argument theory (as presented by these textbooks) that can be addressed by a theory of argument in cultural context.

HOW IS THE CONTROVERSY WE'VE IDENTIFIED
RELATED TO THEORIES OF ARGUMENT?

As Richard Ohmann demonstrated years ago in *English in America,* the authors of argument textbooks seem to assume (although they feel no need to argue the point) that logic governs society and that power yields to its demands. Moreover, Ohmann asserted, textbooks often present theories of argument as composed of invariant trans-historical and trans-cultural concepts. Good reasons, clearly and sincerely presented, will win the day. When reading others' arguments, it is necessary for student readers to attend to their clear presentation of reasons, rather than to raise questions about motives, class identification, ethnic difference, gendered feelings, and so forth. Finally, these textbooks present reading as a process, not of making meaning, but of finding out authorial intention.

The following propositions from Crusius and Channell's section on "Reading an Argument" suggest that little has changed since Ohmann's *English in America.* Taken at face value, they offer commonplaces of reading theory. But these commonplaces are strangely inconsistent. The sentences that follow, for example, imply an uncritical and confusing range of "meaning conditions."

1. "You should read arguments critically [. . .] to decide how well the argument achieves *its aim.*" (17)

2. "Experts have found that readers who have the greatest success comprehending the ideas in any text meet two criteria: (1) They have some prior knowledge of the subject matter, and (2) they are able to see a piece of writing in *its rhetorical context.* Such readers can use *context to determine the meaning of unfamiliar words,* and they are often able to 'read between the lines,' recognizing ideas and assumptions that are only implied." (17)

3. "Critical readers breathe life into a written argument by seeing it as part of a dynamic activity. They think of the author as a human being with hopes, fears, biases, ambitions, and—most importantly—a purpose that his or her words on the page are intended to accomplish. *The argument becomes an action,* aimed at affecting a particular audience in a particular place and time." (17)

The first statement, rather like the New Criticism of the 1950s, seems to locate the meaning of the text *in* the text. Both the aim and its achievement are in the argument, not the author. The third statement, however, locates meaning in the author's intention and appears to assume that the author's "hopes, fears, biases, ambitions" are consciously available and a part of that intention. The intervening statement suggests that the reader plays a considerable role in the process, by bringing to it "prior knowledge of the subject matter," "read[ing] between the lines," and using context. But for Crusius and Channell, the reader's prior knowledge of the subject matter and "ability to read between the lines, recognizing ideas and assumptions that are only implied" might be said to invoke Wolfgang Iser's notion of repertoire but they operate, not to encourage her to call the repertoire into question, but to "comprehend ideas." And knowledge of context would seem to be useful only to "determine the meaning of unfamiliar words."

Of course the three statements are not mutually exclusive; nor do we wish to insist on a spurious consistency. On the contrary, Crusius and Channell's "dynamic activity" seems close to what Louise Rosenblatt would call a transaction between author and reader, in which a reader might try to come to terms with authorial intention while remaining aware that intentions are neither knowable nor always achieved.

But the reader of an argument needs not only to come to terms with the argument as the intentional act of an author but also to decide whether to accept that argument and how, if necessary, to refute it. To that task, Crusius and Channell bring this advice, using terms from reception theory:

> Virtually every piece of writing about an issue is part of an ongoing conversation, involving a number of participants who represent a range of opinions and who have each contributed a variety of ideas, facts, and authoritative citations to the debate. The greater a reader's familiarity with this background, the easier it is for him or her to approach a new argument from a critical perspective, filling in any gaps of information and recognizing a writer's assumptions and biases. [. . .] If you are conscious of the attitudes and ideas you bring to your reading, you can better see an argument in its own light and not so much colored by your own biases. (16)

But whereas for Iser a gap is a space of indeterminacy that prompts a reader to "ideate" or imagine connections and consistencies among disparate moments of reading, the term "gap" here seems merely to designate a lack of information on the reader's part. Crusius and Channell's use of the word *bias* is even more alarming. They don't define the word, but (*as they advise*) we've assumed from context that *bias* means something like "ideology," which we understand as Louis Althusser describes it: a subject's [or reader's] imaginary relation to the real, a narrative, in other words, through which a subject makes sense of the world she or he experiences in terms of preexisting beliefs instilled by various Ideological State Apparatuses—probably not the sense of "bias" they "intended," we'd guess. Rather than explaining to students that no one can be ideology-free (as, for example, in the discussion above) though, Crusius and Channell caution students to be aware of their own "biases" in order to recognize those of the author. They do not explain how this process might work. We are conscious of our "bias" concerning "ideology" but see no reason to discard it in favor of the neutrality they recommend. Since they offer no delineation of how one frees oneself from such biases, we find ourselves stumped. Discussions of reasoning in the research of cognitive psychologists do not assume that persons are capable of bracketing their cognitive frameworks. In a recent textbook on the *Fundamentals of Cognition,* Mark Ashcraft notes that, according to the most recent research findings, comprehension involves not only a "conceptual level" at which persons analyze "the message with respect to general world knowledge" but also a "belief level" where the text is analyzed "with respect to the speaker's and listener's knowledge of each other, and the context of the utterance." In the final analysis, the argument goes, belief depends upon the audience's "belief system" (Ashcraft 277–79).

To show the kinds of problems attempting to follow the advice given in this textbook might occasion, we have tried to read statement 3 (above) as we are advised to do by statements 1 and 2. The claim that "the argument becomes an action" when "critical readers breathe life into" words as part of a "dynamic activity" in which "they think of the author as a human being with hopes, fears, biases, ambitions," invites students to "think" (imagine) another person on the basis of the words in the text. Prompted by our professional and scholarly interests (biases?) as teachers of argument and readers of the works of twentieth-century rhetorician Kenneth Burke, we see "dynamic activity" as Burke's conception of identification, a process through which a rhetor rediscovers the emotions (fears, hopes) that stimulated an utterance. As a consequence, we notice that the list of reading questions Crusius and Channell suggest in their next paragraph are consistent with Burke's description of the "pentad" in *A Grammar of Motives* (1945):

When was this argument written? (If not recently, how might it be helpful to know something about the time it first appeared?)

Why was it written? What prompted its creation?

Who is the author, and what is his or her occupation, personal background, political leanings?

Where does the article appear? If it is reprinted, where did it appear originally?

For whom do you think the author is writing?

What purpose does the author have in writing. What does he or she hope to accomplish through the act of making this argument? (17)

When, Where, Why, Who, and How are the questions that reveal what Burke termed "scene," "purpose," "agent," and "agency" of the "act" of the argument, the five elements of the pentad. In thinking of Crusius and Channell as advocates of Burkean rhetoric, our *response* is legitimized by the instruction we are given as readers. Because we recognize "scene," "act," "agent," "agency," and "motive" in the questions the textbook advises its readers to ask, we again assume that the guidelines are informed by a Burkean sense of indeterminate meaning, constantly in play, constantly under revision in the great discursive parlor.

At the same time, we can imagine this passage being read by students who have never heard of Kenneth Burke. Since the passage does not attribute the position to him, and his name does not appear in the index, a student reader advised to ask questions about an author's intentions ("What purpose does the author have in writing. What does he or she hope to accomplish through the act of making this argument?" [*A Grammar of Motives*, 17]) would be likely to assume that Crusius and Channel are instructing her to look for stable intention and that interacting with the text (as we just did) will lead her to it. However, can we safely assume, especially in the absence of reference to Burke, that symbolic action is what Crusius and Channel have in mind? What has our "transaction" with their text accomplished? Reception theory, then, (if only in the sense of the reader's relation to the text is understood as a transaction) has made its way into this textbook, but the use of its conceptions is reductive and oriented toward the fixing of meaning rather than an analysis of its free play. Our belief system (our biases, ideologies), just as cognitive psychologists predict, is the source of the meaning of the text. At the purely semantic level, the text offers theoroids as a kind of nondenominational belief system that is supposed to replace one's own.

In *Elements of Argument*, Annette Rottenberg writes that, "Critical, or close, reading of arguments leads to greater-comprehension [. . .]—understanding what the author is trying to prove. Then comes evaluation—careful judgment of the extent to which the author has succeeded" (x).

The equation of "critical or close reading" is problematic here. From a theoretical point of view, "close reading," a formalist attempt to comprehend the text as a semantic network (as Rottenberg seems to recommend), is not a "critique." Moreover, if the comprehension to which it supposedly leads is limited to "understanding what the author is trying to prove," then the student is being instructed precisely *not* to be "critical." Such a student has neither incentive nor opportunity to discover *why* (ideologically) the author's point *needs* to be proved, who will profit from that proof, and how. This advice explicitly evades the notion of critical reading that it seems to advocate. Although Rottenberg cautions "evaluation" of "the extent to which the author has succeeded," she eschews (in this passage at least) advice about the context of the success. Consider, however, this passage: "Good readers are never merely passive recipients of the material. They engage in active dialogue with the author, as if he or she were present, asking questions, offering objections, expressing approval" (26). Rottenberg's pronoun reference here is slightly confusing. Is it the author or the reader who asks questions, offers objections, expresses approval? (We don't know what Annette Rottenberg intends here!) The conventions of English usage suggest that the author, as imagined by the student reader, gives approval for comprehension. But if the student reader seeks the author's approval, she or he is not behaving critically. The student reader in this passage is advised to try to imagine what the author intended. And she is persistently guided to do so through a combination of "close reading" and "biographical speculation." For example, under the caption, "Here are a few strategies for close reading of an argument," is the following advice:

> As you read the essay for the first time, look for the main idea and the structure of the whole essay. Make a skeleton outline in your mind or on paper. Remember that your purpose in reading an argument is to *learn what the author wants to prove and how he or she proves it,* and to frame a response to it as you read. At this stage, avoid concentrating on details. Reading is a complex mental operation, and you cannot do everything at once. (26, emphasis added)

In this passage, the student is advised to concentrate on the main idea and her response to it as she reads in order to discover what the author intends to "prove." This invitation to "reader response" is couched in (and in our view reduced to) the discourse of the biographically oriented literary history that New Criticism replaced. A student who successfully follows Rottenberg's advice will allow the text to assimilate her into its ideology—that meaning is stable and determinable. Rottenberg offers another similarly untheorized delineation of the process of reading:

> Don't be timid about asking questions of the text. No author is infallible. Some authors are not always clear. Ask any questions whose answers are necessary to improve your comprehension. Disagree with the author if you feel confident of the support for your view. After you have read the whole argument, you may discover that most of your early questions have been answered. If not, this may be a signal to read the article again. Be cautious about concluding that the author hasn't proved his point. (27)

In this passage, students are advised to conduct a "dialogue" with the text in which they raise and answer questions that occur to them. But unlike the reception theorists who would see this dialogue as indeterminate, the overarching purpose of the Rottenberg dialogue is to discover *whether the author has proved his point.* Student readers may disagree only if they are "confident" about the support of their view. If they still disagree, they are instructed to read again, to be cautious about concluding that the author has failed. As the author describes it, reading is most difficult when the reader is attempting to discern the truth of a complicated issue. Here most explicitly, the reader-response guidelines are negated by an uncritical appeal to truth.

How many thinkers who have changed the world, we wonder, would have met Annette Rottenberg's criteria for disagreeing with its reigning paradigms? The power of feminist, Marxist, and postcolonial readings comes precisely from their refusal to accept the "self-evident" premises of hegemonic texts. Judith Fetterley's reading of "Indian Camp," for example, emerges most forcefully from her refusal to accept the premise that a woman's screams are not important. Fredric Jameson's reading of *Lord Jim* in *The Political Unconscious* is quite explicitly a refusal to assent to its racist and colonialist assumptions.

In our third example, from Ramage and Bean's *Writing Arguments,* as in the first, our responses as readers of an argument text are invited and the implied readers are still the same de-culturalized, disembodied students with an unproblematized reader-response orientation toward arguments. Ramage and Bean invite their student readers to read arguments (a) as believers, (b) as doubters, (c) as analysts, and (d) as judges (20). Thus the reader's attitudes are given a central role as a condition of the meaningfulness of the text. As in the previous two examples, students are instructed to view the process of reading dialogically, as a conversation with the author. They are also asked to "reconstruct" the rhetorical context, adducing the same set of "what, why, where, when and how" questions. The role of readers' strategies is made explicit.

In the recommendation that students read arguments as believers, the concept of empathy as delineated in the work of Carl Rogers[6] authorizes the strategy. As evidence of appropriate (believer) empathy, students are asked to restate (summarize) the argument and "examine all the ways in which you could agree with [the author] by bringing your own experience and values to bear supportively" (31). Ramage and Bean give no indication that this process might be in any way problematic. Instead, instructions about summarizing, paraphrasing, and outlining are given as if students who held beliefs contrary to the one argued could suspend them at will, clearing the ground for a detached engagement of opposing beliefs.

The sentence introducing the "second" strategy seems to suggest that it takes place simultaneously with the first.

> But reading as a believer is only half of being a powerful reader. You must also read as a doubter by raising objections, asking questions, expressing skepticism, and withholding assent. In the margins you add a new layer of notations demanding more proof, doubting evidence, challenging the author's assumptions and values, and so forth. (39)

In their annotated "student readings" of the sample essay, Ramage and Bean show their student readers how to read as a believer and then as a doubter. Inevitably, we think, students are given to understand that reading is a process of belief followed by doubt: "our point [they write] is that you should practice 'doubting' an argument as well as 'believing' it" (41). What we find troublesome about these instructions is that the student reader is never told that she is being asked first to establish a context for meaning and then to question the ideological assumptions of that context. The language of belief and doubt obscures the conflict that occasions the argument in the first place. Belief and doubt are surely central to any theory of argument. Yet the notion that we should "practice" doubt (in the sense of practice makes perfect) seems counterintuitive. To Ramage and Bean, practicing doubt is evidently *not* uncritical, unreflective, or counterintuitive. Yet, our *response* is surely "valid." All responses are valid responses—that is the problem reader-response theory brought to light.

Ramage and Bean introduce their third and fourth reading strategies (analysis and evaluation) by remarking that "sources of disagreement [. . .] often fall into two categories: disagreement about the facts or truth of the case, and (2) disagreement about underlying beliefs, values or assumptions, including assumptions about definitions" (42). But they do not explain how this disagreement occurs. Is it the result of multiple "rational" viewpoints, or is it that rational presentations of incommensurable needs and desires necessarily conflict? Isn't it more often the case that people disagree about who gets to formulate the question at issue and how that question gets formulated? For example, would someone who wishes to repeal *Roe v. Wade* call herself "anti-choice"? Would someone who seeks to preserve the rights Roe granted to U.S. women call himself "anti-life"?

The authors suggest that there are two sources of disagreement: (a) facts or truth, and (b) values, beliefs, or assumptions (Ramage and Bean 42). If we examine these areas, they suggest, we are likely to find the "reason" for the disagreement and thus adjudicate between the disputants. But Ramage and Bean conspicuously omit greed, hatred, power, lust, envy, and lies as reasons for disagreement. Instead, they present arguments as textualized artifacts open to investigation rather than as cultural practices fraught with struggle and pain. To a generation of students who have grown up with TV advertising, the pronouncements of the tobacco and automobile industries, the greenhouse effect, the telecasts of the Gulf War, virtual reality, presidential campaigns, and trash news, the process of "reading" arguments is not the clean-cut, unambiguous, disciplined, and ethical debate they are being asked in these textbooks to take on in conversations with imagined author(s). From a cultural context wherein logic is regarded as reductive and oppressive, argument textbooks would seem elitist and complicit with the conservation of the economic status quo. If so, then streetwise students are likely to find argument textbooks implausible if not laughable.

Furthermore, although arguments are often, even usually, constructed along rational lines, they are not necessarily always conducted by "reasonable people." Rather, we believe, they are conducted by persons whose interests, needs, and desires are likely to be fulfilled by their discursive success. Consider a minority student who has experienced "arguments" that deny her loans, housing, jobs, status, and health care. Consider the tobacco industries' argument that nicotine has not been "proven" harmful. Consider arguments about how welfare provides a safety net for the truly needy but denies cheaters their ill-gotten gains. Consider the arguments of industry spokespersons giving reasons why the harmful effects to a community have occurred despite their best efforts.

We of course agree that our students often read carelessly, imposing ill-considered beliefs onto readings with which they therefore "disagree."

Our point, though, is that pretending that meaning is stable is not a good way to get these students to be more responsible.

The pattern we are tracking is one in which reception theory is loosely assimilated into existing new critical assumptions without changing them. Multiple, various, gendered, and raced readers' responses are invited, that is to say, on the assumption that the text will govern their responses. Virtually no acknowledgment of the cultural diversity of readers is made. Furthermore, no attention is paid to the ways in which economic considerations affect the authors' choice of readings, their explanations, and their theories of argument.

Even though we've never met Crusius, Channel, Ramage, Bean, and Rottenberg, we're prepared to believe that they are neither uninformed nor meretricious. Quite the contrary, we believe categorically that they are intelligent and decent people who have striven in their writing to help their student readers learn to argue better. Furthermore, as the authors of textbooks ourselves, we know on the pulse that the labor of making a textbook is arduous and that authors are frequently asked or even required to produce a common denominator of ideas dumbed down to common sense. We have been in one sense quite unfair to the textbook authors we have used as evidence in our argument. These five authors and countless others have needed to "reduce" and de-complicate their guidance.

Who profits from such reductions? Not students. When a student enters an electrical engineering class, she does not expect that the teacher will offer her a "dumbed down" version of Visual Basic. When a chemist prepares to teach an introductory course, she uses the latest version of the periodic table—the one that includes all the elements she knows about. It seems obvious that if students are capable of learning a highly encoded programming language like C++ or very abstract scientific concepts, then they are capable of learning and deserve to be taught the most recent and most cogent theories of argument.

And because we believe that such reductiveness does everyone a disservice, we've elected to try to show what happens to the intelligent work of decent people when they are treated as de-culturated and disembodied implied authors.

Another way of making our point would be to say that we think of arguments, not as texts, but as cultural practices.

We are not interested in some sort of return to "pure" reader-response theory. On the contrary, we conclude by pleading for more respect for the intelligence students will bring to these texts. As teachers, should we not help our students to see the unreasonableness of certain positions and of the persons who hold them?

NOTES

1. We understand "reader response criticism" as a term used in the United States by such thinkers as David Bleich, Norman Holland, and Jane P. Tompkins to point to psycho-analytic or psychological processes through which readers "make meaning." "Reception aesthetics" is Wolfgang Iser's name for his phenomenological study of the processes through which readers construct an aesthetic object.
2. See, for example, Ralph Cintron's *Angels' Town: Chero Ways, Gang Life, and Rhetorics of the Everyday.*
3. In "The Theory Junkyard," James J. Sosnoski takes up the question of the life cycle of theories in literary studies.
4. We're heartened by the work of such scholars as Elizabeth Miles, whose dissertation, *Building Rhetorics of Production: An Institutional Critique of Composition Textbook Publishing,* earned the James Berlin Dissertation Award from the Conference on College Composition and Communication. Miles examines relations between the textbook industry and the institutional edifice of composition studies.
5. In their *Reception Study: From Literary Theory to Cultural Studies,* James L. Machor and Philip Goldstein trace a different history of studies of reading and readers. Richard Beach's *A Teacher's Introduction to Reader-Response Theories* is particularly useful for its treatment of pedagogical matters.
6. Cf. his notion of "client centered therapy" in *On Becoming a Person.*

WORKS CITED

Althusser, Louis. *For Marx.* Trans. Ben Brewster. New York: Verso, 1990.

Ashcraft, Mark H. *Fundamentals of Cognition.* New York: Longman, 1998.

Barthes, Roland. *S/Z.* New York: Hill, 1977.

Bartholomae, David, and Anthony Petrosky. *Ways of Reading.* 5th ed. Boston: Bedford/ St. Martin's, 1999.

Beach, Richard. *A Teacher's Introduction to Reader-Response Theories.* Urbana: NCTE, 1993.

Bleich, David. "In Case of Fire, Throw in: What to Do with Textbooks Once You Switch to Sourcebooks." *(Re) Visioning Composition Textbooks: Conflicts of Culture, Ideology, and Pedagogy.* Ed. Xin Lu Gale and Fredric G. Gale. Albany: State U of New York P, 1999. 15–42.

———. *Readings and Feelings.* Urbana: NCTE, 1975.

Burke, Kenneth. *A Grammar of Motives.* Berkeley: U of California P, 1969.

———. *A Rhetoric of Motives.* Berkeley: U of California P, 1969.

Cintron, Ralph. *Angels' Town: Chero Ways, Gang Life, and Rhetorics of the Everyday.* Boston: Beacon, 1997.

Crosman, Inge, and Susan Suleiman, eds. *The Reader in the Text.* Princeton: Princeton UP, 1980.

Crusius, Timothy W., and Carolyn E. Channell. *The Aims of Argument.* Mountain View, CA: Mayfield, 1995.

Eco, Umberto. *The Role of the Reader: Explorations in the Semiotics of Texts.* Bloomington: Indiana UP, 1979.

Fetterley, Judith. *The Resisting Reader.* Bloomington: Indiana UP, 1978.

Fish, Stanley. "How to Recognize a Poem When You See One." *Is There a Text in This Class?* Cambridge: Harvard UP, 1980.

_____. "Why No One's Afraid of Wolfgang Iser." *Diacritics* (Spring 1981): 2–13.

Graff, Gerald. *Professing Literature.* Chicago: U of Chicago P, 1987.

Hairston, Maxine. "Breaking Our Bonds and Reaffirming Our Connections," *College Composition and Communication* 36 (1985): 272–82.

Harkin, Patricia. *Acts of Reading.* Upper Saddle River, NJ: Prentice-Hall, 1998.

Hemingway, Ernest. *The Short Stories.* New York: Scribner's, 1995.

Holland, Norman. *Five Readers Reading.* New Haven: Yale UP, 1975.

Ingarden, Roman. *The Cognition of the Literary Work.* Evanston: Northwestern UP, 1973.

Iser, Wolfgang. *The Act of Reading: A Theory of Aesthetic Response.* Baltimore: Johns Hopkins UP, 1979.

Jameson, Fredric. *The Political Unconscious: Narrative as a Socially Symbolic Act.* Ithaca: Cornell UP, 1981.

Machor, James L., and Philip Goldstein. *Reception Study: From Literary Theory to Cultural Studies.* New York and London: Routledge, 2001.

McCormick, Kathleen, Gary Waller, and Linda Flower. *Reading Texts: Reading, Responding, Writing.* Lexington, MA: Heath, 1987.

Miles, Elizabeth. *Building Rhetorics of Production: An Institutional Critique of Composition Textbook Publishing.* Diss. Purdue U, 1999.

Ohmann, Richard. *English in America.* New York: Oxford UP, 1977.

Petrosky, Anthony. "From Story to Essay: Reading and Writing." *College Composition and Communication* 33 (Feb. 1992): 19–37.

Ramage, John, and John Bean. *Writing Arguments: A Rhetoric with Readings.* 4th ed. Boston: Allyn, 1998.

Readings, Bill. *The University in Ruins.* Cambridge: Harvard UP, 1996.

Richards, I. A. *Practical Criticism: A Study of Literary Judgment.* New York: Harcourt, 1929.

Rogers, Carl. *On Becoming a Person: A Therapist's View of Psychotherapy.* Boston: Houghton, 1961.

Rosenblatt, Louise. *Literature as Exploration.* New York: MLA, 1995.

Rottenberg, Annette T. *Elements of Argument.* 5th ed. Boston: Bedford, 1997.

Salvatori, Mariolina. "Reading and Writing a Text: Correlations between Reading and Writing Patterns." *College English* 45 (Nov. 1983): 657–66.

Saussure, Ferdinand de. *Course in General Linguistics.* Ed. Charles Bally and Albert Sechehaye. Trans. Roy Harris. London: Duckworth, 1983.

Smith, Frank. *Psycholinguistics and Reading.* New York: Holt, 1973.

Sosnoski, James J. "The Theory Junkyard." *Minnesota Review* 41–2 (1994): 80–94.

Tompkins, Jane P. *Reader Response Criticism.* Baltimore: Johns Hopkins UP, 1980.

6

Reading the Visual
in College Writing Classes

Charles A. Hill

For about a decade now, scholars have been declaring that the age of printed text is all but over. Jay Bolter claims that we are now in "the late age of print" (2) and in 1994, Sven Birkerts estimated that printed books would be dominant for about another fifty years (121), to be replaced almost entirely with online hypermedia forms of communication. But regardless of whether one agrees with these and other obituaries of the print medium, it would be difficult to deny the importance of electronic and other visual media in today's society. The students now entering our classrooms have grown up with 100 channels of television, and the World Wide Web is no longer a novelty, but part of their social, academic, and working lives. If we include nonelectronic sources of visual communication such as billboards, print advertisements, and the ubiquitous packaging that has taken such an important place in our consumer culture, then we have to conclude that most of the information that our students are exposed to is in a visual form.

There is little doubt that the increasing ubiquity of visual and aural forms of communication is one of the reasons that so many students arrive at the university with apparently little experience with the written word. However, while our students might engage relatively rarely with print text, we should not therefore conclude that their lives are devoid of information or of expression. Quite the opposite is true. Our students may have been exposed to more "texts" than any other generation in history, and many of these texts are dense with cultural information. One might argue that most of these texts are designed primarily to entertain or to sell something rather than to offer information or increase one's understanding of complex issues; nevertheless, our students are exposed to a broad range of information daily. So far, our educational system has failed to take seriously and to adequately respond to the fact that so much of this information is in visual form. As Barbara Stafford notes, "In most American university curricula, graphicacy remains subordinate to literacy" (5).

THE NEGLECT OF THE VISUAL

One might assume—or at least hope—that a major goal of the educational system is to help students develop the abilities necessary to comprehend, interpret, and critically respond to the textual forms that they will encounter as members of the culture. Since so many of the texts that our students encounter are visual ones, and since visual literacy is becoming increasingly important for everyday social functioning and even for success in the workplace (Kress and van Leeuwen 2–3), it would seem obvious that our educational institutions should be spending at least as much time and energy on developing students' visual literacies as these institutions spend on developing students' textual literacy. However, both in the classroom and in literacy research, the amount of time and effort devoted to developing students' abilities to comprehend, analyze, and critique visual messages is relatively miniscule.

As a result, Americans tend to act as passive consumers rather than as critics or analysts of visual messages. While we are all being increasingly exposed to highly manipulated images meant to influence our beliefs, opinions, and behaviors, very few of us are adequately prepared to analyze and critique these images in order to make informed decisions about them. In fact, many people seem unaware of the rhetorical power of images and of their mediated nature. The adage "seeing is believing" is often applied, not just to natural objects that are being directly perceived, but often to visual representations of objects, people, and events, as well. Photographs and video, in particular, are typically treated as "direct copies of reality" rather than as representations designed to influence viewers in particular ways (Messaris, vi).

The field of rhetoric in general, and the subfield of composition in particular, have largely ignored visual types of expression, especially in the classroom. This is true for many reasons, largely historical. It could be argued that visual forms of rhetorical expression have not become predominant until recently, and that the methodological and theoretical work necessary for the analysis of visual rhetoric is in the process of catching up to its increasing presence and importance. But this argument cannot fully explain the scholarly neglect of visual information. From the iconography of the medieval church to the propaganda posters of the two world wars, it cannot be denied that visual forms of rhetoric have always existed and have always served important functions in society (Purves). Why, then, has visual rhetoric been so neglected, especially as its power and influence have grown steadily over the last century?

Perhaps this neglect can be largely attributed to a widespread and traditional dislike and disparagement of mass culture, and from our fears that visual and other modes of communication will overtake, replace, or diminish the importance of the print medium (Stafford; Stroupe; Welch). When most people think of visual media, they think of the "vast wasteland" of television (including the much-derided music video), comic books, picture books (produced for young children who have not yet "progressed" to purely verbal texts), "coffee table books" (usually considered more decorative than informative or scholarly), and Hollywood cinema (though, of these genres, film is generally assumed to have more promise as a "serious" medium). Despite our supposed postmodern rejections of canonical hierarchies that would place literary and scholarly texts above such commercially produced and widely disseminated "texts," we still tend to favor words over images, and we worry defensively that our students are spending too much time watching television and surfing the Web, and not enough time reading books. Stafford describes the present situation in the scholarly community eloquently: "The passionate visualist, roaming the labyrinth of the postdisciplinary age, is haunted by the paradoxical ubiquity and degradation of images: everywhere transmitted, universally viewed, but as a category generally despised" (11).

When educators discuss among themselves the role of visual forms of communication (especially the culturally dominant, mass-produced forms), it is usually to express and reinforce the worry that students are already too reliant on the visual, in many cases almost to the exclusion of written forms, and that educators should be trying to arrest that trend in their classrooms, not reinforce it. Dealing with visual texts in university classrooms might seem like surrendering to the inevitable "dumbing down" of our society's discourse or pandering to our students' lazy tendencies (Stafford 3). However, the avoidance of taking images seriously in general education, and especially in writing classrooms, is based on some assumptions that may not be valid.

The most basic, and perhaps the most misguided, of these assumptions is that we could ever draw a distinct line between the visual and the verbal, or that concentrating on one can or should require ignoring the other. As W. J. T. Mitchell argues, "recent developments in art history, film theory, and what is loosely called 'cultural studies' make the notion of a purely verbal literacy increasingly problematic" (6). Communication has always been a hybrid blending of visual, written, and aural forms, and the new electronic technologies are making this melding of media easier and more common, requiring readers and writers to have a richer understanding of how words and images work together to produce meaning (Stroupe 618; Welch 131, 157). James Elkins argues that "mixed images" (incorporating some combination of pictures, words, and/or notations) are the norm rather than the exception (91). He goes on to argue that, while it may be useful to make a conceptual distinction between a "pure" image (requiring no verbal interpretation) and a "pure" text (with no meaningful visual element), we should recognize that this purity does not exist in the real world, and pedagogical efforts should be aimed toward helping students deal with combinations of picture, word, and symbol. Perhaps Mitchell makes the case most adamantly: "all media are mixed media, and all representations are heterogeneous; there are no 'purely' visual or verbal arts" (5).

Even if we could make a clear-cut and reasonable distinction between purely verbal texts and purely visual ones, it would still be a mistake to concentrate our teaching efforts on reading and writing to the exclusion of other modes of communication and to neglect visual forms. Most students enter the university unable to articulate any principles about how visual messages work and without any of the skills or habits necessary to critically analyze such messages. In fact, largely because they have adopted the prejudices and fears of their educators and of the larger culture, many university students need to be convinced that visual images constitute meaningful texts at all in the sense that people are used to thinking about written texts. The very dominance and ubiquity of visual messages suggests that our students should develop at least a basic understanding of how they work. Students also need to develop both the ability and the inclination to examine their own reactions to such messages, if they are to have any real independence and effectiveness as social agents.

Finally, images should be studied and understood because of the unique epistemic power they possess. As Stafford argues, images are not "just more efficient conveyors of extant verbal information"; rather, they are "indispensable in discovering that which could not otherwise be known" (40). In other words, images are not just another method for expressing propositions that could otherwise be expressed in verbal form. Rather, they are essential for expressing, and therefore for knowing, things that cannot be expressed in any other form. To ignore images is to ignore all of the knowledge that they can help us develop, knowledge that cannot be logically deduced or proven; they "help us to organize and make sense of that floating world, that milieu, stretching considerably below certitude and somewhat above ignorance" (Stafford 39).

The public's general inability to interpret and analyze visual images has not gone entirely unnoticed. At its November 1996 meeting, the National Council of Teachers of English passed a resolution to "support professional development and promote public awareness of the role that viewing and visually representing our world have as forms of literacy" ("NCTE Passes Visual Literacy Resolution"). And educators are developing curricular units and materials on nearly every educational level to help students interpret and accurately respond to visual messages. Still, these initiatives are often treated as add-on units, subordinated to the larger goal of developing students' reading and writing abilities. For a variety of reasons, educators in general, and perhaps those of us in the humanities above all, continue to neglect visual sources of communication in favor of verbal texts.

If literacy development were a zero-sum game, in which our time and energies must necessarily be spent on *either* written *or* visual literacies, then this neglect would be understandable, perhaps even defensible. However, ignoring the visual aspects of rhetoric, even the visual aspects of written texts, hinders our efforts to help students develop an accurate understanding of the nature of rhetorical practice, including an adequate understanding of the potential, as well as the limitations, of written discourse.

TOWARD A PEDAGOGY OF VISUAL RHETORIC

It is one thing to argue that university students should be exposed to more explicit instruction about the uses of visual communication, and it is quite another to develop a workable pedagogy for dealing with visual rhetoric. Such a pedagogy has not yet been developed, partly because no one recognizable discipline has staked a claim around the immense and vaguely defined area that is variously referred to as "visual communication," "visual rhetoric," or "visual literacy." Research and scholarship in the production, comprehension, interpretation, and analysis of visuals continually takes place in fields as diverse as art history, anthropology, education, semiotics, film studies, political science, psychology, and cultural studies, but none of these disciplines can claim the study of visual communication as its own, and there is little coordination among the various fields that study it. Roy Fox proposes an interdisciplinary endeavor that would be called "Image Studies," and that would draw from the sciences, social sciences, humanities, and arts. But until such a formalized collaboration exists, we have nowhere to look for a highly developed pedagogy of visual rhetoric.

In fact, because visual communication does not yet have a formalized disciplinary framework, we do not even have generally accepted definitions and parameters within which to work. For example, what sorts of visual input should be included in a pedagogy of "visual communication"? Or, working from the process of elimination, what sorts of visual input are we willing to say are *not* communicative? Humans process visual input continuously, and much of this input is consciously interpreted as carrying meaning or implying something beyond the specific empirical data being observed. For example, a viewer who sees a tree bending in a sudden wind may interpret the image to mean that a storm is approaching. Similarly, a viewer may see a person in ragged clothing pushing a shopping cart through a downtown area, and interpret these signs as indicating that the person is homeless (Worth and Gross). However, while these kinds of visual images are interpreted as carrying meaning beyond the visual data they provide, they would not generally be considered instances of visual *communication* because they are not images created by an agent for the purpose of communicating some particular information or ideas to others. Worth and Gross call these kinds of events "natural signs"—imagistic events that the viewer might consciously interpret, but without making any assumption that an agent is creating or distributing these images in order to communicate an idea.

On the other hand, a *painting* of a tree bending in the wind would be interpreted, not as a natural event, but as a conscious representation of such an event. The viewer interprets such images with the assumption that a deliberate intent to communicate is driving the production and distribution of the image. Worth and Gross call such image-events "symbolic signs." So, for example, if we are watching a documentary, and we see in the documentary a shot of a person in ragged clothing pushing a shopping cart though a downtown area, we assume that the producer of the documentary has consciously chosen to include that image in the film in order to influence the viewer's reactions. It is this intent (or, more precisely, the viewer's assumption that this intent exists) that makes this shot in the documentary a *symbolic* sign.

These classifications are not objective ones. What distinguishes a natural sign from a symbolic sign is the viewer's interpretation of the image event. For example, if two people see a homeless person walking down the street, the first viewer may determine that the homeless person is merely going about his or her business, unmindful of how the image he or she is projecting may be interpreted by others, while the second viewer may decide that the person being viewed is deliberately "playing up" the image of homelessness in order to affect the reactions of passersby. (A viewer could also suspect that the "homeless" person is a performance artist, a sociological researcher, or an undercover police officer, deliberately creating an image of homelessness in order to produce a specific reaction in passersby.) In this case, the first viewer would see the ragged clothing and the shopping cart as elements of a natural sign, while the second viewer would see the same elements as constituting a symbolic sign (a deliberate attempt to project an image of homelessness).

It is relatively easy to exclude naturally occurring events, those that are not produced or influenced by humans, from the category of symbolic signs (unless one posits some nonhuman entity deliberately attempting to communicate with us through these events). But it seems impossible to say of almost any human action that it is not in any way influenced by a communicative intention. Almost any human action (even sitting still or some other form of nonaction) could be interpreted as resulting from a communicative intent. However, if our aim is to develop a workable pedagogy of visual rhetoric, we will have to draw the boundaries around our subject matter a little more tightly.

Walker and Chaplin follow many theorists in distinguishing between mediated and unmediated vision (23). When we look at a cow standing in a field, we are directly perceiving the cow, unmediated by any outside filter. But when we see a painting or a drawing or a photograph of a cow, or see it in a film, then we are seeing, not the cow itself, but a representation of it. The representation works by instantiating our memories of cows we have seen firsthand, along with any of our feelings or attitudes about cows that the producer of the image would like to instantiate. Even if the viewer has never seen a real, unmediated cow, the viewer understands that such creatures exist, and that they have particular traits and associations that the creator of the image would like to bring to the forefront of the viewer's consciousness.

From a purely theoretical perspective, of course, it is highly problematic to speak of concrete objects as being unmediated images. Too many people make the mistake of insisting on a rigid binary distinction between mediated and "real" objects, in essence positing two separate worlds—the "real" world, which we can walk through or drive through, looking at cows and barns and trees—and the world of created images, consisting of paintings or photographs or drawings of these objects, as well as movies and television shows that include images of them.

In almost every instance in which the physical, "real" world and the world of representations are compared, the physical world is assumed to be the preferable, superior, the more "authentic" of the two, and therefore more epistemologically trustworthy. The assumption behind this hierarchy of values is that, while images are a representation of someone else's perception of an event, and therefore tainted by that person's biases and imperfections, the physical world provides the opportunity for pure, untainted perception. This assumption, though, cannot begin to stand up to the considerable challenges that face it. First, a vast amount of scientific research on the subject of perception makes clear that we perceive events around us very imperfectly and incompletely. Because we cannot possibly process all of the visual information that bombards us on a continual basis, we actively filter and prioritize the visual information we are exposed to, and this filtering and prioritizing process is driven by our own preconceptions, desires, biases, and value judgments.

The second challenge to the assumption of the purity of direct perception consists of a simple recognition that all of our perceptions are influenced by cultural values and assumptions. One of the most succinct and persuasive accounts of this recognition is given in a work of fiction: Don DeLillo's *White Noise*. In DeLillo's novel, Murray Siskind, a professor of popular culture studies, accompanies the novel's narrator to "a tourist attraction known as the most photographed barn in America" (12). The narrator and Murray watch as crowds of tourists take pictures of the barn.

> Murray maintained a prolonged silence, occasionally scrawling some notes in a little book.
>
> "No one sees the barn," he said finally. "Once you've seen the signs about the barn, it becomes impossible to see the barn." [. . .]
>
> "Being here is a kind of spiritual surrender. We see only what the others see. The thousands who were here in the past, those who will come in the future. We've agreed to be part of a collective perception. This literally colors our vision." [. . .]
>
> "What was the barn like before it was photographed?" he said. "What did it look like, how was it different from other barns, how was it similar to other barns? We can't answer these questions because we've read the signs,

seen the people snapping the pictures. We can't get outside the aura. We're
part of the aura. We're here, we're now."
He seemed immensely pleased by this. (12–13)

What the fictional Murray Siskind understands is that no visual perception is a pure apprehension of objective reality. Comprehending and
interpreting any image, whether it is a barn seen through a car window or
a painting of a barn, requires an active mental process that is driven by
personal and cultural values and assumptions. When we look at an object, no matter how mundane, our perception of the object is filtered
through, and transformed by, our assumptions about it and attitudes toward it, assumptions and attitudes that may be highly idiosyncratic or
widely shared within the culture. Seeing a rusted car on blocks in someone's front yard may signal any range of assumptions about the owner,
whether the car is seen in a photograph or painting, or whether one is seeing the actual car. To use a quite different example, it is impossible for
members of our culture to view a sunset without it bringing to mind a
range of associations from literary and other cultural sources. As Murray
Siskind would say, we're part of the aura, and we can't escape it.

Having said all of this, though, I think it is valid and useful to make a
distinction between looking at an object and looking at a representation
of an object. Though both may be activities involving mediating influences, there *is* a difference between the act of seeing an object "firsthand" and seeing a visual representation of it. In the first case, the mediation results from the individual's past experiences with similar objects,
experiences that are largely culturally shared but sometimes idiosyncratic. In the second case, there is an added layer of mediation—the
conscious and sometimes unconscious choices that the producer of the
image has made in order to further his or her own goals as a communi-
cator. These choices can only influence—not determine—the viewer's
interpretation of and emotional responses to the object. But these choices
can determine what the viewer actually sees, and this mundane fact
should not be overlooked.

At some point in their careers, students should come to understand
something about visual semiotics in a broad and inclusive sense, one that
includes consideration of the ways in which even direct apprehension of
concrete objects is influenced by cultural values and personal experiences.
However, in order to deal with more immediate concerns—or at least
ones that teachers of rhetoric and communication are more prepared to
deal with—it might make sense to restrict our efforts, at least initially, to

visual representations—objects meant to "stand in for" or to create in the viewer's mind a representation of something else, whether that something else be a concrete object or an abstract idea. Visual objects that could be studied as representations include paintings, sculptures, murals, photographs, drawings, videos and films, logos, icons, symbols, and multimedia art.

It is necessary, before moving on, to make one more point about the category of visual objects we are dealing with. I have been discussing the difference between concrete objects and visual representations of those objects, but rhetorical images do not necessarily have to portray an object, or even a class of objects, that exists or ever did exist. A picture of a unicorn can carry meaning because the viewer has been exposed to other representations of unicorns, both visual and verbal, and can associate the new representation with memories of those encountered previously. And, like words, visual representations can stand in for abstract ideas. Many symbols (e.g., a swastika or a peace sign) are designed primarily to represent an idea or an institution or an ideology without attempting to look like any concrete object. But just like representations of concrete objects, these abstract symbols depend on the viewer's ability and willingness to attach some particular meaning to them, and they will likely be treated as "symbolic signs"—that is, the viewer will likely assume that the producer of the visual symbol is attempting to instantiate within the viewer some shared cultural meanings that are commonly attached to the symbol (Worth and Gross). (The various controversies over the display of the confederate flag in some southern states powerfully demonstrate the symbolic nature of some abstract icons, and demonstrate also that the meanings of these symbols are not fixed.)

Even after narrowing the range of visual objects to deliberate representations, we are still left with the most basic pedagogical question—what, exactly, do students need to know about representational images? In other words, what exactly should we be doing with visual representations in our writing and rhetoric classes?

Of course, many instructors already deal with visuals in writing classrooms, and textbook publishers are beginning to take visual information more seriously as a rhetorical mode. In fact, a recent first-year composition textbook deals almost entirely with visual communication (*Seeing & Writing*, by Donald and Christine McQuade, published by Bedford/St. Martin's). But there is nothing even approaching a consensus about what types of visuals should be used in writing classrooms or exactly what students should be doing with them. Perhaps, given the nature of the discipline, no such consensus will ever emerge. Nevertheless, as a point of discussion, I offer here some thoughts about how visuals can be profitably used in a writing and rhetoric curriculum. I consider these ideas to be an early step in the development of a coherent undergraduate pedagogy of rhetoric, a pedagogy that combines the visual and the verbal without subordinating either mode of rhetoric to the other.

THE PLACE OF VISUAL INFORMATION
IN AMERICAN CULTURE

First, students can and should be taught about the cultural work of images in our society. Many of our most powerful and influential cultural concepts are encoded within what Richard Weaver called "God words" (e.g., "freedom," "motherhood," and "justice"). But we are a largely visual society, and many of these powerful cultural concepts are encoded within easily recognizable images (e.g., representations of George Washington, the Statue of Liberty, the Madonna and child, and the American flag). And besides these common images, advertisers and others continually create new images designed to exploit many of our society's predominantly held values and assumptions. Visuals are also used both to take advantage of and to reinforce roles and stereotypes defined by gender, race, and socioeconomic status.

Students need to learn to appreciate the power of images for defining and for reinforcing our cultural values and to understand the ways in which images help us define our individual roles within the society. Students also need some understanding of the many ways in which the producers of images take advantage of these cultural values and use them for their own persuasive purposes.

FIG. 6.1.   Insurance company.

The advertisement in Fig. 6.1 is an example of an image that takes advantage of common cultural values for persuasive purposes. The advertisement constitutes an appeal to readers to purchase and maintain an amount of life insurance that is adequate to cover their family members' needs. In the narrative at the bottom of the ad, we are told that, while "life suddenly changed for Mark when his father died," his father's foresight in purchasing adequate life insurance allowed his mother to pay the mortgage so Mark "can remain with his friends in the community where he grew up." The picture at the top of the ad (processed in a blue-gray duotone, to give the scene an old-fashioned, slightly dreamy quality) shows two boys (one of whom is presumably Mark, but we don't know which one) laughing as if sharing a joke. The point, presumably, is to demonstrate the claim that Mark is relatively happy, given the unfortunate circumstances of his father's death. (Clearly, the advertisement is not trying to claim that Mark is unaffected by his father's death—just that having adequate life insurance did not make matters even worse than they had to be.)

Seen as a piece of evidence (albeit a fictional one, given that the picture is obviously posed), the image can be treated rather straightforwardly as evidence to support the author's claims. However, as with any picture, the producers of the image had many decisions to make, and their decisions reflect some of the values and assumptions of the current American culture.

One of these values is racial integration and harmony. The picture portrays a European-American boy and an African-American boy playing and laughing together. (Their stance indicates that they are having a conversation.) While I hope and believe that interracial friendships among children are relatively common, it is almost certainly more common to see close friendships among children of the same race. But the creators of the advertisement are not interested in showing the world as it most typically is, but in creating a scene that will appeal to its target audience—parents, and most specifically, fathers. Portraying children of two races playing together as friends helps fathers of both of those races identify with the children in the picture, and it also makes the scene more positive (if slightly idealized) by evoking one of the more positive values in American culture—a desire for racial harmony.

Given the target audience, it is also no surprise that the creators of the advertisement chose to pose one of the boys with a baseball glove (held up to his chin, in order to situate it prominently in the middle of the frame) and the other one with a baseball bat over his shoulder. When it comes to fathers interacting with their sons, perhaps no activity is more iconic in American culture than baseball. From Hollywood movies like *Field of Dreams* and *City Slickers,* to Ken Burns's PBS miniseries, to the countless novels and nonfiction books extolling its virtues and celebrating its Americanness, the message is clear—if you're a father and you want your son to think back on your time together with fond remembrance, take him to a baseball game.

It is easy for an analysis like this to begin to sound cynical, painting the use of cultural values as a manipulative process. But it's important to point out, especially to students who may be exposed to such an analysis for the first time, that this need not be the case. It may be true that the picture in this advertisement is deliberately designed to portray an idealized version of American boyhood; the point is to present boyhood as a parent *would like it to be* for his or her son. In order to accomplish this, the advertisers must necessarily play to their audience's ambitions, dreams, and values. But this is true for any type of persuasive appeal; visual rhetoric is not unique in this regard.

Certainly, professional persuaders should be criticized when they appeal to some of the more negative aspects of American culture, including our fears and prejudices. And we can certainly find things to critique about the advertisement in Fig. 6.1 if we are so inclined, such as the traditional gender roles that it represents. But we can just as certainly analyze the persuasive strategies being used and point out the use of common cultural values without the analysis turning into a condemnation of the agents behind it, and it is possible to find some instances of this strategy to be relatively benign. (And would we really prefer that the advertisers use surly, tough-looking teenagers, playing violent video games and smoking cigarettes, in a more "honest" attempt to stir fathers' emotions?) An analysis of a persuasive appeal need not always become a criticism of its source, and an analysis of visual messages in which cultural values are reflected and reinforced need not, in every case, become a criticism of those values. These points are especially important to keep in mind when dealing with young university students, who may grow suspicious or weary of rhetorical analysis if they see it as inevitably leading to a criticism of the values they have been raised to accept.

Of course, this does not mean that a critique of widely cherished American values has no place in the classroom. And there are other types of ethical questions in respect to visual rhetoric that we should prompt students to explore. In the case of Fig. 6.1, even if the ultimate goal of the ad is to increase the revenues of insurance companies, convincing parents to

carry an adequate amount of life insurance seems largely unobjection-
able. But we might feel differently if the picture were being used in an advertisement for cigarettes, or for a political campaign in which we thought
that the candidate's policy goals were actually harmful to American children. Such ethical questions are not trivial, and preparing students to deal
with such questions should be a central goal of rhetorical education. But
my point is that an instructor faced with a classroom of students who
have never been asked even to think of images as rhetorical appeals, let
alone to analyze the rhetorical strategies being used in them, does not necessarily have to cover all of this ground in one leap. The first step, the one
that must be taken before such ethical and moral questions can be fruit-
fully addressed, is to get students to understand and accept that, more often than not, images used in persuasive messages both reflect and reinforce common cultural assumptions, biases, and values, and that
examining these images reflectively can tell us a lot about our own culture
that we might not otherwise notice.

Of all the ways in which images could be used in writing classes, writing
instructors as a group are probably most comfortable with examining the
ways in which images reflect and help shape current cultural assumptions.
Many first-year composition readers contain articles in which cultural
critics attempt to do this. Still, despite some individual success stories,
getting students to analyze images for cultural assumptions can be extremely difficult. In a sense, we're asking students to step outside of themselves and to see these familiar images as strange and exotic objects. Unfortunately, the more familiar the image, the more difficult it is for
students to examine it reflectively. (I've shown the image in Fig. 6.1 to
several groups of students and asked them what American values and
icons were being used in it, and not one has mentioned the reference to
baseball.)

One method for overcoming this difficulty is to ask students to look
first at images from cultures that are foreign to them, before asking
them to examine more familiar images as cultural markers. The assumption behind this method is that, once students have gained some practice
looking at images from foreign cultures, experiencing those images as
outsiders of the culture, it may be easier for them to then take an out-
sider's relatively disinterested stance when examining visuals from their
own culture. However, the tendency to see a familiar image or cultural
concept as transparent is a powerful one, and there is no significant
amount of evidence that methods such as these can overcome the difficulty students have in analyzing images that they would normally take

for granted. More effort needs to be applied to the development and assessment of methodologies that will help students make this kind of conceptual leap.

IMAGES AS RHETORICAL CONSTRUCTS

In addition to understanding the importance of images as cultural artifacts, students need to understand the psychological processes by which images persuade. Any advertiser, attorney, or political advisor—in short, anyone who engages in rhetorical practice for a living—knows that images can be extremely powerful persuasive devices. In terms used by Chaim Perelman and Lucie Olbrechts-Tyteca, including an image of an object in a persuasive appeal can enhance the "presence" of the object being represented, thereby enhancing its value or importance in the viewer's mind (117–120). Objects or ideas that are merely discussed, especially in abstract terms, have a low level of psychological presence, whereas objects or ideas that are pictured or represented in concrete, visual terms are given added presence, thereby becoming more real to the reader/viewer. "As far as possible," say Perelman and Olbrechts-Tyteca, "such an effort is directed to filling the whole field of consciousness with this presence" (118). In other words, when particular objects are given enough presence, they can crowd out other considerations from the viewer's mind, regardless of the logical force or relevance of those other considerations.

Perelman and Olbrecht-Tyteca's notion of presence is similar to what has been labeled by psychologists as the concept of *vividness*. In psychological studies, vivid information is identified as information that is emotionally interesting and concrete (Nisbett and Ross). Vivid information, which may take the form of imagistic language, personal narrative, or a representational picture, has been shown in experiments to be more persuasive than nonvivid information (Block and Keller; Smith and Shaffer; Wilson, Northcraft, and Neale). Vivid information tends to overwhelm information presented in abstract or technical language and to be given more weight than a coldly rational analysis would justify. Thus, a picture of a single starving child might move masses to action, while an abstract technical argument about crop yields and nutritional requirements might fail to instigate any action at all.

FIG. 6.2.   U.S. Marines of the 28th Regiment of the Fifth Division raise the American flag atop Mt. Suribachi, Iwo Jima, on February 23, 1945. AP/Wide World Photos.

Kenneth Burke points out another way in which images can be rhetorically powerful. He claims that an evocative image is often associated in each individual's mind with "many kindred principles or ideas" and that, when referring to the image, the rhetor implicitly brings all of these ideas to bear without having to explicitly argue for their relevance (87). (Burke is discussing the use of verbal imagery, as in poetry, but his observations are undoubtedly even more true when applied to the use of actual representational images.) For example, the famous picture of U.S. Marines raising the American flag on the Pacific island of Iwo Jima (Fig. 6.2) may instantiate in an American viewer feelings of patriotism, pride, or even nostalgia. If an institution such as a bank or insurance company includes this picture in its promotional literature, the hope is that the image and the values that it evokes in the viewer (e.g., patriotism, valor, courage, sacrifice) will become associated with the institution itself. No explicit ethical arguments need be made for why the institution might deserve to be associated with such an event and, since the relationship between the institution and the attitudes and feelings associated with the image is not explicitly stated, it is not likely to be questioned or challenged.[1]

This process of building associations between an image and a specified product, institution, political candidate, or ideological concept may be the most common way that images are used persuasively. Whether the image represents a scene from a well-known battle, a sexy model, a cuddly puppy, a beautiful sunset, or a farmer standing in his field, the objective is to prompt the viewer to associate the values and emotions that he or she feels toward the object represented in the image with the product being sold. Unfortunately, we do not yet have a well-developed pedagogy for helping students analyze and evaluate such associative arguments.

Over the past century, we have developed a variety of tools for analyzing and evaluating verbal arguments. We can take such arguments apart piece by piece and show where the flaws are. Recently, several argumentation scholars have argued that at least some persuasive images can be analyzed using the conceptual tools that have been developed to analyze verbal arguments, but J. Anthony Blair and David Fleming offer convincing refutations of that position. Because persuasive images are most often used, not to support arguments with logic and evidence, but to prompt viewers to develop new associations, the logical apparatus that has been developed to analyze and evaluate verbal arguments does not seem to apply to visual forms of persuasion.

The analysis of visual rhetoric does not yet have a detailed vocabulary and methodology on the scale of the ones that have been developed for the analysis and critique of persuasive verbal texts. There is, as yet, not an established and widely disseminated pedagogy for discussing persuasive images with students. But a substantial amount of theoretical work is being undertaken in a variety of fields to try to fill this gap (Walker and Chaplin 1–3), and while that work is ongoing, we can help students understand, at least in broad outline, the psychological processes that are brought to bear while interpreting and reacting to persuasive images, if only to try to build students' awareness of some basic truths about the nature of such images as rhetorical constructs (e.g., that they work through prompting the viewer to develop associations rather than through building linear, rational arguments). Concentrating on such an endeavor can provide several important benefits. First, it can help students understand that images are not just ornamental supplements to written texts, but complex texts in their own right, often relying on powerful and subtle psychological processes in order to be comprehended and to be rhetorically effective. Second, even with the relatively limited analytical tools that we have for working with images, providing students with such tools can go far toward empowering them to analyze persuasive images and to reflect on their own responses to such images—not just in the classroom, but in their daily lives as consumers, political agents, and social beings.

THE VISUAL ASPECTS OF WRITTEN TEXT

When students are faced with the task of interpreting and analyzing images in the classroom, they may resist. At the least, they will face some uncomfortable dissonance, perhaps confusion, when asked to treat images as another kind of "text." This is true for several reasons, all of which have been discussed above. First, students are simply not used to working with images in this way; both in secondary and in postsecondary education, the curriculum in the United States concentrates almost solely on written or oral modes of communication, so the act of dealing with visuals as informational and persuasive texts will be unfamiliar to most students. Second, images have been given a degraded status in our culture. Students may see a move to introduce visuals into the classroom as a "dumbing down" of the content, or they may not understand that the instructor expects serious work and sustained analysis to be applied to these types of texts. Finally, students may feel lost or inadequate when they realize that the familiar methods of analyzing verbal text cannot be applied to images.

One strategy for avoiding such obstacles and initial difficulties is to introduce visual analysis into the writing class by first demonstrating how writing itself is partly a visual medium. Too many people, including many writing instructors, think of the visual elements of written texts as mere ornamentation, or perhaps as aids to comprehension. What many people fail to understand is that visual elements are powerful and essential features of almost any written text. Even when all of the propositional content is expressed in verbal form, the design of the page or the screen on which the text resides, the relative location and proximity of textual elements, and even the font used can not only enhance readability, but be part of the message that is conveyed. Overall, the visual aspects of writing can have as much to do with the effectiveness of one's message as choosing an appropriate tone or sentence structure.

Yet general-education writing courses pay almost no attention to issues of page design. By specifying a particular format and font (almost always the default Times New Roman) in their assignments, instructors control issues of page design, and therefore pretend that these issues don't matter. But by making design elements a nonissue in our courses, we leave students unprepared to analyze visual elements as readers and to use them effectively as writers, and we implicitly send the erroneous message that these visual elements are unimportant. Now that digital technologies have given all writers the ability to easily manipulate design elements in their texts, it is past time for teachers of writing to begin to pay serious attention to the communicative and rhetorical aspects of page and screen design.

One obstacle to the teaching of text design in writing classrooms is that many writing instructors themselves have little or no background in text or page design. Changes need to be made in the education of high school teachers and university writing instructors to remedy this lack of knowledge. However, in the meantime, any writing instructor can learn enough to introduce some basic design concepts to students, if only to trigger in them an awareness that text design issues are not insignificant aspects of the rhetorical process.

There are several good introductory texts that any writing instructor could use to introduce students to text design issues, Kostelnick's and Robert's *Designing Visual Language* being a notable example. Almost any good technical writing or business writing textbook will also contain some information about design, and even first-year composition rhetorics and writing handbooks are beginning to include some information about page design (though their treatment of the subject sometimes makes an interest in design seem like an afterthought). For a basic introduction to some broad design concepts, an interested instructor could begin with Robin Williams's *The Non-Designer's Design Book*. In that book, Williams explains four basic elements of text design: proximity (manipulating and varying the amount of space between and around various text elements), contrast (using design features to indicate a hierarchy of importance among text elements), alignment (varying the alignment of text elements with different rhetorical functions), and repetition (consistently applying the same design features to text elements with similar rhetorical functions). Every general-education writing course could easily incorporate some instruction and practice in basic design elements such as these.

A simple example of how the first two of these elements can be introduced is demonstrated in Figs. 6.3 to 6.6, which are variations of a title slide that I have used when giving presentations on the subject of this chapter.

Reading the Visual in
College Writing Classes
Charles Hill
Department of English
UW Oshkosh

FIG. 6.3.

In Fig. 6.3, the text elements are placed together and are all in the same font and style, with no variation in proximity and no use of contrast.

Reading the Visual in
College Writing Classes

Charles Hill

Department of English
UW Oshkosh

FIG. 6.4.

In Fig. 6.4, students can easily see that implementing the principle of proximity (placing elements close together or farther apart to indicate their relationships to each other) can greatly improve readability even of a very simple page, and Fig. 6.5 demonstrates that varying the color, size, and text style of the different textual elements (thereby enhancing contrast) can increase readability even more.

Reading the Visual
in College Writing
Classes

Charles Hill

Department of English
UW Oshkosh

FIG. 6.5.

*Reading the Visual in College Writing
Classes*

Charles
Hill

Department of English
UW Oshkosh

FIG. 6.6.

But comparing Figs. 6.5 and 6.6 demonstrates that using such format features not only increases readability, but can affect the meaning and rhetorical effectiveness of the verbal text. As my name increases in relation to the type size of the title, my sense of self-worth appears to increase, as well. I overwhelm the subject of the essay.

There may be situations in which emphasizing the speaker's name in such a fashion would be appropriate (e.g., if the speaker is a "star," likely to attract listeners by his or her very identity), but it is clear (and students can easily understand) that it would not be appropriate in many situations, and a speaker or writer who uses format elements inappropriately could elicit highly negative reactions from listeners or readers.

Instruction in text design need not be technical and dry—quite the opposite. In fact, I've found that even discussions about typefaces can be lively, and students enjoy the "eureka" moments that occur when they realize how much meaning is often carried by this most mundane textual element. Working from materials (advertisements, flyers, instruction manuals, labels, etc.) that they collect and bring to class, students begin by discussing the "tone" of different typefaces that they have found, until they come to some agreements about particular examples. (This usually results in vague assertions that a particular typeface seems more "playful" or "serious" or "modern" than others.)

Once students find some examples that they agree on, I have them try to determine why the writer/designer decided to use a typeface with those qualities—which necessarily involves a discussion of the writer/designer's rhetorical goals and assumptions about his or her audience. Only after this discussion do we try to determine the specific concrete elements in the typeface that might be influencing the students' judgments. In this final discussion, we touch on many concepts that experienced typeface designers would find familiar, though we might not use their technical terms.

Given the current state of word-processing programs, students can also easily practice manipulating the design elements in their own texts, and instructors can use these features for a variety of creative purposes, such as allowing students to experiment with typefaces, color, and design in their written work in order to express their reactions to particular texts. For instance, students who have read Mary Shelley's novel *Frankenstein* are often inspired to represent their interpretation of the novel visually through typeface choice. The first example uses a Gothic style font, illustrating the students' sense that the novel is a dark tale of dungeons and death:

𝕱rankenstein

FIG. 6.7.

The second typestyle choice, however, seems to indicate a more favorable view of the text as a "classic" work of literature:

Frankenstein

FIG. 6.8.

Dealing with elements such as typography and page layout may be one way to begin to break down the overly rigid distinction between verbal and visual communication that characterizes both scholarly thought and commonly held assumptions in our society. Another way is to recognize and discuss the many ways in which images and text work together in contemporary communication. Examples to analyze can be found everywhere and could include business correspondence, scientific research reports, cartoons, newspaper articles, and all types of advertisements. (Fig. 6.1 is an example in which neither the picture nor the verbal text, if offered alone, would be rhetorically effective.) Kathleen Welch argues that new electronic technologies are making the hybrid text, in which words and images work together, the dominant mode of discourse in our society (131), and Mitchell argues that nearly all texts have both a verbal and a visual element (5). A brief, random perusal of commercially published texts should be enough to convince students of the truth of these statements.

FIRST-YEAR COMPOSITION AND THE VISUAL

Welch argues convincingly that every university student should be taught to interpret, analyze, and produce texts that incorporate visual elements, and I have taken up that argument here. Welch goes on to argue that the composition classroom is the appropriate place to accomplish this, since it is the primary site "for teaching articulation and power" (134). In a more practical vein, it could be argued that, for many of our students, the general-education writing course is the only real exposure to rhetorical theory and principles that they will have. Arguably, the primary purpose of a rhetorical education is to teach students to respond to the messages that they will likely encounter in their lives as part of this culture. Given this objective, and given that so many of the communicative expressions that our students encounter are and will continue to be visual in nature, it no longer seems viable for the instructors of our students' only rhetoric course to ignore issues of visual literacy and visual rhetoric in their classes.

Another reason for placing discussions of visual communication into the writing class is that the boundary separating text from images has always been little more than a convenient fiction, and as new computer technologies become more sophisticated and more dominant, this fiction is becoming quite inconvenient. For a long time, embedding any kind of visual into one's writing was possible only for professional writers, it often involved the work of several people with distinct sets of skills, and it was a complex and expensive process. Today, anyone who uses a standard word processor can manipulate text faces, styles, sizes, and colors and easily embed graphs, drawings, photographs, and even video clips. And the World Wide Web, which is quickly becoming the standard mode of transmission for many types of texts, relies largely on visual elements for its impact and its attraction. It is true that the typical university writing assignment in many disciplines still requires no design elements beyond discrete paragraphs and a centered title. However, with the increasing availability of digital imaging technology, this situation is changing, and it will continue to change. And outside of the academy, such non-visual texts are relatively and increasingly rare. Ignoring graphics and visual design elements in writing classes, even in first-year composition, is quickly becoming anachronistic.

Still, even given all of these arguments, one could reasonably ask if university writing instructors can realistically take on the task of teaching students to interpret, analyze, and produce visual texts. General-education writing courses are already typically overburdened with goals and objectives, and such courses tend to suffer from "mission creep," taking on more and more responsibilities as notions of critical literacy and empowerment continue to broaden. The goals statement for the first-year writing program at my university includes eight objectives, including the following:

- Teaching students to use new writing technologies.
- Encouraging students to interact reflectively with their peers.
- Developing students' critical reading skills.
- Teaching the conventions of academic discourse.
- Teaching students to evaluate sources of information.

And the goals statement doesn't even discuss issues that nearly everyone in the university assumes will be covered in first-year composition, including research strategies, proper citation and documentation, and grammatical and mechanical correctness. Other composition courses across the country take on tasks such as teaching students to analyze literature, raising students' critical consciousness, and teaching them to argue soundly and logically. Clearly, the expectations placed on the first-year writing course are already too great, partly as a result of our own ambitions as instructors and program coordinators, and partly because of the unrealistic expectations of others in the university community. Why, then, should instructors of such courses accept the additional task of helping students learn to interpret and analyze visual images? More important, can they do so effectively, without resulting in an incoherent and watered-down curriculum, miles wide but an inch deep? Given what writing instructors are already faced with, how can we hope to accomplish the additional tasks of helping students learn to interpret and analyze images, create their own rhetorical images, and manage the visual elements of their written texts?

A UTOPIAN PROPOSAL:
THE RHETORICAL CURRICULUM

In a recent essay in the journal, *Writing Program Administration,* John Trimbur addresses the problem of overburdened general-education writing courses and proposes that such courses be replaced with multi-departmental, multicourse writing *programs.* Each program would look different and involve a different set of academic departments, depending on the needs and inherent strengths present on each campus. Trimbur's proposal is a response to what many in the discipline already perceive as a set of expectations that no one university course could hope to meet.

I would go one step further, and say that we should have multi-departmental *rhetoric* programs—programs built on the recognition that writing, visual literacy, and oral communication are all essential skills, but that, in the real world, they work together in complex ways, not in isolation. Scholarship and research related to visual communication is already being accomplished on most American campuses, in departments such as art, journalism, communication, political science, and anthropology, and we can probably find colleagues in history and even literature professors in English who use visuals extensively in their classes. However, on most campuses, the only required general-education courses in rhetorical analysis or practice are in written composition and speech. Though a considerable amount of expertise exists in various areas of visual analysis and critique, students are exposed to this expertise only if they elect to take certain majors that prepare them for professional work in a related area. In other words, the only students who get exposed to principles of visual rhetoric are those who decide that their careers will largely involve the production of some form of visual communication. This leaves the rest of the students, the ones who will presumably make up the audience for these professional communicators, helpless to analyze or critique their messages. The university system is doing a good job of training a select group of students to produce persuasive visual messages. But shouldn't we be at least as concerned with helping the rest of our students respond to these messages in an informed and critical way? If we can tap into the experience, expertise, and interest in visual communication that exists across campus, then we can build a new paradigm, one that takes rhetorical education seriously and that recognizes it for the multidisciplinary endeavor that it is.

Though it may seem like a drastic step, what is needed is a bottom-up reconfiguration of the notion of rhetorical education. As with Trimbur's proposed writing program, what this reconfiguration will look like in curricular terms will vary from one campus to the next. On some campuses, it might involve sharing resources among departments such as journalism, art, and communication. On others, it might involve the creation of a new, stand-alone administrative unit. On still others, it might be accomplished solely within an existing department. What is important is that the interested people within the university work together to decide what their goals are for their students, identify the available resources on campus for achieving those goals, identify the unique set of institutional constraints that must be negotiated on their campus, and figure out the best way, given these resources and constraints, for addressing the issue of developing students' critical and rhetorical literacy in a multimedia world.

No doubt many of us with a vested interest in the general education composition program as it now stands will feel threatened by such a proposal. However, for those of us who see composition as a course in rhetoric, I think implementing such a proposal would represent a new opportunity—an opportunity to have, perhaps for the first time, a campuswide discussion about what rhetoric is, what it means to make students rhetorically aware and rhetorically proficient, and what students need to know about rhetorical theory and practice in order to thrive as citizens in the information age. Following through on this proposal would be risky because it would force us to confront the myths about first-year composition that we have profited from (such as the myth that first-year composition will "clean up" students' grammar). For perhaps the first time, we would have to lay all of our cards on the table. We should be worried only if we are not sure of our hand.

NOTES

1. A potential problem with such persuasive strategies is that the image being used may not be as familiar to a broad audience as one might expect. For instance, Messaris reports that only fourteen students in a class of twenty-nine undergraduates could name "even an approximate place and time (e.g., a World War II battle) for Joe Rosenthal's original photograph of the flag-raising," one of the most famous American photographs of the twentieth century. Messaris reports similar recognition rates among U.S.-born graduate students (*Visual Persuasion* 94).

WORKS CITED

Birkerts, Sven. *The Gutenberg Elegies: The Fate of Reading in an Electronic Age*. Boston: Faber, 1994.

Blair, J. Anthony. "The Possibility and Actuality of Visual Arguments." *Argumentation and Advocacy* 33 (1996): 23–39.

Block, Lauren G., and Punam Anand Keller. "Effects of Self-Efficacy and Vividness on the Persuasiveness of Health Communications." *Journal of Consumer Psychology* 6 (1997): 31–54.

Bolter, Jay David. *Writing Space: The Computer, Hypertext, and the History of Writing.* Hillsdale, NJ: Erlbaum, 1991.

Burke, Kenneth. *A Rhetoric of Motives.* 1950. Berkeley: U of California P, 1969.

DeLillo, Don. *White Noise.* New York: Penguin, 1991.

Elkins, James. *The Domain of Images.* Ithaca: Cornell UP, 1999.

Fleming, David. "Can Pictures Be Arguments?" *Argumentation and Advocacy* 33 (1996): 11–22.

Fox, Roy F. "Image Studies: An Interdisciplinary View." *Images in Language, Media, and Mind.* Ed. Roy F. Fox. Urbana: NCTE, 1994. 3–20.

Kostelnick, Charles, and David D. Roberts. *Designing Visual Language: Strategies for Professional Communicators.* Boston: Allyn, 1997.

Kress, Gunther, and Theo van Leeuwen. *Reading Images: The Grammar of Visual Design.* London: Routledge, 1996.

McQuade, Donald, and Christine McQuade. *Seeing & Writing.* Boston: Bedford/St. Martin's, 2000.

Messaris, Paul. *Visual Persuasion: The Role of Images in Advertising.* Thousand Oaks, CA: Sage, 1997.

Mitchell, W. J. T. *Picture Theory: Essays on Verbal and Visual Representation.* Chicago: U of Chicago P, 1994.

"NCTE Passes Visual Literacy Resolution." *Kairos* 2.1 (1997). 31 August 2000 <http://english.ttu.edu/kairos/2.1/news/briefs/nctevis.html>.

Nisbett, Richard E., and Lee Ross. *Human Inference: Strategies and Shortcomings of Social Judgment.* Englewood Cliffs, NJ: Prentice-Hall, 1980.

Perelman, Chaim, and L. Olbrechts-Tyteca. *The New Rhetoric: A Treatise on Argumentation.* Trans. John Wilkinson and Purcell Weaver. Notre Dame, IN: U of Notre Dame P, 1971.

Purves, Alan C. *The Web of Text and the Web of God.* New York: Guilford, 1998.

Smith, Stephen M., and David R. Shaffer. "Vividness Can Undermine or Enhance Message Processing: The Moderating Role of Vividness Congruency." *Personality and Social Psychology Bulletin* 26 (2000): 769–79.

Stafford, Barbara Maria. *Good Looking: Essays on the Virtue of Images.* Cambridge: MIT P, 1997.

Stroupe, Craig. "Visualizing English: Recognizing the Hybrid Literacy of Visual and Verbal Authorship on the Web." *College English* 62 (2000): 607–32.

Trimbur, John. "The Problem of Freshman English (Only): Toward Programs of Study in Writing." *Writing Program Administration* 22.3 (1999): 9–30.

Walker, John A., and Sarah Chaplin. *Visual Culture: An Introduction.* Manchester: Manchester UP, 1997.

Weaver, Richard M. *The Ethics of Rhetoric.* 1953. Davis, CA: Hermagoras, 1985.

Welch, Kathleen E. *Electric Rhetoric: Classical Rhetoric, Oralism, and a New Literacy.* Cambridge: MIT P, 1999.

Williams, Robin. *The Non-Designer's Design Book.* Berkeley, CA: Peachpit, 1994.

Wilson, Marie G., Gregory B. Northcraft, and Margaret A. Neale. "Information Competition and Vividness Effects in On-Line Judgments." *Organizational Behavior and Human Decision Processes* 44 (1989): 132–39.

Worth, Sol, and Larry Gross. "Symbolic Strategies." *Studying Visual Communication.* Ed. Larry Gross. Philadelphia: U of Pennsylvania P, 1981. 134–47.

CLASSROOM

John Adams Whipple, photographer. Girl Reading (circa 1868). Wm. B.
Becker Collection/American Museum of Photography.

7

The Rereading/Rewriting Process: Theory and Collaborative, On-line Pedagogy

Marcel Cornis-Pope
Ann Woodlief

To read well, that is, to read true books in a true spirit, is a noble exercise, and one that will task the reader more than any exercise which the customs of the day esteem. It requires a training such as the athletes underwent, the steady intention almost of the whole life to this object. Books must be read as deliberately and reservedly as they were written. [. . .] Yet this only is reading, in a high sense, not that which lulls us as a luxury and suffers the nobler faculties to sleep the while, but what we have to stand on tip-toe to read and devote our most alert and wakeful hours to.
—Henry David Thoreau, *Walden* (101, 104)

The particular importance of network textuality—that is, textuality written, stored, and read on a computer network appears when technology transforms readers into reader-authors or "wreaders," because any contribution, any change in the web created by one reader, quickly becomes available to other readers. The ability to write within a particular web in turn transforms comments from private notes, such as one takes in margins of one's own copy of a text, into public statements that, especially within educational settings, have powerfully democratizing effects.
—George P. Landow, *Hyper/Text/Theory* (14)

THEORY: MODELS OF CRITICAL
REREADING/REWRITING

The act of reading, as defined by Wolfgang Iser, is a process of "becoming conscious": "The constitution of meaning not only implies the creation of a totality emerging from interacting textual perspectives [. . .] but also, through formulating this totality, it enables us to formulate ourselves and thus discover an inner world of which we had hitherto not been conscious" (*The Act of Reading* 58). Critical reading in this perspective is no longer an ancillary activity, passively receiving the "imprint" of the text, but—in Wolfgang Iser's well-known formulation—"a dynamic process of recreation" ("The Reading Process" 279) that allows the reader to formulate "alien" thoughts and perspectives but also to question existing perspectives and norms (*The Act of Reading* 147). In reading reflexively, the reader both actualizes the text, giving it significance, and constitutes herself as a reading subject. The interpretation of a particular text is thus "completed in the self-interpretation of a subject who henceforth understands himself better, who understands himself differently, or who even begins to understand himself" (Ricoeur 194–95).

These theoretical insights have been reinforced and aided by the new hypertext and networked communication technologies developed over the past ten to fifteen years. These technologies have allowed readers to interact with the text more closely, highlighting its associative and dissociative impulses and enriching its structures with layers of annotations, linked intertexts, and "winding paths" of circulating signifiers. Electronically assisted textual analysis can result in "perceptual and conceptual breakthroughs," replacing the linear logic of reading and writing with the creative "logic of patterning" (Travis 9). Hypertextual criticism stimulates interactive authorship, transforming "readers into reader-authors or 'wreaders,' because any contribution, any change in the web created by one reader, quickly becomes available to other readers" (Landow 14). Textual interpretation becomes thus an act of "rewriting," both individual, in which a particular reader mediates the relationship between text, author, and culture, and collective in which an interpretive community negotiates not only its reading of a particular text but also its interpretive habits and ideological views. Ideally, the reader's rewriting will also foreground the text's own "rewriting or structuration of a prior historical or ideological subtext" (Jameson 35).

In articles and protocols based on Marcel Cornis-Pope's book *Hermeneutic Desire and Critical Rewriting* (see Woodlief online papers; also Cornis-Pope "Hypertextual"), we recommend a re-creative pedagogical model of literary interpretation based on strategies of rereading/rewriting as part of a community of readers. Although our focus is on the teaching of literature, these strategies can be adapted to the study of any kind of text, and we have also used it as a model for interpreting "visual types of expression" (see Hill, chap. 6, this volume). These strategies, we argue, can benefit students in several ways: (a) helping them move beyond mere text consumption and channeling their interpretive abilities into more active modes of critical analysis and construction; (b) allowing students to experience the complex dynamic of interpretation in its gradual unfolding from experiential first reading, to critical rereading and formal analysis; (c) making them more aware of the naturalized conventions that participate in their construction of meaning, and of their potential for renewal. Reading and writing become inseparable in this perspective, part of a critical dialectic that both interprets and reperforms the text.

Ideally, the reader should pursue an uninterrupted interpretative process, with an active, transformative rereading already implied in first reading. But that rarely happens for most students, whose first—and last—reading is sequential and naturalizing. First reading can at best yield an incomplete interpretation wherein students "perform one synthesis, rather than various syntheses and tend to settle too soon, too quickly" for a resolution (Mariolina Salvatori 659). First reading is sequential, superficial, and mimetic, according to Michael Riffaterre's account. Difficulties in the text (textual bumps, irregularities, twists, deviations from rules—linguistic, conceptual, structural) are generally overlooked (chap. 9, this volume). Only a second and separate retroactive reading can produce "significance" by identifying and reconfiguring the various perspectives of the text (Riffaterre 81ff). That second reading often requires interaction with a larger community of readers to transcend a strong but superficial first reading.

In most theoretical models of critical reading, the transition from a naturalized, early response, to a self-conscious critical interpretation requires a stage of rereading. In phenomenological perspective (Wolfgang Iser, Georges Poulet) there is a significant difference between the "noetic" aspect of reading (the experiencing of a text in the time flow of reading) and the "noematic" (the work actualized at the end of reading). First reading experiences the work in process, as lacunary, variable, unfinished. Only at the end of reading the work takes on "the relative momentary stability of an overall 'noema' " (Ruthrof 75). Even a "subjective" approach to reading such as David Bleich's involves the reader in two different phases of "symbolization" (actualization) of text. The first phase corresponds roughly to an unreflective (and not yet written down) experiential response; the second phase of "resymbolization" involves a retro-spective negotiation of first-reading responses that makes use of language "as complex explanation" (65–66) and of the input of the interpretive community to fine-tune and understand one's reactions to a text. Like-wise, in Norman Holland's "transactive model," reading has an uncon-scious (reactive-associative) and a conscious (critical-transformative) component. Readers are involved in an ongoing process of (self-)explora-tion whose role is to socialize and transform the fantasy material found in texts and in the reader's mind. In all these models rereading (performed individually or in dialogue with a community of other readers) contrib-utes to a restructuring and deepening of vision.

A pedagogy grounded in activities of rereading/rewriting can convert a naturalized first reading into a creative critical production. The activities of rereading refocus the reader's attention on the text's rhetorical devices and ideology usually missed in first reading. In rereading we are "thrown into language, into its flow and surprises," compelled "to recognize that [they] are part of that flow, of that 'writing' " (Kaufer and Waller 83). While first reading depends primarily on the expectation of pleasure (of a vicarious or hermeneutic kind), rereading draws on critical self-aware-ness, the "appreciation of the story through an analysis of the ways in which it achieves its initial effects" (Leitch 494). Enjoyment is not absent from rereading, but it entails the transformation of the "pure," self-contained pleasure of vicarious experiencing, into the more structured and engaged pleasure of intellectual experiencing that connects the reader to the broader contexts of his or her culture. A successful reading can emerge from this interplay of naive absorption and critical reexamina-tion, participation, and self-reflection. If properly performed, rereading can enrich and pluralize interpretation, establishing a more responsible, collaborative relation with the text. As Roland Barthes (15–16) put it suc-cinctly, rereading "alone saves the text from repetition (those who fail to re-read are obliged to read the same story everywhere)."

Reading critically is a complex activity that requires noticing, relating, and interrogating, all of which entail careful rereadings of various levels of the text. Theorists have traditionally assumed that this is an individual activity. However, even in the most traditional class it is not, as the pro-fessor is drawing the students' attention to details and questions raised by the greater (scholarly) reading community. Often students' own readings are muted in this familiar recourse to "authorities." Networked, hyper-textual criticism encourages students to perform these interrelated opera-tions as a reading community in a nonlinear field, bridging reading with writing, and response with interpretation. Their interpretation can thus

share the advantages of multilinear organization, open-endedness, greater inclusion of nontextual information, and interactive collaborative authorship.

PEDAGOGY: ENACTING A HYPERTEXTUAL AND COLLABORATIVE READING PROCESS

The best reading is a recursive process in which the reader returns to a text after a first reading, focusing on significant passages and details, tracing patterns and developing ideas, asking probing questions, and building on fertile ambiguities and gaps. Dealing with the words of the text, the effective reader must also generate his own words to capture some of this process, as writing and thinking are vitally linked. He must work to surmount his own biases, to find ways of noticing new details and patterns that go beyond his own personal and cultural experiences and join a community of readers.

The practical and pedagogical question is how can this process of rereading be modeled and enacted to a significant degree by each student in the composition or literature class? There are powerful limits of time and attention, and most students resist going beyond the quick first summative reading. What we have discovered is that this reading process can be enacted better than one might expect, with the aid of Web or network-linked computers, well-developed teaching protocols, and extensive response writing.

In his thoughtful chapter on reading in *Walden*, Henry David Thoreau insists that the best reading "requires a training such as the athletes underwent, the steady intention almost of the whole life to this object." For him, reading skills are best created by careful translation of works in Greek and Latin, the "originals," paying intense attention to language, yet the reader also transforms or rewrites them (Christiansen, chap. 4, this volume). The path we recommend to "athletic reading" is different in kind—involving teamwork rather than the classical languages—but not in spirit.

In our experience, (re)reading reflectively and collaboratively comes close to that "athletic" desideratum. The time-honored image of the scholar in his closet or library corner, surrounded by books and carefully preparing his own responses for a future audience, does not work for most students, especially as they begin the rereading process, although it may work well for their professors versed in literary discourse and well-aware of ways to unearth the complex possibilities of meaning. We must remember that even the lone scholar is not alone, for she or he can imagine many different interpretive voices, based on their previous readings. This resource is not available to students who generally hear only the dim voices of teachers who may have presented oversimplified interpretations for the sake of later testing. But without hearing multiple voices pointing out different passages, different questions, and different readings, students have difficulty unearthing their own voices, or seeing what sort of agendas may be governing—and limiting—their own readings. Theoretically, a teacher can generate a number of readings in a discussion class. Practically speaking, this does not happen as well as we hope, and many readings never come to light.

In our effort to define a more adequate pedagogy of (re)reading, we have started from the following assumptions:

- Students need to read, write, reread, and rewrite, exploring questions related to each genre/work in order to think critically about a text.
- To keep this reading/writing process from becoming too subjective (and wandering far from the text), it needs to be done collectively and comparatively, negotiating questions and meanings within a larger interpretive community. Students come to understand the strengths and weaknesses of their individual readings gradually, when challenged by other readings and responses to their own reading, and so learn to develop stronger and more persuasive interpretations.

- Every student must participate fully in order for the class dynamic to work, and in order to develop the strongest, most detailed readings of a work.
- Students must have as much information about biographical, socio-cultural and historical contexts and as many explorative questions related to the text as possible, but presented in a voluntary, timely fashion (e.g., they should have it available when they "ask" for it). These materials, however, should be used to open up and enrich interpretation, rather than simply focus reading on "authorial intention as the stable meaning of texts" (Harkin and Sosnoski, chap. 5, this volume).

The teacher's role in this pedagogy is not that of an "authoritative interpreter" but rather that of a coach and facilitator who can deliver useful information and respond as one member of this community of readers.

The computer offers a number of ways in which readings of a work can be heard/seen, considered, compared, and even discarded, and meanings can be negotiated by every member of a class, not just by a few vocal ones. It also offers a prime tool for accomplishing what we all consider crucial—one cannot think through the reading of any work clearly without putting those thoughts into words, preferably written words, which can be polished and revised. Reflection requires putting thoughts into words, and the sharing of those words in turn leads to further reflection, "piggybacking," explaining, and clarifying those thoughts. Many teachers have long thought that collaborative writing is essential for learning how to write, yet it is just as essential for learning how to read, and the computer offers an effective collaborative environment for the reading-rereading-writing-rewriting process to develop.

In a typical undergraduate literature class taught by us over the past six years, students meet one to three times a week in a LAN-networked computer lab to read, write, and converse mostly electronically, achieving a level of interaction that cannot be reproduced in a traditional classroom. Our tools for navigating the world of "hypertrails" were first a Window-based hypertexting program, GUIDE, and now the Internet, with Netscape Composer and more recently, with an annotating program from the University of Texas called Critical Tools (http://www.cwrl.utexas.edu/~criticaltools/). Our tools for electronic interaction have been W. W. Norton's CONNECT (see www.wwnorton.com/connect) and discussion forums (see Blackboard at www.blackboard.com), but any kind of threaded discussion format, such as WebCT, will work. These formats enable the class to function as an interpretive community, exchanging interpretations that are individually persuasive and collectively aware of the larger conventions at work.

The electronic technologies encourage students to read in a multi-sequential and exploratory fashion, producing "hypertextual" criticism (annotating, cross-referencing, and linking texts), and communicating among themselves throughout the reading and writing process. The thematic structure of our introduction to literature course follows two "natural" progressions that are gradually "denaturalized": a progression of texts, from those we "naturalize" more easily such as narrative and visual images, to those that elicit more complex processing, such as poetry and drama; and one of criticism, moving from naturalized first readings, to reflexive rereading, critical analysis, and self-analysis. By segmenting the critical process into discrete steps, students are made aware of their choices and helped, through carefully designed reading and writing protocols, to readjust their interpretive approaches after each stage.

First Readings

The first reading is the point where most students begin and end, except for the few who have already learned how to begin rereading on a first reading. Students who come to understand just how a first reading works for them—and for others—are generally ready to perform an experiential reading and move on to more critical rereading.

As a rule, a first reading is emotional, selective, and generally uncritical. The reading process relies heavily on sequential and holistic procedures, on "naturalization" (Jonathan Culler), "consistency-building" (Iser), "selective attention" (Louise M. Rosenblatt). Readers look for closure and coherence, singling out solid clues and eliminating problematic ones. Especially with fiction, students smooth over contradictions and follow the narrative to settled conclusions even when they distrust the narratorial voice. On the other hand, they find stories that thwart such expectations disappointing, obscure, and "dry." Responses often begin with "I like" or "I don't like" as the reader accepts or resists the situation, characters, or ideas. Sometimes the first reading is performed purely for pleasure, both of a vicarious experiential kind and of an ideological kind, as the reader finds a desirable position he can identify with and through which he can "inhabit" the world of the text. Plot or the reconstruction of "what happens" is of primary importance at this stage. In the process of constructing the "story line," much is often missed or read over as a distraction.

Although superficial, this first reading is essential. If words or actions are misunderstood or missed, the story may be distorted. Making personal connections is equally crucial, as this is the kind of drive that makes for devoted readers. And yet, such a reading is only a beginning. Making it a basis for a more thoughtful rereading requires that the student put his or her response into words, and share those words with other readers in a supportive, collaborative environment. In short, even at this stage, it is necessary to be an active reader/writer. Writing online, whether in a forum discussion format or an e-mail list, means that each student "speaks" and is "listened to" as he or she responds to the reading.

On a practical level, writing first-reading responses online requires preparation, especially at the beginning of a class, as students are unaccustomed to having to take this responsibility. We've programmed them well to come to class and wait to "see what it means." Frequently students have to be reassured that it is acceptable to acknowledge what "I think." It is equally important for students to write under their own names, in our opinion, not anonymously or with a pseudonym, taking responsibility and credit for their own ideas. The computer format seems to offer enough feeling of anonymity for the shyest students, even under their own names.

Bad "chat" habits are discouraged from the beginning—no abbreviations, full sentences with appropriate capital letters, etc. Generally it is reasonable to ask students for at least a "screen's worth" of response and ask for a subject line (generally an option in the forum format) that is a question or a topic. Students should be encouraged to quote key passages in their responses (copying from an online text can help).

It is useful to offer leading questions to students, either generic or focused on the work, to consider during first reading, especially at the beginning of the course. There will be far fewer "I like" and "I dislike" responses with such direction. Our questionnaires sometimes begin with a "pre-reading" section that requires the students to focus on their expectations, experiences, and preconceptions they bring to the process of reading. According to "reception" theorist Hans Robert Jauss, studying the "horizon of expectations" (20ff) that readers and texts activate is crucial to the process of interpretation. The term "horizon of expectations" designates an area of "collective" assumptions, genre conventions, and cultural ideologies shared by texts and readers. In reconstructing a work's original "horizon of expectation," our reading can foreground the cultural contexts activated by a work and participate in their reformulation. Similarly, by examining their own expectations as readers, students can begin to understand the interests, experiences, and preconceptions that they bring to the process of reading.

Here is an example of a prereading questionnaire for the reading of literature:

TEXT:

- What assumptions do you have about the author of the text? Have you read any of his/her other works?
- Knowing when, where, and by whom this story/poem was written, what are your expectations of theme, character treatment, techniques?
- What type of story do you expect, judging from the title of this piece? What suggestions/expectations does the title convey? Read the first page (stanza, etc.) and comment on the probable direction of this literary text. What new meanings has the title acquired for you?

READER:

- What are your dominant feelings before reading this text? Are you looking forward to reading a text by this particular author? Does the author, genre, type of literature appeal to you?
- What are your general expectations from reading? Does it matter if you read for pleasure or for "study"? Do you use different techniques and assumptions in reading "for pleasure'?
- Are you aware of any of your strengths and weaknesses in reading?

The prereading questions help students "locate" themselves as readers. These questions are followed by first-reading protocols that help students locate themselves as readers in a particular text. These protocols are designed to slow down and disrupt the linear progress of first reading, enhancing the students' self-consciousness about reading. The types of questions students are invited to consider are designed to foreground points of tension both within the text, and between the text and the interpretation we impose on it. The first-reading questionnaires encourage students to pay more attention to textual details, gaps, rhetorical strategies, and language "clues," moving them beyond a naturalized first reading. Students may be given questions to consider as they read, such as this general protocol on poetry:

General: What is the poem about (in a rough paraphrase)? What is its story or argument? What is happening, where, when, and to whom? Who is speaking, about what and to whom?

Free Association: What personal associations come to your mind as you read? What associations with other literary readings? What words, images, or phrases stand out to you? What do you identify most with? What do you "recognize" as parallel to your own experience? What conflicts with your perspective or experience?

First Questioning: What seems to be unclear? Are there lines you have to reread in order to untangle their implications? Any words or allusions you can't decipher easily? Any words or phrases that don't seem to fit or are surprising in the context? Are there gaps in the story or argument you've reconstructed? Is there anything you would like to know that you think would help in understanding the poem?

Preliminary Interpretation: What (in fairly simple terms) do you think the poem/poet is trying to argue/do?

The first-reading questionnaires for fiction need to be equally detailed, alternating between text-specific questions and more general interpretive tasks. Mariolina Salvatori's model of asking students to find "moments of difficulty" is another good approach. As an example, here is a reading protocol focused on Flannery O'Connor's "A Good Man Is Hard to Find":

- What details of plot interest you and why; what is your response to them? Are there parts of the story that do not seem to fit? Are you shocked by the ending? At what point did you see a change of tone and foreshadowing of the violent end?
- What is your response to the different characters in this story, especially the grandmother? How much of the family interaction and plot action is she responsible for? Do you feel sympathy for her? Did you identify with any character during reading? How did this identification affect your understanding of the story?
- What "gaps," contradictions, unresolved questions in the story's plot, characterization, or overall structure have you found?
- What expressions and clusters of images stick in your memory; what is their role in foreshadowing and building theme?
- What associations (with personal experiences and other readings) has the text triggered?
- Are you aware of a narrator in this story; how reliable or biased is he/she?
- What would you say are some of the more important ideas and attitudes expressed in this story? How important is the Southern setting

for understanding the characters and their motivation? How much are the grandmother's pretensions of "being a lady" and her attachment to the past keys to the action?

- What techniques or aspects of style have you enjoyed most; which have caused most problems for you? Would you consider this a "dark comedy"? Do you find the family's interactions realistic or funny?

Such lines of questioning need be explicit only in the beginning of a semester, as students develop more active reading habits. The first-reading process can be rehearsed in class, with the students being asked to take notes during their reading, perhaps on an electronic "Notepad." In a later phase, students can be asked to respond to the reading protocols on their own and bring to class their written responses to post online. Verbalizing one's reading is crucial. As David Bleich has argued, "Our knowledge of our behavior can become available only through language and thought. We are thus motivated to acquire self-awareness, which in turn gives us the capacity to regulate and to produce further, more complicated, more adaptive motives to govern growth" (64). As part of the ensuing discussion, students are required to read through and respond to other students' responses, whether in the group as a whole or in smaller groups.

Clear-cut "credit" for this activity is generally necessary; old habits are hard for them to break. The teacher should be active but not too "loud" in these online discussions once they begin, pointing out productive ideas, asking questions, suggesting directions or supporting quotes, and waiting for students to jump in and answer questions or respond to clear misreadings. Previous (edited) forums from other classes can be posted during the discussion to give students ideas about how to proceed into the often-novel territory of active reading. In our experience, students will soon begin to "stretch" to match the more articulate responses, even if the teacher says very little online.

Perhaps the most important task enacted in a first-reading discussion, whether online or in person, is to push against premature interpretive closure and to open new possibilities that students can explore in their rereading. Just the range of responses (and offering a forum from another class certainly enhances that range) accomplishes much of that. However, at the beginning of a class—when students are preferably responding to shorter works—it is useful for the teacher to write an overview of the session after it is complete. Not only can ideas be pulled out for further exploration, but the way in which the discussion is accomplishing the usual goals of first reading can be explored in some detail.

Rereadings

The reading process has to be experienced in all its complexities which, for Stanley Fish, involve "the making and revising of assumptions, the rendering and regretting of judgments, the coming to and abandoning of conclusions, the giving and withdrawing of approval, the specifying of causes, the asking of questions, the supplying of answers, the solving of puzzles" (158–59). The whole purpose of rereading is to allow these complexities, both in the text and in our interpretive dynamic, to come to the fore.

Many students, especially in lower-level undergraduate courses, have rarely reread a work except to find patterns, theses, or research questions for assignment papers; yet without productive and conscious rereading, these papers are likely to be thin and oversimplified. First reading often yields an incomplete, impressionistic interpretation that tends "to settle too soon, too quickly" the text. Having little more than first-reading responses to depend on, readers will resort in their written "explications" to a literalist, "blocked" pattern approach: "they lift various segments out of the text and then combine them through arbitrary sequential connections (usually conjunctions)—a composing mode that is marked by a consistent restriction of options to explore and develop ideas" (Salvatori 659).

Rereading, on the other hand, allows us to retrace and analyze our first-reading responses, relating them back to the text's generic and cultural features, but also to the assumptions and experiences that we bring to the text. Rereading should be more self-conscious, explorative, reformulative. At its best, rereading is a slow-motion, imaginative experience that involves reading "into" the work for discovery and interactive recreation. To some degree, this kind of reading is a form of rewriting, teasing out new implications, finding "otherness" as well as self-discovery, connecting with other texts and experiences. Rereading makes us conscious of the presentational aspects of a text—literary and visual rhetoric (Hill, chap. 6, this volume), discursive techniques and arrangements—and how they affect us.

One way of making rereading more conscious is to organize it around specific questions that call for a written comparison between first and second reading, between response and critical interpretation. Readers can be asked to reexamine their position toward the story after second reading, to ponder some of the exclusions, distortions, misreadings they have perpetrated during first reading. They can also be asked to speculate on how successfully they have attended to details, how closely they have monitored the progress of the story through inferences, predictions, and connections.

This is an example of a general rereading protocol on fiction that might be handled either in a reading journal or, more collaboratively, in an online discussion:

- How did the story's general purport and orientation change after second reading?
- What aspects of the story have you "misremembered," adapted to conform to your first reading?
- What possibilities of the text have you ignored (not accounted for) during earlier reading?
- What "mysteries" or "gaps" in the narrative have you tried to settle and how successfully?
- What aspects in the story are still unresolved, what questions unanswered?
- Who did you identify with during first reading, and how did this identification change in subsequent rereadings?
- Have your generic or thematic expectations about the story changed?
- Is the story more or less satisfying after second reading, and why?
- As you begin to sort out the textual "evidence" in support of an interpretation of the story, which details do you find useful, and which seem difficult to resolve with your interpretation?
- Has this approach to reading given you more confidence in your judgments and helped you understand the intricate details of the text better?

Another rereading protocol, focused in this case on a poetic text, can be built from questions such as these:

1. EXPLORING THE TEXT: Read the poem slowly and "outloud" several times. Look up any words you are unsure about, noting different meanings, synonyms, antonyms, linguistic roots as relevant, including allusions you don't know (such as references to classical mythology or the Bible). Note any images in the poem and experience them in sensory as well as intellectual terms.

2. EXPLORING PATTERNS: What is/are the metrical pattern(s) of the poem? Where are there breaks in the pattern? Are there any repeated words, phrases, or images? Does the poem rhyme? Is it a regular rhyme scheme? Are there any approximate or off-rhymes?

3. QUESTIONING THE TEXT: Where are the gaps or ambiguities of syntax or meaning in the poem? Are there any hints of a subtext that conflicts or questions the surface text?

4. EXPLORING THE AUTHOR'S AND WORK'S GENERAL REPERTOIRE (adapted after McCormick, Waller, and Flower, 16–27): What do you know about the author and the personal conditions under which he/she wrote? What can you deduce from the poem? How do you think age, gender, race, social, or financial status of the author might be relevant to the poem? What else do you know about the time, the place, and social, cultural, and/or political conditions of the work? Which of these might be relevant to this particular text?

5. EXPLORING THE AUTHOR'S AND WORK'S LITERARY REPERTOIRE (adapted after McCormick, Waller, and Flower, 16–27): What are the literary conventions and expectations of the time that affect this work in terms of genre and form, rhetorical strategies, imagery, meter (or lack of it), etc.? Do you know any other works by this author? If so, what patterns and ideas seem to recur in those works that you think may be in this one?

6. MATCHING UP YOUR OWN PERSONAL, LITERARY, AND GENERAL REPERTOIRES: What expectations do you have for the genre and the subject represented by this poem? How does it meet or disappoint those expectations? How do your relevant personal experiences (as recorded in your free association) match or clash with those suggested in the poem? Are they so strong that they might block your ability to respond to the poem? What differences (from the author) in age, race, gender, social or political status, etc. might color and shape your reading of this poem?

One traditional sign of a careful rereading is underlining and annotating copiously a text. But what if a text had unlimited margins in which more than one reader could write, question, respond, mark patterns, make comparisons? What if each of these readers could also explore—in the vicinity of the text—his or her own changing responses to the story, stepping back to look at what is happening in this process? In other words, what if a text offered unlimited space for a community of readers, acting alone and in concert, to explore its nuances and patterns, to propose interpretations and pose open questions?

The tools for enacting such a re-creative and interactive rereading/rewriting in the vicinity of a text are available on the computer and the Internet, especially if one begins with a text in electronic form. Readers can write notes, responses, and questions in a file and link them electronically to elements in the text and share them with other readers, whether in online papers or interactive forums. A similar process can also be done, albeit more slowly and awkwardly, with response papers and notebooks shared by students. Technology can help refine the student's techniques of note taking. Hypertext programs like GUIDE, *StorySpace, Common Space,* and Netscape Composer allow students to annotate the text directly, embedding definitions, comments, and questions in linked files. This technique provides ample opportunity for commenting (practically every word can be associated with an annotation, becoming a "yielding word"), but also can allow the clustering of annotations around particular key words, or a reading of all class annotations together to assess the density of comment that a particular passage has received. We urge students to annotate in a way that invites audience participation, asking thought-provoking questions and suggesting explorative tasks rather than providing answers.

Again, most students need models to understand how they may enact the rereading process on their own. We have had success in offering students online study hypertexts (annotated and interlinked literary pieces), which they read and respond to, sorting out their information, asking questions, noticing patterns, and making new connections as more experienced readers are wont to do. For example, a first reading of Kate Chopin's "The Story of an Hour" would provide for student response in a forum, in which students would be asked to pull out (copy and paste) key words, passages, and images to discuss and pose questions. Then they would read through a study hypertext, which presents frames with a highlighted text on the left and linked notes and open questions that offer different interpretive possibilities for the story. There are also linked files that present related information about the author, her time and place, as well as several Chopin stories with similar themes and a range of student comments about the story. After reading this, students join in an online forum in which they add their own comments and rationales for their own readings. The range of ideas suggested by the students in the forum is at least as important as the hypertext itself.

It has been our experience that students quickly learn from reading such hypertexts and the accompanying discussion the kind of noticing and questioning of information that they need to do on their own. They also learn that critical writing is in itself a form of hypertexting, combining annotating with reconfiguration, linking, relating, and intertextual comparison. The computer technology allows students to experienced the critical process in all its complexity, moving from readers to creators of hypertexts.

Hypertextual Critical Writing

The interactive critical pedagogy we have been describing should give students ample opportunity to move from reading to writing, and from understanding to reformulation, so as to experience a stronger mode of cultural construction. Writing is already involved through first reading and rereading, from (hypertextual) annotations and short explorations of repertoires to more elaborate written responses that reflect on the reader's questions, reactions, and interpretations of a text. Moving from reflexive response to more formal interpretation, students are encouraged to engage the text through a "multisequential" approach, which enables them to explore the rich internal linkages that a literary text develops, and to further connect this text to other relevant "intertexts" (biographical, historical, narrative). They are taught, in other words, to do "hypertextual criticism."

This type of criticism shares the advantages of hypertextuality: multilinear or networked organization, open-endedness, greater inclusion of nontextual information, interactive authorship, etc. More important, hypertextual criticism is a form of "participatory" criticism, bridging reading with writing, response with interpretation, questioning with argument. In that sense, hypertextual criticism has been anticipated by a number of directions in "poststructuralist" theory. Even before hypertextual programs became available, Jacques Derrida wrote his criticism in the form of elaborate "notes" and parallel commentaries, often sharing the page with the literary text itself. Feminist critics like Julia Kristeva, Hélène Cixous, or Adrienne Rich developed a mode of criticism that is part autobiography and part interpretation, part argument and part narrative; postmodern writers like Robert Coover, Raymond Federman, Grace Paley, and Joanna Russ developed hybrid genres they called "critifiction" (novel-essays). These hybrid, multileveled texts make it more difficult to establish where the literary text ends and criticism begins; boundaries are called into question, genre features rethought, the creative play of language allowed more freedom. The techniques of hypertextuality can also be recognized in modern literature: in the free associations and complex referencing (linking) of T. S. Eliot's poems, in the parallel (simultaneous or contrastive) narratives of Joyce, Virginia Woolf, and Graham

Greene, in the collage assemblages of W. C. Williams, e. e. cummings, and Henry Miller, and so on. Hypertextual criticism allows students to interact with the text within its structure or in its immediate vicinity: annotating and interrogating it, surrounding it with information and other intertexts, linking its images into patterns, navigating its various semantic paths. Another effect of hypertextual reading/writing is that it allows students to explore a text on their own, by clicking on italicized words or phrases to see what is embedded in them, or by navigating linked texts at their own leisure. The teacher is still sharing information, insights, and questions, but he is much less intrusive or "authoritarian," remaining essentially "behind" the text.

The nuts and bolts of hypertexting are still somewhat awkward and dependent on available software. We began with the GUIDE program, in which students could easily take an online text and create a critical hypertext in stages, beginning with thematic and lexical annotations (in pop-up notes) on first reading, continuing with internal links on rereading, and finishing with more complex "expansions" that contained linked "intertexts" and the students' own critiques. However, this program was not compatible with either WORD or html files, and so could not take full advantage of Web resources or be easily used outside of the computer classroom. Adding the collaborative element or forums was also awkward, requiring other programs, such as Norton's CONNECT, whose use was again generally limited to the computer classroom.

However, as more students have good personal access to the Web, outside of the constraints of time and place of the class, it has become clear that the Internet is the best platform for this kind of community rereading and hypertextual critical writing, especially with the advent of discussion forums and intuitive html editors such as Netscape Composer and Front Page. The specific ways in which students annotate, create, and link files, or work in groups changes each semester, depending on many factors such as level of expertise, the specific computer classroom setup, software availability, and need not be discussed here (we anticipate that the software for such operations, as well as available texts in electronic forms, will be improved and more available in the near future). What is important, however, is to continue finding ways for students to read and write in a "multilinear," hypertextual mode, and share their rereadings/rewritings of a work in an interactive community of readers. However awkward or complex, the hypertextual and interactive technology allows students to experience the three modes of textualization described by Robert Scholes (24), blending "text-within-text," "text-upon-text," and "text-again-text" in complex critical products that would satisfy visually as well as intellectually. In spite of the difficulties involved in mastering complex programs, students are often willing to move rapidly from reading to writing in hypertext. They prefer the opportunity of creating their own annotations, links, and trails over reading those produced by former classes. They do, however, appreciate the fact that their various projects became part of a corpus of critical hypertexts to be shared with future classes.

It is difficult to discuss hypertextual reading and writing in this linear medium without online examples. Anyone interested in seeing both teacher- and student-generated hypertexts can look at a number of them at http://www.vcu.edu/engweb/webtexts.htm. Since these are often used in conjunction with online forums or class discussions, most are missing one important element—the ongoing contributions of students. Daniel Anderson at the University of North Carolina has created hypertexts with online interaction with several hypertexts, such as "The Country of the Pointed Firs" at http://sites.unc.edu/storyforms/pointedfirs/. Wood-lief has also developed reading protocols based on these principles for the LitWeb site associated with *The Norton Introduction to Literature* (7th and 8th editions).

By themselves, hypertextual and networking technologies do not necessarily guarantee satisfactory critical results. As long as they are used to reinforce old habits of reading/writing or to ask "fairly traditional questions of traditional texts" (Olsen 312), they will deliver modest results. Used imaginatively, however, as part of a new interactive-transformative pedagogy that emphasizes the creative role of a reader, these technologies can be very productive. Even with the awkwardness of present technology, it has become clear for us that students who reread "into" and "behind" a text by filling unlimited margins with their questions and thoughts and then share their interpretations with other readers create a powerful learning process difficult to enact in the ordinary classroom setting. In the words of Molly Abel Travis, the electronic technologies can provide us with the "interstitial space" where links to others and to alterity can occur. The electronic classroom and hypertextual criticism encourage otherwise often passive students to "careful [interactive] reading," writing and "listening" (132), the kind that would allow them to redefine their identity and agency, reinserting them on the Web. This is "athletic reading" in twenty-first-century style.

WORKS CITED

Barthes, Roland. *S/Z*. Trans. Richard Miller. New York: Hill and Wang, 1974.
Bleich, David. *Subjective Criticism*. Baltimore: Johns Hopkins UP, 1981.

Cornis-Pope, Marcel. *Hermeneutic Desire and Critical Rewriting: Narrative Interpretation in the Wake of Poststructuralism*. London: Macmillan; New York: St. Martin's, 1992.

————. "Hypertextual and Networked Communication in Undergraduate Literary Classes: Strategies for an Interactive Critical Pedagogy." *Learning Literature in an Era of Change: Innovations in Teaching*. Ed. Dona Hickey and Donna Reiss. Sterling, VA: Stylus, 2000. 152–67.

Culler, Jonathan. *The Pursuit of Signs: Semiotics, Literature, Deconstruction*. Ithaca: Cornell UP, 1981.

Fish, Stanley. *Is There a Text in This Class? The Authority of Interpretive Communities*. Cambridge: Harvard UP, 1980.

Holland, Norman. *The Dynamics of Literary Response*. New York: Norton, 1968.

Iser, Wolfgang. *The Act of Reading: A Theory of Aesthetic Response*. Baltimore: Johns Hopkins UP, 1978/1980.

————. "The Reading Process: A Phenomenological Approach." *New Literary History* 3 (1972): 278–95.

Jameson, Fredric. *The Political Unconscious: Narrative as a Socially Symbolic Act*. Ithaca: Cornell UP, 1981.

Jauss, Hans Robert. *Towards an Aesthetic of Reception*. Trans. T. Bahti. Minneapolis: U of Minnesota P, 1982.

Kaufer, David, and Gary Waller. "To Write Is to Read Is to Write, Right?" *Writing and Reading Differently: Deconstruction and the Teaching of Composition and Literature*. Ed. G. Douglas Atkins and Michael L. Johnson. Lawrence: UP of Kansas, 1985. 66–92.

Landow, George P., ed. *Hyper/Text/Theory*. Baltimore: Johns Hopkins UP, 1994.

Leitch, Thomas M. "For (Against) a Theory of Rereading." *Modern Fiction Studies* 33.2 (1987): 491–508.

McCormick, Kathleen, Gary Waller, and Linda Flower. *Reading Texts: Reading, Responding, Writing*. Lexington, MA: Heath, 1987.

Olsen, Mark. "Signs, Symbols, and Discourses: A New Direction for Computer-Aided Literary Studies." *Computers and the Humanities* 27 (1993): 309–14.

Poulet, Georges. "Phenomenology of Reading." *New Literary History* 1(1969): 53–68.

————. "The Self and Other in Critical Consciousness." *Diacritics* 2 (1972): 46–50.

Ricoeur, Paul. "Qu'est-ce qu'un texte." *Hermeneutik und Dialektik: Festschrift in Honor of H. G. Gadamer*. Ed. Rödiger Bubner. Vol. 2. Tübingen: Mohr, 1970. 181–200.

Riffaterre, Michael. *Semiotics of Poetry*. Bloomington: Indiana UP, 1978.

Rosenblatt, Louise M. *The Reader, the Text, the Poem: The Transactional Theory of the Literary Work*. Carbondale and Edwardsville: Southern Illinois UP, 1978.

Ruthrof, Horst. *The Reader's Construction of Narrative*. London and New York: Routledge and Kegan Paul, 1981.

Salvatori, Mariolina. "Reading and Writing a Text: Correlations between Reading and Writing Patterns." *College English* 45.7 (1983): 657–66.

Scholes, Robert. *Textual Power: Literary Theory and the Teaching of English*. New Haven: Yale UP, 1985.

Thoreau, Henry David. *Walden*. 1854. Princeton: Princeton UP, 1971.

Travis, Molly Abel. *Reading Cultures: The Construction of Readers in the Twentieth Century*. Carbondale and Edwardsville: Southern Illinois UP, 1998.

Woodlief, Ann. *Index to Online Papers on Computers and the Reading Process*. <http://www.vcu.edu/engweb>. Includes article with Marcel Cornis-Pope. "Notes on Critical Literary Philosophy and Pedagogical Practice." <http://www.vcu.edu/engweb/home/theory.html>.

8

(Re)Reading and Writing Genres of Discourse: Creative Writing as General Education

Mary Ann Cain
George Kalamaras

A MULTITUDE OF GENRES

David Bleich, in *Know and Tell: A Writing Pedagogy of Disclosure, Genre, and Membership*, argues for the value of recognizing and making use of the multiple genres that traverse both written and oral language use in the classroom. He writes,

> The materiality of language also pertains to the value of disclosure [. . .] which urges us to recognize that different genres [. . .] of talk, language use, and writing emerge from all of us at different times and situations, and that these genres are welcomed in the writing classroom. (xvi)

Bleich puts great emphasis on the writing classroom as providing the time, space, and means for students and instructor to generate new genres, not simply to try to imitate the conventions of more familiar, seemingly static genres. In this way, new knowledge may emerge, and students become active participants in the making of such knowledge. It's not as if students aren't already using diverse genres, Bleich notes, but that the classroom has typically not been a place in which students are encouraged to extend what they already know and use into less familiar forms. Instead, they are treated more as *tabulas rasas,* empty slates waiting to be filled with the knowledge necessary for their "progress."

We wish to extend Bleich's argument for the multiplicity of genre into the issue of reading. Just as Bleich argues for the need to consider and make use of a multitude of genres, both spoken and written, we argue for equally diverse forms of reading (or, to be more specific, interpretation) to be recognized, valued, and ultimately put to use in the writing classroom. Such interpretations cross back and forth between spoken and written forms. Rather than assuming that the English classroom is a place to "discipline" (as in enforcing a set of textual conventions, both explicit and explicit, around which English as a discipline is structured) the diversity of interpretations that may occur, or even the subject of those interpretations, we prefer Bleich's invitation to make use of what we and our students already use in our lives, then generate new forms that more consciously address the needs of a particular moment of learning. This is not to say that we do not value any disciplinary constraints, any limitation on what can be interpreted or how. It is to say that such constraints are, in practice, much more mobile, context-bound, and specific to a given moment in the course of a semester's work, rather than a fixed focus throughout. We think that the difference lies not in what interpretations occur in practice but in the degree to which such diverse interpretations are named, discussed, and consciously used, as opposed to remaining tacit and thus outside of critical awareness. Earlier in this collection, Patricia Harkin and James Sosnoski have commented on how various positions within critical theory now assume that ideological contexts shape interpretation, yet these insights have yet to significantly influence studies in writing. But as other parts of this essay show, there is ample evidence to illustrate the existence of such diverse forms of interpretation.

*   *   *

Reading
    background and information and, 293, 296–97
    books versus history, 79–80
    centripetal, 230
    close, 133–34
    cognitive model of reading, 296–99
    critical, 294
    dialogue and, 294
    expressive model of reading, 299–302
    individually vs. culturally, 190, 299–308
    institutionalized, 153–69
    integrated with writing, 270–90, 330
    interpretation and, 64–74
    literature vs. criticism, 245
    objectivist model of reading, 297–99
    passivity and, 283
    readers as writers, xvi
    reading theory versus literary theory, xvii, 292–308
    role of reader in, 295–308
    role of text in, 295–308
    rough drafts of, 281
    social-cultural model of reading, 302–8
    social subject/product and, 293–308
Reality
    reflection vs. selection vs. deflection, 28–29
    Reception theory, 215–16
    Recruitment of faculty, 119
    Redistribution of wealth, 93–119
    Relativism, 137–38, 200
    Representation, 184–85
    Resistance theory, 72

*   *   *

OPEN ADMISSION(S)

Janelle responds to my (Mary Ann's) question as carefully as a litigator. "What have I learned so far this semester?" she repeats the question I have posed to all the W103 Introduction to Creative Writing (a general-education requirement in the arts) students who have come to my office for their midterm conferences. She takes a deep breath, adjusts herself between the arms of the upholstered chair while I, seated on an armless wooden desk chair, lean my left elbow on the corner of my desk. We are seated across from each other, my desk not between us but to our sides. Only I am close enough to use it as a prop for my elbow. There is a small space between us, just enough for either of us to cross our legs without causing the other to move.

I think I already know what she wants to say. I tense, wondering if she will be so daring. But time is against us. I was running ten minutes late when I called her in after the previous student. We both acknowledged our need to end on the half-hour, so the conference would be only twenty minutes long.

When I look at her now, I don't know if her frowning and sighs are because our conference has been cut short or because it already seems too long.

I don't remember exactly how she answered my question. I remember she said how familiar everything in the course already was, how she wrote voluminously on her own before this class, how she wrote for herself and not for others. Mostly what I remember is how I leaned on my desk and said very little, waiting for her pauses to tell me when I might respond, finding that her pauses were the only punctuation in a long, long monologue. While she spoke, I found myself feeling that I had switched to the role of a therapist, nodding, listening, but letting the "patient" talk long enough so that she might begin to actually hear herself.

Maybe I just want her to come out and say what I was pretty sure she really felt: She hadn't learned a thing; she was already a good writer before this class; she was "stuck" in a required class that was "below" her abilities and talents; she just wanted to write what she wanted to write and not have to follow assignments, guidelines, or any other "rules."

I think about how I started noticing fewer smiles and more frowns, even eye rolling from her in class after I'd returned an exercise and raised some questions about the action, or lack thereof, in her story. I had offered possible alternatives to more conventional plot structures, but her only response was to say she didn't know what else she was supposed to do, and thus she did not revise. In fact, her entire midterm portfolio showed no revision, only new writing, the kind that she really wanted to do, not anything "assigned."

As she speaks, it's as if I have become hypnotized by the sound of her voice, and whenever she pauses, I simply wait for her to go on, so powerful is the onrush of her words. She has not said, "I learned nothing so far," probably because she understands that learning is what the grade depends upon, and she still wants a good grade. I tell myself that she wants a grade based upon what she already knows, and that it appears that she thinks she knows quite a bit, more than the other students, which likely translates into an "A" in her mind.

Watching her speak, no, monologue, for ten, fifteen, twenty minutes, carefully avoiding what she believes is true but cannot say for fear of risking a good grade, I take in her presence: her round blue eyes, pale skin, baggy jeans, tightly bound red hair. *I remember that she may have crossed an ankle or even leaned back at some points. But she definitely did not close her body off from the surrounding space. She claimed it, while I tried to hold a neutral position, not react. I may, in fact, have come across to her as bored, as I continued to lean my elbow on my desk, my "authority."* It's as if she's turned me into another therapist, in the line of them that she has seen over the years. But in fact, I am conflicted, frustrated that she wants me to grade her on what she already knows, wants acknowledgment for her talents and won't discuss other possibilities since she writes only "for herself." Wondering if, in some way, the class has failed her, or if I am trying too hard to make her conform to a prescribed course of development. Maybe, I hope, if I listen I will be able to get through to her. I fantasize how she will come to trust me and want to share her drafts with me, eager for my tactful, sensitive response.

When I recounted this episode to a visiting writer from another university, he said, simply, "If she wants to write for herself, why is she in your class?" I responded, "It's a gen ed requirement," and that ended the discussion. No surprise, really—few who teach creative writing must teach it as a general-education requirement, as I do. One of the biggest "privileges" that creative writing teachers claim is not having to teach writing to students who don't want to learn. That is why teaching composition, in contrast, feels so much more draining to teach. Attitudes against writing are difficult to contend with, let alone change.

And yet, Janelle is not a "problem" writer insofar as she writes without prompts, without deadlines, but, as she says, "for therapy." Only at the end of the term, in our final exit conference, does she reveal a prior diagnosis of dyslexia. In the meantime, her prose recounts episodes of family turmoil—an evil stepmother, a brother brought to court, a runaway teen on the road—and youthful drama—the death of a friend, a romance between two misfit teens who marry and defy the adult world by staying together against the odds. She scorns the "hearts and flowers" themes embraced by her writing group peers. Although she is the youngest in the group, her cynicism and suspicion runs much deeper. They, oddly enough, speak in reverent tones about the "deep" subjects she ventures. But for some reason, I have become a roadblock, not a facilitator, to Janelle's work. I don't know how I became this, any more than I know how I became an impromptu therapist. I don't like the roles I fall into, but I feel helpless to work against them, mainly because I'm not entirely sure the casting is wrong.

Does she somehow pick up my inner conflict about how to respond? The conference ends after twenty minutes with no discussion about her midterm grade-in-progress (what was supposed to be "negotiated" between us), no resolution to the question of what she learned, just a litany of reasons why she did not attempt revision of any of the works included for a portfolio grade. Perhaps it's because she does, indeed, sense my inner conflict that she refuses to reschedule another conference, claiming she does not have the time, given her work schedule, to come in and try again. My guess is that she saw me as yet another adult in her life who did not set clear boundaries, whose silence was suspect, a cover-up for insecurity and weakness. For such adults, her fear had blossomed into open disdain. I was not worth bothering with.

After the conference, she leaves a note on my door telling me she thinks she deserves an "A" for her portfolio grade-in-progress. She justifies her lack of revision (a major criterion for the grade) as her choice as an artist to leave her words intact. Her justification emphasizes her feeling that to change her work would make the writing worse, not better. I find myself continuing to fantasize that I can somehow "break through" to her, even as I am increasingly frustrated by her refusal to discuss her work in any other terms than a power struggle for ownership: either her version or mine will prevail. She's testing me, I think, to see if, indeed, her words will prevail.

I write back on her note that we still need to talk to resolve the question of what she has learned, especially because she has not revised her work. A series of e-mails follows, initiated by her, that become increasingly volatile, even hostile, toward me. I interpret them this way: Because *I* was late in starting the conference, because *my* assignments block *her* creativity, because *I* sat and said nothing in the conference while *she* was forced to keep the conversation rolling, she will not waste her time in another conference. So I am forced to assign a grade without further discussion: B, for lack of revision. In the process, I feel violated, victimized, on the verge of complaining to some higher authority how this student has verbally abused me.

* * *

"I want my students to have some of the uppitiness of writers towards readers—to be able to talk back—to say, 'I'm not just writing for readers or teachers. I'm writing as much for me—sometimes even *more* for me.' I want them to fight back a bit against readers" (Elbow, "War" 273).

* * *

OPEN ADMISSION(S) REVISITED

To fight back a bit against readers, what might that entail? In our case, we debated whether to include an explanation of this essay's admittedly "alternative" structure in the beginning. But we fought back a bit, resisting our training as readers to first state our ideas and then exemplify them. Instead, we chose to first perform what we mean, and within that performance offer the exposition of our structure. We find that in changing the genre—performing our argument—we also change the nature of what is said as well as our and the readers' relationship to it, foregrounding the dialogic aspects of our inquiry. This is, in short, a way of "walking our talk"—not only to argue for the need to let genre and interpretation evolve in the classroom but to demonstrate what happens when that occurs in scholarly inquiry such as this chapter. To fight back a bit against the domination of "reading" a classroom over "writing" a classroom, we have fought back a bit against ourselves so that we might expand the complexities of genre and its meaning-making capacities.

* * *

INTERPRETATION AND COMPOSITION

W103 Introduction to Creative Writing occupies a paradoxical space in the general-education curriculum as an "unnecessary requirement." Its intention is to ensure that students receive the proverbial "well-rounded education," including aesthetic appreciation and (to a lesser extent) artistic skill. Few W103 students believe they are, or ever will be "real writers" (in other words, literary writers), and few have any ambitions to write beyond the requirements. Yet because creative writing is widely perceived as nonessential, and, as Nancy Welch has noted, of little social consequence, some students are actually less fearful of such writing, in contrast to composition courses that claim to prepare them for "real" writing in the academy and (sometimes) in the professional world. From this perspective, creative writing may do little harm (except for the possibility of a bad grade), but it also does little good. On the other hand, some students are even *more* fearful in required creative writing than in composition classes because they claim they are not "creative," and composition courses, they claim (ironically), require no creativity.

To the extent that little of the reading and writing students do in W103 will be used in other courses or even in the world, the course is of little social consequence. However, W103 holds a potential for something more consequential, especially when students are given a chance to inquire into forms of interpretation with which they are already familiar, even possess some skill in, and are invited to do something *more* with them.

This *doing something more* marks not a bridge to but a point of departure from many literature classes in which specific genres of writing and forms of interpretation are emphasized, mainly because, as in Paulo Freire's banking model (in which students are regarded as banks into which teacher knowledge is deposited then withdrawn upon examination), students are constructed as lacking such knowledge. Our experience is that students tend to agree that they lack such knowledge, that they are, in fact, taking such a course in order to "learn something new." Janelle, for instance, felt that she already knew what W103 had to teach her, and thus it was largely a waste of time. Yet ultimately what is "new" to students like Janelle is not something of students' own making but rather their introduction to unfamiliar disciplinary conventions. At the same time, students always bring some assumptions about what any course is "about" and their relationship to what they picture as the course content and methods. In Janelle's case, she assumed that the conventions around which the course was based would not help her write what she wanted to write.

Doing something more begins with what is "old" in terms of what students assume to be true about a course, in this case, creative writing. For instance, what is "old" knowledge to some students is that such writing requires acts of imagination, even genius, individual expression, and "hidden meanings." As Harkin and Sosnoski illustrate, these assumptions include a form of interpretation that assumes a stable, determinate meaning that can be deduced from authorial intention, a view to which, they argue, many textbooks ascribe. Other forms of interpretation that come from such assumptions often focus on what feelings or impressions a given work might generate, memories or associations, as well as interpretations that employ concepts such as symbolism, theme, and plot sequence. Such concepts harken back to the New Criticism of the 1940s and 50s, a school of literary criticism in which the text was regarded as an autonomous object whose meanings were encoded in literary form. The role of the reader was to extract meanings from such texts using an objective method similar to that of scientists, separating the reader's own feelings and perceptions from what the "text itself" communicated, as well as deferring the question of the writer's intentions in favor of formal analysis.

Reading with an eye toward diversity, then, begins with *naming* these forms of interpretation *as forms* by observing them. Such observations structure the metadiscursive dimension of classroom conversation, the talk about the talk about the writing. Observations are "enabling constraints," a concept borrowed from Judith and Geoffrey Summerfield. Enabling constraints use literary form as a prompt for investigating what is possible to say within a given constraint (such as the number of words in a sentence). Writers then use those constraints to expand the possibilities of what can be expressed. Thus, observations, when used as "enabling constraints," interrupt the "natural," seemingly formless progression of making meaning. Through observation, students begin to notice how their interpretations do, in fact, have a form, make connections to other people's interpretations, and (ultimately) point toward other possible meanings.

Without observation, and, in turn, without the "readings" that it enables, the formal constraints of composing in literary genres can feel oppressive, and students (like Janelle) may construct form as an inflexible rule or boundary that is not subject to their own meanings. For instance, an exercise on metaphors and similes can become a way of "following the rule": using "like" or "as" versus implying a comparison. The meaning that results from generating a comparison is thus overshadowed by how well it conforms to the form. However, observation brings form back into the context of making meaning by asking students to attend not only to literary form but also to forms of interpretation. For instance, when reading comparisons, we discuss the difference between reading comparisons that are striking or unusual versus how students read clichés (which can also be comparisons). We discuss how the value of clichés changes from one rhetorical context to another—from an encoded familiarity among group members to something that obscures meanings to outsiders. As a result, interpretation becomes an integral part of composition via observation of its forms.

Observing forms of interpretation leads to another point emphasized by Bleich—diversity of genres, both spoken and written. W103 depends upon such diversity, well beyond the disciplinary constraints that mark the formal boundaries of the course. Janelle's story reveals the complexities, as well as the risks, in negotiating these genres. Thus, interpretation and composition are not armchair leisure activities nor are they formal exercises with little connection to "real life." Instead, they become crucial to social connection and learning. Harkin and Sosnoski also note how such readings require more, not less, responsibility on the part of students, compared to more "stable" forms of reading. Indeed, a great deal is at stake, including the consequences that follow an end to the making of meaning, in this case between teacher and student. For the teacher, there is verbal violence from the student; for the student, there is isolation from other, perhaps more powerful, rhetorical, intellectual, and creative positions from which to speak and write.

The use of reading has been argued for and against within composition studies (including in this collection) as a gap that exists to be bridged, or is unbridgeable, a transformation or reconfiguration, a reunion of disparate, even antagonistic, forces within the discipline. While we do emphasize the value of reading as interpretation within W103, we hesitate to say that W103 itself represents such a bridge or transformation. We do not see this convergence of interpretation and composition as in any way seamless or smooth, at least in terms of bringing forth a disciplinary coherence out of a carnival of difference. Instead, W103 marks a moment of turmoil, challenge, and change in a curriculum and disciplinary tradition that seeks to contain and constrain it.

*   *   *

centripetal
dialogue and,
passivity and,
reading theory versus literary theory,

role of reader in,
rough drafts of,

*   *   *

In W103, when we discuss "genres," we (like Bleich) consider not only spoken but written discourse, including the overarching dialogues ("talk") that occur between instructor and students, students and students, and students and those texts in the "world" (and the worlds in those texts) they read and write. The genres of "talk" that we encourage go beyond spoken discourse, finding connections between what is written and what is spoken, between *how* one uses language and *what* one says. Simply put, we consider "talk" what students write and speak to each other and to the instructor: about what they write; about what others in the class write and say; and about and into the world beyond the classroom. Talk, then, is crucial to the making of meaning (interpretation) which, in turn, facilitates composition (which also crosses between spoken and written discourse).

Talk occurs in particular genres, most of which are already common to many writing classrooms. Classroom discussion, for example, can employ several of these genres on a given day. These include responses to student writing, responses to readings, invention exercises, journal assignments/writer's notebook, self-evaluations, and conferences.

In these genres, the role of interpretation goes far beyond disciplinary constraints, reaching into those areas of "new" composition that Bleich extols. Writing fifteen years prior to Bleich, Nancy Comley and Robert Scholes describe such compositions in the context of using poetry writing to teach interpretation in a freshman English course: "What [students] produce is neither 'creative writing' nor 'composition,' in the usual sense of those expressions, but simply writing—writing that illustrates their growing command of this essential skill" (108). We find that interpretation occurs not only about the written texts of student and published writing but about the talk about that writing, too, which includes the worlds from which their spoken and written texts have come. Thus, "reading" the social dimensions of classroom talk (as exemplified by Janelle's story) becomes an integral part of learning also to *compose* discourse. Interpretation, then, is not only about learning what meanings that disciplinary forms of interpretations can yield (which we still value) but also how such forms help make visible the otherwise unseen forms of interpretation that students already use. In making such forms visible, it places them into a critical context, one available for revision and (perhaps most important) transformation. This is what we mean by dialogue—knowing one form of interpretation in relation to another, as one among many possibilities.

                                        *   *   *

GENRES OF "TALK"

The following section describes the genres of "talk" that tend to occur in W103 and how Marie Ponsot and Rosemary Deen's methods of observation, interpretation, and evaluation provide the necessary "enabling constraints" for composition to emerge from interpretation.

Responses to Student Writing.   The main goal of response in W103 is the development of perceptive readers—not just of texts, but also of the world—as opposed to the development of ideal texts. This is not to say that we believe teachers should neglect the development of student work. However, it is to say that what gets valued as "good writing" should be closely tied to the contexts that shape it. This is possible because of the constraints imposed on classroom "talk," specifically Ponsot and Deen's concepts of observation, inference (interpretation), and evaluation. The course can begin by discussing the uses of what Judith and Geoffrey Summerfield call "enabling constraints," asking students to consider examples, from both inside and outside the classroom, of how language use is always constrained. Then the instructor can introduce observation, interpretation, and evaluation as a way to facilitate students' (often anxious) attempts to find something to say about another writer's work.

Many students are already familiar with a form of response that seeks to "bury Caesar, not to praise him." Some associate this with comments and/or grades received by former teachers. The mirror opposite of this mode is praise, which many students associate with student responses to each other, assuming all writing that is personally expressive cannot be evaluated. Praise, then, is not, strictly speaking, evaluation, but rather a means of asserting the impossibility of it and a way of valuing one another's individuality. Neither criticism nor praise guarantees that interpretation will occur as a result. In fact, in practice, both of these forms of response tend to yield the opposite—an end to interpretation. This is where observation plays such a crucial role: it helps make visible the limits that such forms of response place upon interpretation.

Observation is noticing the elements that shape a written text, that is, naming what materials go into a piece of writing. The key to understanding observation is the *what*—what can be pointed to, quantified, classified, as patterns or anomalies in a given work. For example, on a local level, one might point to the repetition of the word *red*, images related to the sky or sunlight, capitalization of words in the middle of a sentence or line, nouns used as verbs, the length of paragraphs or stanzas. More globally, one might note changes in patterns of imagery and form, characterization, and modes of action (from inner to outer, or vice versa).

Interpretation builds upon observation. In "unconstrained" talk, observation and interpretation are often simultaneous, but for the purposes of developing a greater awareness of these concepts, we ask students to keep them separate, especially early in the semester. The *what* of observation now includes a discussion of *how* it means. For example, if several students observe how predominantly soft vowel sound patterns in a poem change into largely hard consonant sounds, then a useful interpretation might include a discussion of the metaphorical dimension of "soft to hard"; the change in consciousness reflected in a shift in the speaker's voice; and the ways those sounds change in relation to other aspects of the poem such as speaker's voice, dominant imagery, and narration.

The final concept, evaluation, builds upon the first two. In fact, a true evaluation depends upon observation and interpretation, yet students often feel compelled to assert an evaluation, sometimes to relieve the ambiguity they face with the proliferation of meaning (a new experience for many of them, who are used to language meaning one thing only and not another). However, observation and interpretation often demonstrate the value of ambiguity, not as mystification but as a way to deepen one's understanding of textual complexity. Evaluation asks what value we might place on what has been written. Saying whether one likes or relates to a piece of writing is not the point of evaluation; instead, it is to show how readers experience the text: to locate and describe moments of confusion and understanding; to ask critical questions (about shifts in textual patterns, for example); to illustrate how an emotion or thought they experienced is constructed through what they have observed and how they have interpreted it. Evaluation ensures that the discussion of interpretation does not remain relativistic but instead is grounded in what can be observed.

The formats that a course like this one models for both oral and written responses are part of the overarching constraints of classroom response, a necessary context for the reading of literary and social texts and contexts. For classroom discussion, several different formats are useful; instructors can seek students' input to determine the best ones for a given class. Formats include asking each student to respond, one at a time, to a written text (student draft or professional) with little or no conversation, and to offer their observations, interpretations, and evaluations. A variation of this "monologue-style" format is to ask each student for brief observations, followed by each student offering interpretations. The instructor's role here can include keeping track of the observations noted, helping students articulate them more fully, and asking for interpretations of the most noticed observations. Sometimes after a series of "monologues" we open the floor to dialogue between respondents, although we, as the facilitators, can bring back initial observations and interpretations for further reflection and analysis.

Written responses to student writing can include letters that students write to each other about drafts of their work. These letters, which are modeled after ones instructors write by way of responding to student work, should be written before class, with one copy turned in to the student writer and one to the instructor. On occasion, we ask students to respond to the responses they receive, including those we have written. Part of our work as instructors is to respond to the students' responses, so that respondents receive feedback on how well they are responding.

Response is, of all the writing workshop's activities, central to how the class's talk is focused and shaped. However, the following assignments are also important. For many writing teachers, these are nothing new; what is, perhaps, different, is the context of "enabling constraints" in which we use them:

- Journal assignments/writer's notebook (including responses to professional readings, observations of language outside the classroom, reflections on their writing and processes).
- Invention exercises/collaborative invention (to generate new writing and/or the discussion of writing as social and contextual).
- Formal self-evaluations (to accompany portfolios for midterm conferences and final evaluation/grade).

* * *

OPEN ADMISSION(S) REVISITED

role of reader in,
rough drafts of,

* * *

11/17/99

Mike,

Your poem, "Mick Taylor," is interesting. I'm a Mick Taylor fan, my-self. I began listening before he joined the Stones, when he was part of John Mayall's Bluesbreakers, and I met him this summer when he was in Fort Wayne. Did you attend his concert?

At any rate, this is a tough poem to write—one reason I asked students not to try to write through the voice of a famous person but, rather, to create a character. It's hard to capture the voice of someone famous. But you still bring up good details in places, especially in the fourth, fifth, and sixth stanzas. Other areas are more vague and/or cliched (see what I've marked as examples). Try to show "permeate my being," "go through / the motions," etc. I think you're ultimately trying to say he's burned out, but this poem might be enhanced if you showed this while also showing something positive. This might make him more believable and complex. At any rate, I especially enjoyed reading this since I like his music. Thanks!

George

* * *

BRIDGING THE GAP?

Reading and writing can work productively together as equals to benefit each other and the profession. Both parties can be on top. We can create a better balance and relationship between reading and writing. [. . .] To do so, we will need to give more emphasis to writing in our teaching and our curricular structures and use writing in more imaginative ways. (Elbow, "War" 270)

* * *

John Trimbur's discussion of Freshman English in his article, "The Prob-lem of Freshman English (Only): Toward Programs of Study in Writing," is helpful in further articulating the problems and possibilities posed by a course such as W103. Trimbur's emphasis, of course, is on first-year com-position courses; however, W103 straddles that boundary as a freshma' writing course that is required, although not "necessary" in terms of ' perceived service to the rest of the curriculum. Furthermore, students may choose from other, nonwriting options to fulfill this requirement in the arts. Practically speaking, however, many students take the course not because they want to write, but because it fits a scheduling slot, or because the alternatives are even less familiar and thus more intimidating than creative writing. Thus, W103 represents many of the same tensions that surround freshman composition, tensions that, as Trimbur explains, mark Freshman English as both "oversaturated" and "overdetermined" in its perceived function and usefulness.

Trimbur makes a compelling point, especially in the context of a collection such as this one, about the dangers of trying to unify apparent oppositions within English studies. Admittedly, until now, we, the authors, have not closely examined on what terms we seek to bring reading and writing, rhetoric and poetics, together within the contexts of our teaching and research. We've previously used the term *dialogue* as well as *nexus* and *reconfiguration* (borrowing from sources such as Mikhail Bakhtin, Stephen North, and James Berlin), and have leaned on the metaphor of "bridging" here and there, too, as we've theorized our work through the years (Cain, Kalamaras). However, Trimbur's article has caused us to take a closer look at exactly what we mean when we say that interpretation and composition work together in W103. Trimbur writes,

If anything, I believe that current theories to reconfigure English studies by unifying the opposites—composition and literature, rhetoric and poetics, writing and reading—may well represent a serious obstacle to the development of the programs of study in writing I am pressing for. (27)

Trimbur goes on to note that writing studies' relationship to English departments is "both accidental and overdetermined" (27), and that the question of whether writing and literature "belong" together is ultimately dependent upon local conditions. But the larger question of whether and how reading and writing, interpretation and composition belong in the same classroom is seen by Trimbur as a question of challenging a disciplinary focus that has been, throughout American education, one of "English-Only." Trimbur sees "English-Only" in terms of writing instruction's "institutional affiliation and the languages in which students write" (13). His use of "English-Only" refers not only to the use of English as the primary language of the university but also to English Studies' historical link to "a racialized curriculum and turn of the century First Worldism" (27). Comley and Scholes also allude to a similar problem:

"We must destroy our own mental idols if we are to escape the idolatry of English under which we now labor" (108–109).

We appreciate Trimbur's recasting of what has heretofore been seen primarily as an "English-Only" problem because it points toward a curriculum that can more readily absorb and make use of the multiple genres of reading and writing for which Bleich argues. We prefer to think, then, of W103 as a course that marks a potential point of entry toward such a curriculum as well as a point of departure from the "English-Only" focus that still undergirds all of our efforts in English Studies, whether or not one's home department is in English, rhetoric, composition, or elsewhere.

The story of Janelle and Mary Ann's conference might, then, be understood as emblematic of the problems and possibilities of diverse approaches to interpretation as part of the work of composing. Not only were they trying to compose the texts contained in Janelle's portfolio, but they were also composing each other, their respective roles as teacher and student (and beyond), and the social contexts of their interaction. As Bleich points out, personal disclosure and affect play a role in most acts of interpretation. For Janelle, such disclosure included her feelings about her work and what it meant to her. For Mary Ann, her feelings toward Janelle and her work led her to conclude that Janelle was unaware of what Mary Ann perceived her work revealed about her learning. Janelle's "mistakes" (what she had ventured but rejected as failures) were what she needed to reconsider instead of resorting to more familiar, less critically aware, habits. However, professional and academic contexts tend to impose strong constraints upon the presence of such "mistakes." The conference story illustrates how reading and interpretation matter in ways that Bleich would like to further exploit. Unlike the images of leisurely, armchair, pleasure-driven reading, on one hand, or the agonizingly painful apprenticeship of learning a new discourse, on the other, this story shows how crucial interpretation is to learning. So crucial is interpretative freedom (or what Harkin and Sosnoski refer to as "play") that, as the story shows, when it is thwarted, it yields a potentially violent outcome.

*   *   *

As I (George) write this, it is early August and there is a "W233 crisis" on our campus. Several part-time faculty have either resigned or been reassigned to teach beginning composition classes, and enrollments in the intermediate expository writing course (W233)—a course taught through the English department and billed throughout the university as "research writing in the disciplines"—are once again burgeoning, without sufficient staffing. At the same time, I receive word that my W203 poetry writing course is "vulnerable" since its enrollment is currently in "single digits." The department chair tells me that if W203 is canceled through Arts & Sciences, W233 would be my "fate" because of the W233 "crisis."

It's simple math, right? Simple economics? Anyone in his or her right mind would want to fill as many sections of W233, with its twenty-two students, as possible? I even wonder what I would do if I were Dean and the decision was mine. But—staring down at my beagle who anxiously stares out the porch window at the squirrel whose bushy tail sweeps across the fence in rhythm with the anxious hopping of a robin near our backyard bird feeder—I quickly dismiss any uncertainty. No way I'd cancel W203, even with enrollments in single digits.

As a feeder class for W303 and W403 (poetry writing and advanced poetry writing), and as a beginning creative writing course that often serves as an introduction to English for majors and nonmajors, W203 is invaluable, even if the immediate bottom line does not demonstrate this. I watch the robin suddenly gather its courage and lift itself to the feeder, suspiciously eyeing the squirrel, then trying a few seeds in a backward tilt of its head that momentarily exposes its throat. The squirrel flicks its tail briefly but otherwise does not move. Still, it's enough to make the robin hop over to a neighboring tree before coming back to the feeder. My beagle is simply beside herself with all this activity, all this lolling and sprawling of neighboring creatures in her own backyard as if they thought they owned the joint. Her head tilts in a way that makes her velvet hound ears look even longer yet alert, her entire body tense to pounce, even though there's a window between her and her counterparts.

I consider my arguments in the event that W203 is suddenly put on the chopping block. How invaluable W203 is not only to the success of creative writing but also to the major. Numerous students have told me how the course, with its emphasis on Ponsot and Deen's "observation, interpretation, and evaluation," helps them learn to "read" for the first time, and how as a result of taking "creative writing" they are now more discerning, "creative readers" in their literature courses. But I consider how such anecdotes might sound to my literature colleagues, some of whom pride themselves on teaching "real" literature as opposed to what I do as a mere teacher of writing. I rehearse, instead, pleas I might make to the administration if the course continues to stagnate in single digits, say, at eight or nine students. How enrollments in upper-division poetry courses might falter in later semesters as a result. How canceling W203 could work against the need to attract prospective majors. How given our non-

traditional student population we're bound to pick up a student or two during drop/add week if the course were only given that much of a chance. How W233, though valuable, skews the priorities of the department toward "research" and classification. Part of me feels like my beagle—eager, tense, curious, perhaps even a bit annoyed at this sudden flurry of activity. As if we'd both just been stirred from our summer afternoon nap, our respective situations seem to demand our attention, but all either of us can do is examine the feeding through clear porch glass, tinted a little from the coming and going of summer storms.

For the sake of one or two more bodies, I think, feeling for the first time something of what Lot must have felt when he was told by the voice of God that Sodom could be saved if he could find "one good man." I examine the current class roster, which is filled with students whom I've either had in W103 or even those few who previously tried W203 but because of personal difficulties had to drop—students who enthusiastically signed up during preregistration as far back as last March. I think about how Mabel seems to be writing for her life—to give her a sense of sanity after working the night shift at the mental health ward, as well as ways to retrace her African-American Cherokee heritage; how Adrian had to drop the course last spring because his medication for his depression had been too strong, making him—as he told me—feel like he'd "rather die" than be on medicine; how last term as well Angie had health problems and is trying W203 again now that she can concentrate on the course. I consider Jeremy, who after dropping the course last fall re-enrolled last spring and was one of the star pupils and now plans to continue writing poetry. Though W203 is a "required" course in general education, I have this overriding sense that the dominant "requirement" for these and other

students is to figure out how to live; for many of them, learning to write
poetry represents an opportunity to do just that.

If the course gets canceled, my "fate" I'm told is W233. That's not a
bad "fate." I've taught that course numerous times and enjoy it, even
helped implement some important changes into the course's curriculum.
So, it's not that I don't want to teach composition. There's something
deeper here, something telling me that the university is out of balance,
that its priorities are not always mine. Does the administration read enrollment figures the way a teacher does—the way I do? Are there other
factors to consider besides numbers? My beagle whines, looking up at me
pleadingly, as if to ask why the bird and squirrel have entered her yard,
why they sit in her territory eating and ignoring her, why she can see them
clearly but can't seem to make a difference? I'm not a beagle, I think. I can
indeed do more than whine and sniff at the window. So I spend the weekend calling twenty-five to thirty former W103 creative writing students,
notifying them about the W203 class. In the end, I get two more students
to make the necessary minimum of ten—but it's close, those two being a
70-year-old retired woman I'd recently met at a poetry reading and who'd
asked me to keep her on a mailing list for poetry events (she needs to go
through the formality of being admitted to the university first before we
can officially add her to the roll) and another former student whose student loan check will not arrive until the first day of class (well past the
date courses are usually canceled). Still, with such guarantees the administration is sympathetic. The department chair informs me that I "saved"
the class, that the Dean was sympathetic and agreed that, though capped
at fifteen, he wanted the class to "make," and that an enrollment of ten
ensured that. I'm elated, of course, thinking of students like Mabel,
Adrian, and Angie. I'm relieved that W203 will fly, that it can serve to introduce students to the major, that it can act as a reservoir for upper-
division creative writing, even provide a necessary anchor for those most
in need of writing poetry during turbulent times in their lives. At the same
time, I'm still troubled that such a "crisis" existed, that I had to spend an
entire weekend phoning former students, that the fate of so many rested
on the difference on the roster between a "nine" and a "ten."

My beagle seems more relaxed now, too. We'd been traveling for a
month out west, and now that she's settled back into home she's becoming increasingly used to other animals passing through her yard. On some
level, she seems to understand that the bird feeder is not there for either
her enjoyment or her displeasure, but for some other purpose. She seems
content to watch the flurry of feather and squirrel tail come and go.

* * *

THE ROLE OF THE READER

role of reader in,

* * *

During fall exit interviews with W103 students, I (George) offer M&M's, chocolate chip cookies, and, for Mike, a signed poster of Mick Taylor that I thought he'd enjoy seeing. I want students to feel their semester's work has added up to something; comments and grades alone can't carry the full import of what they've learned. Neither do M&M's and cookies, of course, but I still want to give students something more than they've come to expect.

Most students seem relaxed—even relieved—to wrap up the semester and receive grades on their final portfolios. I'm told by more than a few that I have a "reputation" as being "tough" and "challenging." Most are anxious for any parting words of advice, comfortable enough in our fifteen-week bond to confide, "The writing was tough, but I'm also grateful for what you had us read. I mean, I never would've thought a poem or story could be that *deep*."

But Mike seems more nervous than most, something I don't understand immediately because he often stays after class to chat about things, to tell me about his life. "I liked your final poem on Mick Taylor," I say. "I thought you might enjoy seeing this." I hand him the signed poster. I figure Mike might feel odd that he chose a character to write about that he assumed his teacher might not know, or conversely, that he's fearful that in this case the teacher knows "too much," so I'm anxious to let him know it's OK—that, even though he didn't follow the instructions of "making up a character," I actually enjoyed someone writing about one of my heroes for a change.

But before even looking at the poster, he clears his throat. "I think you misread my poem," he says. "I mean, I think I better tell you that I didn't even know there was such a guy as Mick Taylor. I just thought the name captured a burned-out rocker. I didn't want you to think I hadn't followed instructions. I really thought I'd made him up."

WORKS CITED

Bakhtin, M. M. *The Dialogic Imagination*. Ed. Michael Holquist. Trans. Caryl Emerson and Michael Holquist. Austin: U of Texas P, 1981.

Berlin, James. "Rhetoric and Ideology in the Writing Class." *College English* 50 (1988): 477–94.

Bleich, David. *Know and Tell: A Writing Pedagogy of Disclosure, Genre, and Membership.* Portsmouth, NH: Boynton/Cook, 1998.

Cain, Mary Ann. "Problematizing Formalism: A Double-Cross of Genre Boundaries between Creative Writing and Composition." *College Composition and Communication* 51:1 (September 1999): 89–95.

Comley, Nancy R., and Robert Scholes. "Literature, Composition, and the Structure of English." In *Composition & Literature: Bridging the Gap.* Ed. Winifred Bryan Horner. Chicago: U of Chicago P, 1983. 96–109.

Elbow, Peter. "The War between Reading and Writing—and How to End It." *Critical Theory and the Teaching of Literature: Politics, Curriculum, Pedagogy.* Ed. James F. Slevin and Art Young. Urbana: NCTE, 1996. 270–91.

Horner, Winifred Bryan. *Composition & Literature: Bridging the Gap.* Chicago: U of Chicago P, 1983.

Kalamaras, George. "Interrogating the Boundaries of Discourse in a Creative Writing Class: Politicizing the Parameters of the Permissible." *College Composition and Communication* 51:1 (September 1999): 77–82.

North, Stephen M. *Refiguring the Ph.D. in English Studies: Writing, Doctoral Education, and the Fusion-Based Curriculum.* Urbana: NCTE, 2000.

Ponsot, Marie, and Rosemary Deen. *Beat Not the Poor Desk: Writing: What to Teach, How to Teach It, and Why.* Portsmouth, NH: Boynton/Cook, 1982.

Slevin, James F., and Art Young. *Critical Theory and the Teaching of Literature: Politics, Curriculum, Pedagogy.* Urbana: NCTE, 1996.

Summerfield, Judith, and Geoffrey Summerfield. *Texts and Contexts: A Contribution to the Theory and Practice of Teaching Composition.* New York: Random, 1986.

Trimbur, John. "The Problem of Freshman English (Only): Toward Programs of Study in Writing." *WPA: Writing Program Administration* 22.3 (1999): 9–30.

Welch, Nancy. "No Apology: Challenging the 'Uselessness' of Creative Writing." *JAC* 19.1 (1999): 117–34.

9

Reading Matters for Writing

Mariolina Rizzi Salvatori

It's early morning. I sit at the computer to write. As is my ritual, before I begin, I take in and lock in my mind the view of the lake framed by the window. The air, various hues of shimmering gray, silhouettes a white cranelike bird (a heron). A car rolls by; the bird, "con l'ali alzate e ferme" (wings raised high and poised), glides away through the air.

I am fifteen. I stand, frightened but erect by my teacher's desk reciting Paolo and Francesca's story as told by Dante in Canto V of The Divine Comedy. I hate having to do it. I would rather ask about "the book" Paolo and Francesca are reading. But I have been schooled to silence and to doubt the voice within me. So I breathe in and, before repeating what well-known historians of literature said about it, I recite:

Quali colombe dal disio chiamate
Con l'ali alzate e ferme al dolce nido
Vegnon per l'aere, dal voler portate

As doves summoned by desire,
with wings raised high and poised, glide
the air guided by will to the sweetness of the nest

And so on, toward the canto's climax, the scene of reading I cannot interrogate:

Noi leggiavamo un giorno per diletto
Di Lancialotto come amor lo strinse;
Soli eravamo e senza alcun sospetto.

Per piu' fiate li occhi ci sospinse
Qualla lettura, e scolorocci il viso;
Ma solo un punto fu quello che ci vinse.

Quando leggemmo il disiato riso
Esser basciato da cotanto amante
Questi, che mai da me non fia diviso,

La bocca mi bascio' tutto tremante.
Galeotto fu il libro e chi lo scrisse:
quel giorno piu' non vi leggemmo avante.

One day, for pleasure,
We read of Lancelot, by love constrained:
Alone, suspecting nothing, at our leisure.

Sometimes at what we read our glances joined,
Looking from the book each to the other's eyes,
And then the color in our faces drained.

But one particular moment alone it was
Defeated us: the longed-for smile, it said,
Was kissed by that most noble lover: at this,

This one, who now will never leave my side,
Kissed my mouth, trembling. A Galeotto, that book!
And so was he who wrote it; that day we read
No further. [. . .][1]

"Galeotto fu il libro e chi lo scrisse." [Galeotto = Galehot, traitor] *I re-cite the line as if it were an invective, as if I were uttering a curse against the book that "meno' costoro al doloroso passo." ("led these two to such a fate-ful step.") I want to ask: Can a book do that? Can a book make you do what it describes, and then punish you for that (for being an active reader?)* [I should also say that, weighing heavily on my mind at the time, was the fact that I had just stealthily read, in translation, a "libro all'indice," a book indexed as "do not read" on a sheet of paper posted on the portals of Catholic Churches, *Lady Chatterly's Lover.*]

I loved the story of Paolo and Francesca, but had difficulty making sense of it. I knew I was expected to abhor their *sin;* I knew that was the lesson I was supposed to learn from reading (and publicly declaiming) their tale. But their death seemed so unjust. Why was I afraid *to like* them, and also *not* to like them? Why was the language that described their plight so beautiful? I wonder, had I been able to formulate these questions, would my teacher have "disciplined" me to suppress them?

* * *

What's the point of going public with this memory? Let me *make* the point from my position as a university professor of English, a passionate compositionist, whose understanding of reading and its connection to writing, and the consequences of such an understanding for [her] teaching at the undergraduate and graduate level was fundamentally and forever transformed by Gadamer's *Truth and Method,* and *Philosophical Hermeneutics,* Iser's *The Act of Reading,* Rosenblatt's *The Reader, the Text, the Poem,* Berthoff's *The Making of Meaning, Forming, Thinking, Writing,* and *Reclaiming the Imagination,* Barthes's *S/Z: An Essay, The Pleasure of the Text,* and *Image, Music, Text,* De Man's *Allegories of Reading,* Poulet's "Phenomenology of Reading," Steiner's *On Difficulty and Other Essays.*

In the scene of instruction I reconstructed, the questions I could not, did not know how to raise about the representation of reading it enacted *did not matter.* Orally as well as in writing, I had been schooled *to recite:* I had been taught to interpret what I read by weaving together (a considerable skill) the interpretations of established scholars. My "own" interpretations, as those of any of my classmates, did not count: they had no place in scholarly discussions of the canto, nor could they be the subject matter of writing, my own, and even less, my teacher's. I am not trying to demonize my teacher. I am suggesting, instead, that in light of the dominant theories of reading in circulation in Italy at the time, she could not frame my "difficulty" as anything other than the result of my inadequate preparation, or of my irrelevant, arrogant, preposterous "response."

Decades later, and in another country, I was enabled to see things differently.

In the 1980s, in the field of composition, poststructuralist understandings of reading and writing, and of their interconnection, produced electrifying innovative curricula. The destabilizing force poststructuralism exerted on canonicity, intentionality, reader's function, and reader's relationship to writer, text, and context, would make it possible, and even imperative, for some teachers and scholars in certain pockets of English studies (especially composition and women's studies) to validate and to study novice readers' steps toward interpretation. In the 1980s, as a teacher, I had the good fortune of working in a department of English where, because of a felicitous convergence of theoretical, historical, institutional, and economic forces, the composition and literature programs could initiate and sustain a vigorous and respectful dialogue with each other, one that led to productive, and lasting, changes in approaches to teaching and to understandings of learning. The project of placing reading at the center of writing instruction, keeping reading and writing together, and nurturing their nexus by theorizing and making visible their interconnectedness, was enacted for the most part, though with differing intensity, in every program and at every level, and it became, and remains, a distinctive marker of the work some of us still do. It is arduous, highly reflexive, intricate work; but it is well worth the time, the mental engagement, and the commitment it demands.

Not surprisingly, within our department, as well as elsewhere in the nation, the goal of setting and keeping the activities of reading and writing in a mutually enriching rather than ancillary relation met with considerable resistance. One of the most frequently invoked arguments against the inclusion of readings in writing instruction (particularly the inclusion of *difficult* texts), was that many students read little and/or poorly; therefore, having students read and respond to texts was unfair to them and to their teachers who had to invest most of their time *explaining* to them the assigned readings so that they could fulfill their writing assignments. Time invested in trying to teach students how to read, the argument went, is time taken away from necessary writing instruction. This kind of argument does not envision the possibility of imagining the interconnectedness of reading and writing in mutually enriching ways.

As the contributors to this collection make clear, there is still much work to be done in this area, and the relevance of this work is not limited to the teaching of freshman composition.

In the rest of this essay, I will reenter the debate about the place of reading in the teaching of writing through a discussion of "reading difficulties," of different "readings" of reading difficulties, and of the extent to which different readings of reading difficulties occlude or generate writing and a deep understanding of its inextricable connection to reading.

READING DIFFICULTIES AS SOURCES FOR WRITING: A MODEST PROPOSAL

In "The Difficulty of Reading," Helen Reguerio Elam argues that American education does not take well to the idea of difficulty and suggests that a penchant for easy and immediate solutions leads many to expect and demand in all areas of life—including reading—an ease of achievement that is antithetical to the complexities of our thinking process. I want to complicate her argument. My experience teaching courses at the most basic undergraduate level ("Basic Reading and Writing") and the most advanced graduate level ("Literacy and Pedagogy," "Reception Theories") and at all levels in between, and my exposure to the scholarship of the fields, lead me to suggest that in most departments of English (or in other higher education contexts), concepts of and approaches to difficulty too often function as a sort of "Great Divide." On one side of it, the side of so-called "novice" or "reluctant" learners, difficulties are complications that it is not profitable, or economically viable, for students to identify, to address, let alone to resolve. As Elam says, they go against the grain of educational efficiency. However, on the other side of the divide, the side of "consummate" and "passionate" learners, difficulties and the ability to understand, to process, and to live with them are markers of learners' high culture, sophistication, and intelligence. Here difficulties are nur-

tured and kept in circulation by means of a highly specialized, exclusionary discourse that speaks to and for those who already know how, or know how to learn to handle them.

My intent is not to deny the value of difficulty but rather to suggest that more of a teacher's time and energy be spent teaching *all* students to deal with difficulties in sophisticated and productive ways.

For reasons that have to do with my cultural dislocation as well as my personal and intellectual proclivities, I have been long interested in the role of difficulty in the learning process (Salvatori, "Towards a Hermeneutics of Difficulty," "Difficulty: The Great Educational Divide"). Over the years, I have taught myself to frame and reflect on students' "moments of difficulty" for their hidden potential to produce understanding and to instruct. This practice of sustained attention has made me realize that for a student, indeed for any learner at any level of learning, to perceive or to name something as difficult is to demonstrate a form of knowledge, incipient perhaps, inchoate, not (yet) fully communicable, but knowledge nevertheless, and one that it is both profitable and responsible to tap into—whether to further develop or to "readjust" it.

It has become increasingly apparent to me that as students are taught to engage (rather than move away from) their reading difficulties, the writing that records the various phases of their investigation often displays observations, perceptions, considerations similar in kind (if not in degree) to those that enable fluent readers to come to terms with difficult texts. Consider this case. Several years ago, in an introductory literature course ("Introduction to Critical Reading"), a student (whom at the time I might have described as recalcitrant) vehemently complained that Shakespeare unnecessarily complicated the story of King Lear. When I asked him to be more precise about his complaints, he mentioned the two plots (he felt he could not tell with certainty which story line he was in at any given time) and the similarity of names (Edgar/Edmund). He had noticed two signal features of the play, but judging them according to criteria of simplicity, clarity, and linearity, which the specific context defied, he understood them as unnecessary difficulties rather than difficulties worth reflecting on. Well-intentioned, expecting my gesture would produce instant enlightenment, I provided him with an example. I referred him to the following assessment of Shakespeare's technique by Una Ellis-Fermor:

> Each aspect of technique, then, plays its part in revealing the dramatist's apprehension of life, but plot may fitly follow character here since they

merge naturally into each other through the continuous interplay between individual character and even within a given play.

Plot, indeed, whether simple or complex, single or multiple, may be said to have two aspects, the spatial, which is concerned with character-grouping, and the temporal, which has regard to the order and relation of events. ("Character Grouping and Plot," 77–78)

The example, proffered without a clue, did not enlighten the student. I kept talking, ignoring the incipient understanding his difficulty revealed.

I wish I could take back that moment. If I could, I would try to help that student retrace the steps that led him to his negative valuation of the salient features of *King Lear*. I would try to help him hypothesize the steps the critic took to formulate her valorization of them. And I would try to help him acknowledge and reflect on the presuppositions of knowl-edge and the reading strategies that led each to such differing conclusions. The intrinsic difficulty of this approach to teaching is how to promote the student's process of introspection without doing the work for him, with-out taking away from him ownership of what he knows, and can use, to move forth toward further knowledge.

In the next section, I will focus on the writing that Genevieve Evert, an undergraduate writer, produced as she read and engaged difficult texts. Before I proceed, however, I want to call attention to the problematics that inevitably attend to the kind of scholarly piece I am trying to com-pose. It's a hybrid genre. It bears traces of the language, rhetorical moves, and strategies of several sub-genres: the philosophical investigation, the theoretical essay, the classroom experience piece, the reflexive meditation. It is a genre that inevitably calls attention to the inherent, intractable dif-ficulty of its trying to foster scholarship about *student texts,* texts that our discipline, intitutions, and culture at large, frame as non-scholarly.[2] Con-sider, for example, our discipline's convention (a convention that from now on I will no longer follow) of referring to the students whose work we study and write about by first name only. Consider the widespread as-sumption that the value/worth of scholarship is usually measured in terms of the status of the texts it investigates: scholarly writing about Shake-speare, in other words, grants its author prestige that scholarly writing about "remedial" students, or undergraduate students, simply cannot. And consider the fact that our discipline is only now systematically ad-dressing the very serious issue of how to quote, in scholarly publications, student writing that is not in the public domain.

Future historians of our discipline will no doubt acknowledge and cite the work that Joseph Harris, editor of CCC, did on behalf of student writ-

ing in his "forewords" to the journal's issues. In our scholarship, we need
to enforce the rules of conduct he established therein, by fostering and
sustaining a culture that treats student writing with intellectual integrity
and respect.

Considerations of this kind, I know, have deterred and still deter
young scholars in fields other than composition or education from writing and publishing on what teaching and learning in their fields calls for.
That this is not the case in the fields of composition and education is laud-
able (see, for example, Bartholomae and Petrosky, *Facts;* Bartholomae
"Inventing the University"; Lawson, Sterr Ryan, and Winterowd, *En-
countering Student Texts;* Helmers' *Writing Students;* Goleman's *Working Theory;* Donahue and Quandahl's *Reclaiming Pedagogy*). But until
these practices become common in other disciplines, scholarship that
pays attention to student texts will continue to be constructed as dubious,
or second-rate. We need to expose the implications of abiding by theoretical and disciplinary assumptions that make student work dispensable or
invisible (Levine, "Two Nations").

UNDERSTANDING DIFFICULTIES

*You can expect to write regularly in this course. In preparation for class dis-
cussion and writing assignments, you will write short (1/2 to 1 page) "difficulty papers": these are papers in which you identify and begin to hypothesize
the reasons for any possible difficulty you might be experiencing as you read a
text. Each week, all of you will write a difficulty paper. Each week, I will select one or two of them as unusual or representative examples of the readings
you produce. I will photocopy, distribute, and use them to ground our discussions. My goal, in doing so, is to move all of us from judging a difficulty as a
reader's inability to understand a text to discerning in it a reader's incipient
awareness of the particular "demands" imposed by the language/structure/
style/content of a text.*

The excerpt above, or a variation of it, now regularly appears in my
course descriptions. This assignment, and the work it entails, has come to
function as the spine of every course I teach, graduate or undergraduate
(Salvatori, "Understanding Difficulties"). In this section, I want to focus
on the effect that the focus on difficulty had on Genevieve Evert's work—
specifically, on the kind of writing that her increasingly sustained engagement with reading difficulties produced.

The context of her writing is a freshman composition course* in which students were assigned to read *The Dig,* a collection of poems by Lynn Emanuel, and *Landscape for a Good Woman,* by Carolyn Steedman. The work of the course was arranged around students' explorations of difficulties, both the difficulties of reading and writing one's and others' life stories, as enacted in Emanuel's and Steedman's texts, and students' own difficulties reading and writing about those texts, and about their life. The ten sequenced assignments, which Dave Bartholomae and I designed, were conceived as assisted invitations: they both acknowledged the difficulties of the assigned texts and put students in a position to engage them and to reflect on the value of that kind of work.

Evert, a good and academically successful student, had considerable trouble, at first, identifying and responding to "difficulties as sources of understanding." She had an arsenal of literary strategies she could deploy to quickly circumvent whatever prevented her from achieving interpretive closure. She wrote well. She read with interest. Her written assignments were always on time. She made smart contributions to class discussions. And yet I sensed her perplexity with the course's unusual directives. Uncertain about her work, perhaps for the first time in her life as a student, in her third Difficulty Paper (DP) she produced the following rationalization of the difficulty she felt she was experiencing.

Difficulty paper # 3

11 September 1996

My greatest difficulty with the work that we are doing is not so much in the reading, but in the writing. In fact, the sentence I just wrote is a perfectly acceptable opening for a difficulty paper in General Writing, but such an elementary opening phrase would not have been acceptable in my former English classes. Opening statements had to be bold and enticing, tempting the reader to continue reading. *One* never used "I" or "we" in a composition, these pronouns were considered improper in written work. Using the past tense *was* also considered a sign of weakness in writing by my former teachers. For the past three years I have been trained to read texts for meaning and discuss that meaning in a very professional way. This style of writing has become more and more inhibiting as time has passed. Because I was never allowed to change tenses in my writing, my stories always occur over a brief period of time. My first assignment was about the changes in

---

*The course is called General Writing.

how I viewed the people around me over a period of years; however, the actual story I wrote gives specific detail of a day's time and the rest of the story is covered in a broad introduction and conclusion. Knowing what I want to convey to my reader, I am excited to cut loose from the binds of mechanical detail and to just be able to tell my story.

The point about the limits imposed by the dogmatic prohibition not to change tenses is brilliant, I think. But the assumption that "cut[ting] loose from the binds of mechanical details" might solve the difficulty is a bit facile. At this point in the term, however, Evert, a professed lover of poetry and avowed interpreter, cannot quite come to terms with the fact that, as she reads *The Dig,* the text keeps thwarting her desire to pull "together the little pieces and bits of understanding that Emanuel presents in order to create a coherent story" (DP # 1, 3rd September 1996). The fact is that *The Dig* does not spin a coherent story. Evert notices as much, which is an indication of her perceptiveness as a reader. But having learned to expect a *telos* in every text, she reads her inability to construe one as a sign of the text's chaos, or meaninglessness.

Significantly, as Evert circumvents her reading difficulty, she sketches an intellectual landscape in which the activities of reading and writing unfold along parallel rather than intersecting lines. There is reading, and the writing that marks her performance of that task (the difficulty papers); and then there is that other kind of writing, the writing of her personal narrative,[3] which she sees at this point as not comparable to and unaffected by Emanuel's "narrative." The theoretical and practical interconnectedness of the activities is the goal of the course, but at this point Evert has not yet realized this complex and complicating conceptualization.

Steedman's *Landscape* put into motion a long process of revision culminating in a final essay (titled "This Piece") that, read against the background of the writing she produced throughout the course, stands as a remarkable example of what Gadamer calls a learner/reader's "application" of understanding (*Truth and Method,* 274–78; 295–305), the phase in which a reader/learner extends, applies to a different context (that is a new context, or an old one known differently), the kind of knowing that is produced when one identifies and reflects on what and how one knows. (In *Understanding by Design,* Wiggins and McTighe call this "deep understanding.")

As stunning as that essay is (it earned the University of Pittsburgh OSSIP Award), and in spite of the pleasure that sharing it with my readers would give me, I will focus instead on what led to it, on those moments of confusion and struggle, those bits and pieces of emerging understanding and reflection that, engaged rather than glossed over, made "This Piece" possible. In other words, I want to focus on the kind of reading Evert learned to do to enable herself to write the way she did.

In her description of the difficulty she experienced with the first chapters of *Landscape,* she says:

> My difficulty with the first section of this book was the style in which it was written. Pages three to twenty-four read like a critical article and not an introduction to a story. Steedman opens her book with a lengthy essay explaining and defending her text. "Stories" is a good introduction for the book because it tells me what I will be reading about in the body of the book, but it almost seems to beat me over the head with ideas of class and development. I found it very difficult to concentrate on the passage because it seemed very repetitive in its ideas. This difficulty worked against me because Steedman's scholarly language demands careful attention in order to follow her train of thought.
>
> In spite of the fact that the writing style was somewhat boring, it was thought provoking in some ways. [. . .]

The writing Evert produced in response to Steedman's "thought provoking" text is itself thought provoking. In the difficulty paper cited above, and in the subsequent ones, she identified with almost surgical precision the various elements of the text that obstructed the easy flow of her reading: the use of scholarly references; the writer's use of scholarly epigraphs even in the sections where she tells the story of her life ("I find it somewhat difficult to understand how these passages relate to her life. I wonder why she does not explain their significance and tell why she believes these excerpts are important to her own story," DP # 5); the nonchronological narrative; the blurring of facts and imagination; the lack of symbols that could function as explanatory keys. But she also described the strategies of reading she developed, on her own, to link epigraphs to story, to control her expectations of immediate involvement in the story line, and to forge connections with the text. A pivotal point in the story of reading that subtends this student's work is her changed understanding of how to read the gaps between the "bits and pieces" of a text, and of one's life. This understanding coincides with her increasing realization that to be able to tell/to write one's story is not just a matter of observing or cutting loose "from the binds of mechanical details" (DP # 1). At this time, her personal narrative begins to undergo radical changes in terms of chronology, linearity, multivoicedness. One way of accounting for such changes is simply to suggest that this very smart student had identified stylistic features in Steedman's narrative that she was able to transpose into her own. In and of itself, this would be a valuable, productive use of reading in the writing classroom.

But, I want to argue, something different is at work here. Having gone through the experience of engaging some of the difficulties of Steedman's text, having analyzed, reflected on, and thought through them, Evert begins to close the distance between the reader (herself) and the writer (Steedman) as she begins to adopt in the writing of her own narrative some puzzling textual features from Steedman's text the force of which she had come to understand in her reading. What she learns to do as a reader begins to affect what she does as a writer. But something else happens: while her reading (of Steedman's experience) shapes her writing (of the "personal narrative"), her writing (of the "personal narrative") grounds and orients her reading (of *Landscape* and of her own text).

In her last difficulty paper on *Landscape,* Evert gives an assessment of the challenges (she no longer calls them "difficulties") the text poses for its reader. I will reproduce it in its entirety and I will discuss the essay into which it developed.

Difficulty paper # 9

19 November 1996

From the beginning of the book to the end, Steedman focuses her writing on the approval of the reader. In the first section, "Stories," she defends her reasons for writing a story that seems to have been written so many times before. She wants to represent her history correctly and completely. In "Histories" the final section of the novel she returns to her discussion of approval. Her epigraph from William Labov about "SO what?" exemplifies her concern as a writer because "every good narrator is continually warding off this question" (125). But really, by introducing the question in the text, Steedman is challenging us, as her readers, to ask ourselves 'what' and 'so what' and *'why'*? She wrote her book for herself as a way for her to work through her own history to the point where her curiosities and concerns are dealt with to her satisfaction. And now she asks, "So what?" What are we, the readers, supposed to gain from *her* life, *her* story, *her* analysis? Her language and form have taught us a particular and unconventional way of reading. And, of course, we have learned about her past as well. But, we have also learned a great deal about history in general. We have learned to think about the past and not just to read it. We have learned that the past lives on in each of us in "bits and pieces." And, most importantly,

Steedman's work challenges us to look back at our lives and the lives of our ancestors and to rediscover where we have come from. "So what" [. . .] is my history?

Evert's original personal narrative, the text she wrote at the beginning of the term and that she subsequently revised, was a story of alienation from a clique of so-called friends whose approval she eagerly sought. By the end of the term, the "one day in the life of a teenager" narrative developed into a text ("This Piece") in which, by means of prose and poetry, epigraphs scholarly references and dialogue, reminiscences and meditation, she tried to capture what she saw as the essence of her life.

As I read difficulty paper # 9 again, I feel again Evert's excitement at what she made Steedman's text mean to her, especially how this understanding impinged on her understanding of the question that would drive and give shape to "her history."

I am struck by the light that her personal experience casts on her reading of *Landscape*. She connects with Steedman as she recognizes in her (or attributes to her) the same desire that had motivated the history of her relationship to the high school "clique." This could be a reductive moment. It is worth noticing, however, that the personal connection does not just lead to a "narrative by association" (see Nancy Miller 1991). It is a point of entry that marks the beginning of a critical investigation. It is a "transitive beginning," which she transverses repeatedly until what could have just been a plausible desire to be liked becomes a critical tool, the question "every good narrator is continually warding off." The cosmic question "why write?" which might prompt the cosmic answer "because we are humans," is kept at bay by the purposefulness and potentially debunking force of "so what?" And this question, which subdivides into "what" do I choose to write about, "so what" if I make this choice or that, and "why" might this make a difference, becomes the nexus between writer and reader and marks the interconnectedness of reading and writing in her thinking practice. Evert-the-writer, having retraced (through reading) and recaptured the motivating questions of her writing, having engaged them, must at the end pose one more crucial question: how can all this be meaningful to me? (How can I make it so?) "So what?" becomes a question of responsibility for Evert-the-reader as well: "Steedman's work challenges us to look back at our own lives and the lives of our ancestors and to rediscover where we have come from. 'So what' is my history?"

The difficulty paper I just cited precedes the work Evert did in response to Assignment # 9.[4] In the essay she wrote and included—revised and ti-

tled "So What?"—in her final portfolio, she does, as she is asked to, systematically work through and from most of the difficulties she had previously identified and described, turning them into interpretive tools.

Here is the work of reading and writing the "so what" question enables
her to do in the second half of the essay:

> So, how does a writer bring closure to a book that tells a story that has not
> ended, that will *never* end? With a conclusion, perhaps? Perhaps not.
> Steedman discovered her difficulties and introduced them in the beginning
> of her book. She told us that she wanted to learn her story and share her
> story and teach us about histories and childhood. She outlined her ideas,
> researched her topic, and brought it all together in this book, *Landscape for
> a Good Woman*. Steedman refuses to put so much work into her *work*.
>
> This is not a story, an anecdote; Steedman has indeed been successful in
> resisting "the compulsion of narrative" (144). She realizes that a division of
> literature has been established to define the work that she has done: "the
> enterprise of working-class autobiography" (144). Yet she also refuses to
> let us classify her book under this heading and walk away from it. She has
> done so much work with the text herself that she completes it by handing it
> over to the reader as a difficulty:
>
> I must make the final gesture of defiance, and refuse to let this be ab-
> sorbed by the central story, must ask for a structure of political thought
> that will take all of this, all these secrets and impossible stories, recognize
> what has been made out on the margins; and then, recognizing it, refuse to
> celebrate it; a politics that will, watching this past say "so what?"; and con-
> signs it to the dark (144).
>
> In the final sentence of her book Steedman challenges her readers. She
> tells us not to classify her book in any particular way. She asks us not to let
> her story melt into the menagerie of stories that we have heard before. She
> asks us not to file away or forget what she has told us. But, most impor-
> tantly, Steedman tells us that we should not say "so what?" But really, her
> challenge is that we *should* ask ourselves this question.
>
> "So what?" in its negative sense refers to the idea that the reader does
> not care or that the work does not matter, and the question itself is rhetori-
> cal. Steedman refuses to let her readers close her book with a shrug and a
> question that does not expect any answer at all. I believe that Steedman
> uses "so what?" so that we realize we *can* put the book down and walk away
> and forget it, but we should not. As readers and as students we cannot as-
> sume that when we run out of pages the lesson has ended. Steedman's work
> is no exception. On the contrary, when we finish her book the assignment

has only just begun because now each of us must ask ourselves "so what?" And this time we are expected to respond.

* * *

In tandem with the freshman composition course Evert was taking, I was, that year, also teaching the "Teaching of Teaching" seminar with David Bartholomae. The function of the seminar is to prepare and to assist new Teaching Assistants and Teaching Fellows to meet their obligation to teach, in the same term, an entry course in reading and writing. This scene of instruction is fraught with ideological, theoretical, and institutional tensions, many of which risk remaining undefined, unnamed, hence beyond the reach of analysis, unless they are acknowledged, legitimized, and brought into the open (Salvatori and Kameen).

But to bring the various presuppositions of knowledge that subtend and drive differing positions into the open, and to do so relentlessly yet tactfully, cogently yet generously, is a most difficult intellectual practice to nurture. It requires that teacher and students learn to be vigilantly reflexive about their most cherished theoretical assumptions and courageously committed to assessing the implications and the effects of those assumptions for teaching and learning. It requires that teacher and students ask, and ask again, the "so what?" question Evert so ably deploys. It is, sometimes, a painful, difficult inquiry to sustain. But it can issue remarkable rewards, and understanding.

Traditionally, in our department, whoever teaches the seminar also teaches a section of freshman composition, using the same texts and sequence of assignment TAs and TFs are required to teach. Traditionally, each new teacher writes, if he/she so desires, his/her own course description. All course descriptions, including those of the seminar leaders, are made available to everybody else in the group, and some of them are discussed in class. That year, the difficulty paper requirement, included in my course description, was adopted by several of the new teachers, who even opted to substitute it for the required "position papers" (one on each text to be read and discussed) when course materials and discussions "troubled" them.

The focus Bartholomae and I selected for the seminar was an exploration of "the personal," of its limits and possibilities especially in terms of teaching. Here is an excerpt from our course description:

Our goal in this seminar is to imagine teaching (the teaching of reading and writing) not simply as part of a field of research, or as an arena for the rep-

resentation of our research, but as always and inevitably in reflexive relationship to everything we do in our disciplinary activities. To structure our
work together this year we have chosen as a nominal theme (we might want
to re-name it) for our discussions an issue that is being widely and diversely
discussed in our profession: the "personal" as a source/site/mechanism of
knowledge.

For reasons that beg to be interrogated, the "personal" has often been
deployed in uncritical ways (naive, nostalgic, romantic?) in composition
curricula. Our goal is not to enter and prolong the debate (though some of
you might want to write about it). In keeping with the function of the seminar, our goal is to foreground what might be said to run before, after, and
around the debate. We want to trace the forces that drive competing theoretical constructions of the personal and we want to anchor them, strategi-
cally, to issues of teaching and writing. We want to test these theoretical
constructions in terms of how they make it possible to teach and to learn
practices of reading and writing that honor and incite a subject's agency. In
other words, we are less interested in advancing this or that theory of the
personal (which does not mean that we take a neutral stance on the subject), or in developing their applications, than in testing such theories in
light of the work they call for and make possible.

Given the constitution of the group—students of creative writing, film
studies, composition, cultural studies, and literature—discussions of the
personal and related concepts like, say, originality, creativity, individuality, style and culture, politics, subject position, knowledge production,
false consciousness were for the most part very heated and highly coded.
Among the readings we had assigned (Miller, *Getting Personal,* Brodkey,
Writing Permitted in Designated Areas Only, Flannery, *The Emperor's
New Clothes,* Levine, "Putting the 'Literature' Back Into Literature Department", Tompkins, "Me and My Shadow", Lentricchia, "Last Will
and Testament of an Ex-Literary Critic", Williams, "The Tenses of the
Imagination", and others), those that foregrounded the implications of
one's theoretical apparatus for teaching caused (perhaps the most) turmoil and revisions. Flannery's analysis of style as never innocent, and the
insidious consequences for education ("so what?") when its normative
force goes unacknowledged, proved difficult both to "consign to the
dark" and to fully engage.

Here is a telling example. MFA student, Nancy Krygowski, a poet and
committed teacher of composition, was particularly unsettled by the force
and the implications of Flannery's argument. She could no longer "inno-
cently" uphold her cherished notions of style as "je ne sais quoi."

When I taught before, I consciously shied away from discussing style in my writing classes because, frankly, I saw style in all its "je ne sais quoi-ness" and figured if I couldn't find a good way to talk about it, I shouldn't talk at all. However [. . .] I did give students Bs and As somewhat assuredly (though hesitantly in a moral kind of way) when I felt their writing was missing that certain "je ne sais quoi." And, as I explore these ideas, I'm suddenly having memories of reading aloud sections of Tobias Wolff's, *This Boy's Life,* and saying things like, "Listen to how beautiful this sounds; listen to the way those sentences come together," which is, of course, style talk, and which makes me question what I was promoting while being unconscious, while, in fact, I thought I wasn't promoting any style issues at all.

(Reading this excerpt, I am struck by Krygowski's reliance on the modeling and hortatory modes. Significantly, I made a similar move in the case of the student who thought *King Lear* was unnecessarily difficult. Both Krygowski and I seem to see and to understand something that, we think, our students don't quite know they know. But we don't know how to make their incipient knowing visible. So we feed our students examples, and exhort them to see and hear what the examples mean to us, trusting in the osmotic power of these modes of teaching. Seymour S. Sarasan highlights this teacherly move in his commentary on *Mr. Holland's Opus,* 49.)

Krygowski's reflections make clear the possible insidious effects of the "je ne sais quoi" construct of style for teaching. Since she could not quite define it for her students, she would not talk about it. Yet, she realized, the force of that construct crept in surreptitiously and affected her evaluation of her students' work. Her difficulty paper indirectly, but dramatically, foregrounds the exclusionary effects of the "either you have it or you don't" educational approach, and raises compelling questions about a teacher's responsibility toward those who *don't* already have "it," whether "it" be a cultivated or a "natural" predisposition to appreciate style, literary values, difficult texts, or the ability to learn how to do so.

This is, of course, one of the points that Flannery's *The Emperor's New Clothes* argues, with blinding force and unsettling clarity. And Krygowski stands up to the challenge:

So, Flannery's book, which is designed to make educators think about how our pedagogy may, indeed, be supporting "values, practices, and institutions" (202) we don't intend to, worked for me. It has made me think, and think, about my current teaching and past teaching practices, which is useful. However, sometimes all this thinking just makes me confused. [. . .]

Because my confusion is centered mostly on what I may unconsciously be pushing, style-wise, on my students (I know I never write margin notes about clarity or brevity, but I wonder in what ways I do address style), I pull out, pretty randomly, a sample piece of a GW student, and an idea that is somehow grounded in Flannery resonates in me. I've been feeling frustrated by my students' attempts to reduce Steedman's project to a story about escape and triumph or to one about a mother who lives through her daughter, etc., etc. I find a sentence in my student's writing that exhibits this sort of reductiveness: "I believe that Steedman's mother was trying to make the most out of her life."

This is how Krygowski goes on to read her students' reductiveness:

> I have been seeing this urge for students to take these 'sorts of truths,' these complex ideas boiled down to their most simplistic and common element, as 'thinking problems' (whatever that means). In their urge to understand complexity, they grab hold of their tiny, near-articulations of near ideas and state them confidently in terms they know. Flannery gives me the chance to see this as: a) a result of, perhaps, the history of style pedagogy, which helps give me a way to think about *why* my students may do this, or b) at least, something that they do do, which helps me think about the *what* (or is it the *how?*) of this reductiveness.
>
> Therefore style, that slippery stuff, becomes more concrete in my mind (as a responsible use of language, of a way of thinking how form and content need to mingle responsibly) and I get to feel better about my students by seeing their 'thinking problems' as a result of an educational flaw.

The possibility of reading, through Flannery, her students' reductive moves as a problem of American education is not, for Krygowski, license to think that the difficulty of teaching in general, and of teaching "style" in particular, is resolved. In the final paragraph she acknowledges that "Flannery has been useful in helping [her] understand that difficult texts aren't necessarily exclusionary" (3). "But," she concludes, "this is not a conversion narrative. I am still confused, still thinking. [. . .]" Thinking about what? One of the answers is contextually provided: "what do *I do*, practically, in the classroom or in my margin comments?"

The question is important, and difficult to engage, if we look for something other than tips, things to do, and decontextualized "best practices." My sense is that Krygowski wants to understand how to intervene in classroom discussions, in the margins of her students' texts, so as not to repeat, albeit unconsciously, potentially exclusionary moves. She finds no answer to this query in Flannery's text, not so much because, as she claims, this question falls outside Flannery's framework, but because within Flannery's framework, the question cannot be answered a priori. Flannery's practices are an extension and an enactment of *her* particular understanding of what a particular student at a particular moment might need, and *her* understanding cannot stand for or replace anybody else's understanding.

If this is so, why should Krygowski's practice, which is not unreflexive, be in need of revision? Which criteria do we invoke to answer this question? Since all teacherly interventions are ultimately normative, how does one come to trust one normative intervention rather than another? This is not a question to be settled with the noncommittal answer, "everybody is entitled to his/her own [practice]."

So what *do we* do? How do we responsibly examine, carry out, and revise our work of teaching? How do we know what to do, when, and how?

"Begin where the student is." "Place the student at the center of the educational experience." "Make the classroom dialogical." These are some of the maxims that energized so many teachers in the 1980s, as well as before and after. They seem so obvious, so commonsensical—but how do we move beyond their hortatory force? How do we make them work?

In this essay, I have gone further than ever before in making public and submitting to peers' review my work on difficulty.[5] It is a calculated move: a lot is at stake in it—intellectually, emotionally, and physically. It is a risky move: but I have decided to take the risk so as to invite reflection on educational approaches that, by streamlining and providing answers for difficulties, nurture continuous dependence on a hierarchy of experts most of whom are unwilling or unable to share with others the processes that enabled them to acquire and amass their cultural capital. The approach I have described is one way of placing and keeping students at the center of the educational experience—and not by word alone, or seat arrangement. It is not an easy approach. But it is one that makes it possible for students to make visible, to articulate knowledges and forms of understanding that would otherwise be "consigned to the dark," and for teachers to engage them, and in light of them, "to respond" by systematically revising assumptions about and approaches to teaching that put a ceiling on the learner's intellectual capabilities.

This is the real difficulty, the challenge, of teaching and learning.

NOTES

1. My translation, based on Musa's and Pinsky's.
2. Valuable work on the scholarship of teaching is being done at and supported by the Carnegie Foundation for the Advancement of Teaching (www.carnegiefoundation.

org). The project to define and to promote the "scholarship of teaching," launched by Ernest Boyer, President of the Foundation (*Scholarship Reconsidered: Priorities of the Professoriate*), has been expanded and sustained by his successor, President Lee Shulman ("Knowledge and Teaching: Foundations of the New Reform"; "Course Anatomy: The Dissection and Analysis of Knowledge Through Teaching"; "Teaching Alone, Learning Together: Needed Agendas for the New Reforms"), Vice President Pat Hutchings ("The Scholarship of Teaching: New Elaborations, New Developments," with Lee Shulman; *The Course Portfolio*, Editor; *Opening Lines*, Editor), Senior Scholar Mary Taylor Huber (*Scholarship Assessed: Evaluation of the Professoriate*, with Glassik and Maeroff; "Disciplinary Styles in the Scholarship of Teaching: Reflections on the Carnegie Academy for the Scholarship of Teaching and Learning"; *Disciplinary Styles in the Scholarship of Teaching and Learning*, editor, with Morreale).

3. Evert is alluding here to the writing she produced at the beginning of the term in response to a "personal experience" assignment. This essay she would later revise twice, according to the course's design, as she filtered and re-assessed her assumptions about how to tell a story in light of what she had learned by working through her "reading difficulties" with *The Dig* and *Landscape*.

4. Assignment # 9

> *I know that the compulsions of narrative are almost irresistible: having found a psychology where once there was only the assumption of pathology or false consciousness to be seen, the tendency is to celebrate this psychology, to seek entry for it to a wider world of literary and cultural reference; and the enterprise of working-class autobiography was designed to make this at least a feasible project. But to do this is to miss the irreducible nature of all our lost childhoods: what has been made has been made out on the borderlands. I must make the final gesture of defiance, and refuse to let this be absorbed by the central story; must ask for a structure of political thought that will take all of this, all these secret and impossible stories, recognize what has been made out on the margins; and then, recognizing it, refuse to celebrate it; a politics that will, watching this past say "So what"; and consign it to the dark.*
>
> *Landscape for a Good Woman* (1440)

This is a difficult passage in a difficult final chapter. And it describes what is presented as difficult work, a difficult assignment for a writer—to resist the "compulsion of narrative," to ask for "a structure of political thought," to refuse celebration.

In Assignment # 8, you began to think about the opening sections of *Landscape*. For this assignment we would like you to write about the whole of Steedman's book and her project. What is it about? What has she set out to do? What has she accomplished? What are the key terms and methods for her work? What are the issues? To whom is she speaking? What does she hope to find or learn or do? What argument does she hope to make? (These questions are meant to suggest ways of thinking about the text. They don't need to be answered and they should not be used to organize the essay.)

These are, of course, the questions we asked in an earlier assignment. At this point we are asking where you stand now, at the end of the book. At this point, how would you answer these questions?

You should begin by returning to what you wrote for Assignment # 8, when you were writing about the opening chapter. And you should look back through the book—at notes you have taken, passages you have underlined, sections that remain for you as difficult or memorable. And you should think about the book as a device that enabled Steedman to do this work. Or as a device that enables a reader to think about the project as a project. Think about the book as a work in writing, but think of it also as a set of conventions or formal devices—endnotes, section and chapter headings, epigraphs, introductions and conclusions.

5. I want to take this opportunity to acknowledge the support I received, in doing so, by the Carnegie Foundation for the Advancement of Teaching and by my colleagues (in my department and elsewhere): David Bartholomae, Pat Donahue, Kathryn Flannery, Judith Goleman, Paul Kameen. I am especially grateful to Genevieve Evert and Nancy Krygowski for permission to use their writing and their full names in this essay. Their work has deepened my understanding of the relationship between reading and writing.

WORKS CITED

Barthes, Roland. *Image, Music, Text.* Trans. Stephen Heath. New York: Hill, 1977.

———. *The Pleasure of the Text.* Trans. Richard Miller. New York: Hill, 1975.

———. *S/Z: An Essay.* Trans. Richard Miller. New York: Hill, 1974.

Bartholomae, David. "Inventing the University." *When a Writer Can't Write: Studies in Writer's Block and Other Composing Process Problems.* Ed. Mike Rose. New York: Guilford, 1984. 134–65.

Bartholomae, David, and Anthony Petrosky. *Facts, Artifacts, and Counterfacts: Theory and Method for a Reading and Writing Course.* Upper Montclair, NJ: Boynton/Cook, 1986.

Berthoff, Ann, E. *Forming, Thinking, Writing: The Composing Imagination.* Upper Montclair, NJ: Boynton/Cook, 1982.

———. ed. *The Making of Meaning: Metaphors, Models, and Maxims for Writing Teachers.* Upper Montclair, NJ: Boynton/Cook, 1981.

———. *Reclaiming the Imagination: Philosophical Perspectives for Writers and Teachers of Writing.* Upper Montclair, NJ: Boynton/Cook, 1984.

Boyer, Ernest L. *Scholarship Reconsidered: Priorities of the Professoriate.* Princeton, NJ: Carnegie Foundation for the Advancement of Teaching, 1990.

Brodkey, Linda. *Writing Permitted in Designated Areas Only.* Minneapolis: U of Minnesota P, 1996.

De Man, Paul. *Allegories of Reading.* New Haven: Yale UP, 1979.

Donahue, Patricia, and Ellen Quandahl. *Reclaiming Pedagogy: The Rhetoric of the Classroom.* Carbondale and Edwardsville: Southern Illinois UP, 1989.

Elam, Helen Reguerio. "The Difficulty of Reading." *The Idea of Difficulty in Literature.* Ed. Alan C. Purves. New York: State U of New York P, 1991.

Ellis-Fermor, Ulla. " Character Grouping and Plot: The Nature of Plot in Drama." *Modern Shakespearean Criticism: Essays on Style, Dramaturgy, and the Major Plays.* Ed. Alvin B. Kernan. New York: Harcourt, 1970. 77–92.

Emanuel, Lynn. *The Dig and Hotel Fiesta.* Pittsburgh U of Pittsburgh P, 1995.

Flannery, Kathryn T. *The Emperor's New Clothes.* Pittsburgh: U of Pittsburgh P, 1995.

Gadamer, Hans-Georg. *Philosophical Hermeneutics.* Trans. and Ed. David E. Linge. Berkeley: U of California P, 1976.

———. *Truth and Method.* New York: Continuum, 1975.

Glassick, Charles E., Mary Taylor Huber, and Gene I. Maeroff. *Scholarship Assessed: Evaluation of the Professoriate.* Special Report of the Carnegie Foundation for the Advancement of Teaching. San Francisco: Jossey-Bass, 1997.

Goleman, Judith. *Working Theory*. Westport, CT: Bergin, 1995.

Helmers, Marguerite. *Writing Students: Composition Testimonials and Representations of Students*. New York: State U of New York P, 1994.

Huber, Mary Taylor, and Sherwyn P. Morreale, eds. *Disciplinary Styles in the Scholarship of Teaching and Learning: Exploring Common Ground*. Washington, DC: The Carnegie Foundation for the Advancement of Teaching and the American Association of Higher Education, 2002.

Huber, Mary Taylor. "Disciplinary Styles in the Scholarship of Teaching: Reflections on the Carnegie Academy for the Scholarship of Teaching and Learning." In *Disciplinary Styles in the Scholarship of Teaching and Learning*. 25–43.

Hutchings, Pat. *The Course Portfolio: How Faculty Can Examine Their Teaching to Advance Practice and Improve Student Learning*. Washington, DC: American Education for Higher Education, 1998.

———, and Lee Shulman. "The Scholarship of Teaching: New Elaborations, New Developments." *Change* (1999) 31, no 5: 10–15.

———. *Opening Lines: Approaches to the Scholarship of Teaching and Learning*. Menlo Park, CA: The Carnegie Foundation for the Advancement of Teaching, 2000.

Iser, Wolfgang. *The Act of Reading*. Baltimore: Johns Hopkins UP, 1978.

Lawson, Bruce, Susan Sterr Ryan, and W. Ross Winterowd. Urbana: NCTE, 1989.

Lentricchia, Frank. "Last Will and Testament of an Ex-Literary Critic," *Lingua Franca* (September/October 1996).

Levine, George. "Putting the 'Literature' Back into Literature Department," *ADE Bulletin* (Spring, 1966).

———. "The Two Nations." *Pedagogy: Critical Approaches to Teaching Literature, Language, Composition, and Culture*. 1 (2001): 7–19.

Miller, Nancy. *Getting Personal*. New York: Routledge, 1991.

Musa, Mark. Translator. *The Divine Comedy*. New York: Penguin, 1984.

Pinsky, Robert. *The Inferno of Dante: A New Verse Translation*. New York: Farrar, 1977.

Poulet, George. "Phenomenology of Reading." *New Literary History* 1 (1969): 53–68.

Rosenblatt, Louise M. *The Reader, the Text, the Poem: The Transactional Theory of the Literary Work*. Carbondale and Edwardsville: Southern Illinois UP, 1978.

Salvatori, Mariolina. "Towards a Hermeneutics of Difficulty." *Audits of Meaning*. Ed. Louise Z. Smith. Portsmouth, NH: Boynton/Cook Heineman, 1988. 80–95.

———, and Paul Kameen. "The Teaching of Teaching: Theoretical Reflections." *Reader: Essays in Reader-Oriented Theory, Criticism, and Pedagogy*. 33/34 (Spring/Fall 1995): 103–24.

———. Mariolina Rizzi. "Difficulty: The Great Educational Divide." In *Opening Lines*, Pat Hutchings ed. 81–93.

———. Mariolina Rizzi. "Understanding Difficulties: A Heuristic." In *Teaching/Writing in the Late Age of Print*. Eds. J. Paul Johnson, Carol Peterson Haviland, and Jeff Galin. Hampton Press, forthcoming.

Sarason, Raymond. *Teaching as a Performing Art*. New York: Teachers College P, 1999.

Shulman, Lee. "Knowledge and Teaching: Foundations of the New Reform." *Harvard Educational Review* (1987) 57, no 1: 1–22.

———. "Course Anatomy: The Dissection and Analysis of Knowledge Through Teaching." In *The Course Portfolio*, edited by Pat Hutchings, 5–12.

———. "Teaching Alone, Learning Together: Needed Agendas for the New Reforms." In *Schooling for Tomorrow: Directing Reform to Issues That Count*, edited by T. J. Sergiovanni and J. H. Moore. Boston: Allyn and Bacon, 1988, 166–87.

Steedman, Carolyn Kay. *Landscape for a Good Woman*. New Brunswick, NJ: Rutgers UP, 1987.

Steiner, George. *On Difficulty and Other Essays*. New York: Oxford UP, 1978.

Tompkins, Jane. "Me and My Shadow," *New Literary History* 19 (1987): 169–78.

Wiggins, Grant, and Jay McTighe, *Understanding by Design*. Alexandria, VA: Association for Supervision and Curriculum Development, 1998.

Williams, Raymond. "The Tenses of the Imagination." *Writing in Society*. London: Verso. 259–68.

Afterword

Dale Bauer

As Peter Elbow declares, the war between reading and writing in the composition classroom is not over. But now the battle is not so much between different theorists or ideologues in the profession as an assumed war with our institutions and standards movements. As one of the contributors to this book *Intertexts* writes, the "battleground" is a spiritual one. Or, as other contributors contend, the battle is over what we are expected to teach versus what we want to deliver. And, as Maryann Cain and George Kalamaras argue (chap. 8, this volume), too often the battle occurs between students and teachers.

This collection details the kinds of assumptions about reading that students bring to our classes, exploring instructors' assumptions about student reading practices: why do our students read? To what end and with how much difficulty? One of the most crucial kinds of reading debated here is how teachers read their students. As I read the essays in this collection, I reflected that our own dispositions engender pedagogical assumptions that are both personal and discipline-wide. My response will focus on these *assumptions,* especially as they have informed our practices too unconsciously or unwittingly. As Jeff Smith argues in "Students' Goals, Gatekeeping, and Some Questions of Ethics," we often mistake students' aims in our classes—when we don't ignore them altogether—as ones we need to change or transform to the teachers' "truer" assumptions. So their desires are replaced with ours. Yet as Smith asks, "What do teachers owe their students?" (308). He suggests that "much of what is taught and advocated by today's compositionists is too far removed, its relationship to students' reasons for being in college too abstract" (313). Much of the early debate about what to read is a cover story for questions and confusions about what students want and need from their teachers. As this collection shows, that debate is still ongoing and important. Much of it is based on our mysteries about students' goals.

To the end of bringing the discussion closer to students' reasons for being in college, Marguerite Helmers has assembled this volume in which the contributors have contextualized the many scenes of reading that they encounter in and outside of the classroom. As Helmers's Introduction (chap. 1, this volume) makes clear, the setting and attitude of reading change the assumptions about the text and the practice itself. Lizabeth Rand, for instance, here (chap. 3, this volume) and in *CCC*, analyzes what it means to read *from an evangelical perspective*. Compositionists have tended to theorize teachers' committed voices, ignoring our students' ongoing commitments to politics and values other than our own. Some of the essays included here chronicle the mistakes we make when we assume our students are, as Freire might say, empty vessels of meaning. We have debunked the banking model, but left untouched the more troubling one of students as blank slates. As Rand argues, teaching at a Seventh-day Adventist Christian school compelled her to step "out of [her] comfort zone" and "to notice how completely [she] embraced a secular approach to thinking about the world and how much [she] took that kind of approach for granted" (52). What she took for granted was the assumption that students always share her secular worldview. Being exposed to the Adventist subculture demonstrated the "rich and detailed history that clearly sanctions particular kinds of textual and interpretive approaches—often different than my own."

This difference compelled Rand to question her own reading practice rather than to launch an assault on her students' "carefully trained Christian reading" practices. She came to ask the following questions: What happens when "faith" informs reading? And reading novels and fiction goes against the grain of faith-based claims? Christian subjectivity informs, even dictates, "right reading" so that reading itself becomes a "spiritual struggle." (I know that I have theorized teaching as a political struggle, or sometimes a personal one, but my "conversion" narrative is far different from this one.)

We often encourage an identificatory reading, whereby students suspend their belief systems in order to feel the pleasure of assenting to the experience of a text without granting it "final authority" (63). But faith-based reading, as Rand shows, is all about giving the Word the final authority, submitting to it rather than creating or resisting it.

On the contrary, Christiansen (chap. 4, this volume) assumes that students and teachers alike need to value *facilitas,* or eloquence, in classical education. Imitation, therefore, is the highest form of teaching and learning. Without models to follow, students will never learn the difference between "sophisticated" and "immature" texts. Christiansen also posits that students need precepts. "Leaving students to describe their own analytical processes without introducing to them already known features of text and context asks them to continually rediscover the wheel, a slow and chancy endeavor, when by showing them the wheel, we can then enable them to invent the turbine" (81). Our goal in teaching is to make students "self-conscious" about acts of invention and the consequences of shaping one's responses in relation to the "master frames" of discourse. But the essay also begs the question of what students' assumptions are about "effective" texts, and it may be impossible to argue for the value of classical imitation when their more "popular" imitation means copying and transforming such "texts" as *Buffy the Vampire Slayer* and Missy Elliot. Students might argue that they are not trying to persuade, but to express self (which for them is not persuasion or imitation, but a sense of distinction or individuation). That is, we might best modify classical education by showing how much popular culture is an attempt at imitation, or a persuasion to imitate. But the ends are not eloquence, but consumption.

Harkin and Sosnoski (chap. 5, this volume) deal most directly with the division between classical argument and popular texts, particularly those embedded in textbooks. As they see it, certain argument textbooks reinforce a commonplace assumption that the aim of reading is to find "authorial intention as the stable meaning of texts." Their argument discloses the significant subtext of current argument texts: "the authors characterize reading as a neutral process of decoding authorial intention. They teach their student-readers that close and careful reading will reveal authorial intention, that finding authorial intention is the purpose of reading, and that the meaning of an argument is readily available to any close reader who is willing to respond" (104). This is one of the key assumptions that readers *do* bring to texts and that the first-year composition course has to debunk. Students resist the idea that they are to make their own meaning, preferring to "dig" deeper and get the meaning that is "hidden" in the text itself. Students don't need this assumption reinforced, but rather challenged.

Harkin and Sosnoski offer a powerful argument for how students read emotionally rather than through the logic and reason that textbooks ostensibly sell. Students may assume—and rightly so—that they don't need to know reason in a corporate world dominated by affect. They contend that what has been abandoned in the course of incorporating reader-response theory into textbooks has been the sense of "exploring litera-ture" (as Louise Rosenblatt would have it) or the critical notion that read-ing differs "from person to person, from context to context, from culture to culture." By ignoring affect and emotion, for instance, students get the idea that they are not supposed to bring anything to the text, that the text fully guides a (or *the*) response. This assumption makes students wary of the "transaction between author and reader," fearing that what they have to offer is not good enough. It reinforces the unfortunate notion that there is an ideal reader, and the student is not it. Harkin and Sosnoski ex-plain that the textbooks make the term "gap" from reader-response texts not a theoretical, but a guilty one: the gap is the students' knowledge, not the textual gap that Wolfgang Iser, among others, theorized. More im-portant, as Harkin and Sosnoski suggest, "To a generation of students who have grown up with TV advertising, the pronouncements of the to-bacco and automobile industries, the greenhouse effect [. . .] the process of 'reading' arguments is not the clean-cut, unambiguous, disciplined, and ethical debate they are being asked in these textbooks to take on" (119). Rather, the students find the "reasonable" and "classical" ap-proaches to be "implausible if not laughable." The same problem with trying to "sell" classical education as imitation to students obtains in teaching the logic of argument: students have been taught to eschew argu-ment in favor of the alternate values at work in a capitalist culture: "greed, hatred, power, lust, envy, and lies."

"Athletic reading" is the solution that Cornis-Pope and Woodlief pro-pose (chap. 7, this volume); their invention describes the difference be-tween the kinds of readings students perform at first and then in reread-ing: "The best reading is a recursive process . . ." (157), but one students often resist. How do we get students beyond "the quick first summative reading" (157)? If students assume that there's nothing in it for them to reread (and what in the corporate culture reinforces this assumption that second or multiple readings "pay off"? what in our culture validates the "slow-motion" activity of second readings?), how can such participation be compelled? As they claim, "making personal connections is equally crucial" (161) as a "drive" to create "devoted readers," but how can this devotion be engineered? Cornis-Pope and Woodlief dismiss these per-sonal responses as "superficial, distorted," only a beginning; second read-ings, they claim, are often "thin and oversimplified [. . .] incomplete [and] impressionistic" (165). Let us take their assertion as a warning that this is exactly the kind of assumption about our students that misleads us as teachers. It puts our pedagogy at risk.

Cornis-Pope and Woodlief want students to examine their "preconceptions" about reading, but it is crucial that we examine our own about students. We may assume that the students' first reading is not "active" when in fact it may perform the most crucial activity of all—establishing interest, motivation, direction. Students are not the only ones with problems over "premature" interpretation. Are only the students responsible for "stretching" their responses? Their essay leads me to ask what an "athletic *teaching*" would look like, something like the "interactive critical pedagogy" that they propose for "hypertextual criticism" and online classes.

This collection offers a dazzling response in Mariolina Salvatori's essay on "reading difficulties" (chap. 9, this volume). Rather than assuming how or what our students find difficult, Salvatori's invention is to make this question the terms of a brilliant assignment. Hers is very much a response to previous assumptions about what students know as *beginning* readers: "The common educational practice of the national standards movement is not for a teacher to genuinely ask her students, what do you know? But to say, this is what you are supposed to know. If the students do not know, the teachers give it to them as 'the basics.'" As Salvatori argues, our culture abjures difficulty, in much the same way that Harkin and Sosnoski argue that our culture distrusts logic and reason. Our pedagogy, then, must be aimed at teaching students—against the grain of culture—how to handle difficulty, how to accept it as an effect of reading. For Salvatori, acknowledging difficulty is a form of knowledge, inchoate perhaps, but not "thin or oversimplified," but "profitable and responsible." Obviously, I like the way that Salvatori has redefined the students' roles and practices here. I admire her assumption that reading is difficult for teachers and students alike.

Her hybrid essay considers the confluence of beginning and fluent readers, that is, what they share in their efforts to make meaning. As Salvatori reminds us, it is also important to mine the meaning of difficulties. In doing so, she gets her students to identify "the kind of work that a specific text demands on them as readers." In short, her students produce meditation on interpretation, the kind that Harkin and Sosnoski believe is foreclosed by textbooks that insist there is an authorial intention to be discovered by inexperienced readers. Her method is to abjure the "continuous dependence on a hierarchy of experts" (213) whose processes remain mysterious to students. As many of these essays illustrate, the teachers' ways are inscrutable to students, and vice versa.

Part of this inscrutability, as Charles Hill suggests (chap. 6, this volume), emerges from the generation gap: a generation of teachers trained in textual literacy versus a generation of students immersed in visual literacy. In order to bridge this gap, as much as it can be, Hill argues that our writing classes must revolve around reading visual rhetoric. Instead of the "Critical-Logical" model, which emphasizes the types of expression that *would* be effective in a more perfect world, Hill contends that we need to get real. Seconding Harkin and Sosnoski's stance, Hill posits a pedagogy of visual rhetoric, consisting of inquiries into page design, textual elements like fonts, and hybrid texts of all kinds. Students could then go on to "produce texts that incorporate visual elements" (146). Without this pedagogy, Hill claims that students will be "helpless to analyze or critique [professional communicators'] messages" (148). I'm not so sure they are so helpless, since as Salvatori suggests, students do already have a repertoire of skills; ultimately, it is the difficulty of "decoding" or switching codes that we need to teach students.

Cain and Kalamaras (chap. 8, this volume) imagine—better than any other essay in this collection—what students want. Mary Ann Cain, for instance, assesses what her students are really thinking during their mid-semester conferences: "I have become a roadblock, not a facilitator, to Janelle's work. I don't know how I became this, any more than I know how I became an impromptu therapist. I don't like the roles I fall into, but I feel helpless to work against them, mainly because I'm not entirely sure the casting is entirely wrong" (178). In assessing her own role playing in the performance of teaching, Cain gets at the gap between our students' knowledge and the teachers' that our classes are supposed to bridge. This is the "difficulty paper" that Salvatori theorizes, but applied to the teachers' difficulty in reading students' rather than students' difficulty in reading texts. This self-reflective practice, as Robert Yagelski writes in "The Ambivalence of Reflection," can lead to self-doubt and a mostly uncomfortable, maybe even masochistic questioning of the identity of the teacher. The flip side is that when we challenge students' interpretive freedom, "it yields a potentially violent outcome" (189). Such crises force us to imagine what risks are worth taking in the writing classroom.

Arguably the most optimistic essay in the collection is Kathleen McCormick's "Closer than Close Reading: Historical Analysis, Cultural Analysis, and Symptomatic Reading in the Undergraduate Classroom" (chap. 2, this volume). She argues that we can advocate pleasure and critical skills as part of our pedagogy, *if* we incorporate students' "street knowledge" in our classrooms. The usefulness of McCormick's pedagogy is its assumption of what students already know and practice:

"that [students] themselves are divided and contradictory subjects, caught between embracing a particular position advocated by the popular culture and critique or disdain for it" (32). By assuming that students are already fluent, resistant readers, McCormick can reinforce their "street knowledge" with her conception of academic knowledge. She sees herself as "coach," one not "pretend[ing] to be introducing [students]" (35) to critical reading practices. Her teaching presents students with historical, cultural, and symptomatic (reading the unspoken or unsaid) interpretations as central to embedding their knowledge into different, perhaps larger, contexts. The success of this approach is self-evident: it gives context to students' knowledge rather than invalidating what they know because it doesn't "fit" in the academy. McCormick's method "gives agency" where it belongs.

George Kalamaras deserves the last word: "I still want to give students something more than they've come to expect" (193). Perhaps more than any other, this claim also suggests what *Intertexts* offers: a way of seeing interactions and making transactions between students and texts, and between their assumptions and ours about what teaching is and who teachers are.

WORKS CITED

Rand, Lizabeth. "Enacting Faith: Evangelical Discourse and the Discipline of Composition Studies." *CCC* 52.3 (February 2001): 349–67.

Smith, Jeff. "Students' Goals, Gatekeeping, and Some Questions of Ethics." *College English* 59.3 (March 1997): 299–320.

Yagelski, Robert. "The Ambivalence of Reflection." *CCC* 51.1 (September 1999): 32–50.

Contributors

Dale Bauer . . .

Dale M. Bauer is professor of English and Women's Studies at the University of Kentucky. She has published *Feminist Dialogics* (SUNY 1988), *Edith Wharton's Brave New Politics* (Wisconsin 1994), and edited volumes on Bakhtin and feminism, Charlotte Perkins Gilman's "The Yellow Wallpaper," and the *Cambridge Companion to Nineteenth-Century American Women's Writing* (with Phil Gould). Along with essays on pedagogy and the rhetorics of teaching, she is currently writing *Sex Expression and American Women,* about women's sexuality in American literature from 1860 to 1940.

Mary Ann Cain . . .

Mary Ann Cain is Associate Professor of English at Indiana University-Purdue University Fort Wayne where she teaches writing studies including rhetoric, creative writing, and composition, as well as Women's Studies. Her book, *Revisioning Writers' Talk: Gender and Culture in Acts of Composing,* was published by SUNY Press in 1995. Her articles have appeared in *CCC, Dialogue, Composition Studies,* and *Written Communication,* among others. Her fiction has appeared in journals such as *The North American Review, Thirteenth Moon, The Sun, First Intensity,* and *LIT.*

Nancy Christiansen . . .

Nancy L. Christiansen is an assistant professor of English at Brigham Young University, Provo with specialties in Renaissance Literature and Rhetoric. Besides teaching, she is currently serving as Director of BYU's Reading Center. Her particular research interests are in rhetorical criticism, theory, and pedagogy and in Shakespeare. She has published on all these topics, including "Rhetoric as Character-Fashioning: The Implications of Delivery's 'Places' in the British Renaissance Paideia" in *Rhetorica* 15 (Summer 1997) 297-334, and "Synecdoche, Tropic Violence, and Shakespeare's Imitatio in *Titus Andronicus*" in *Style* 34 (Fall 2000).

Marcel Cornis-Pope . . .

Marcel Cornis-Pope is professor and chair of English at Virginia Commonwealth University. His teaching and research interests focus on contemporary literary theory (reader oriented and new historicist), postmodern fiction, and narratology. He has received a Fulbright teaching grant (1983–1985), an Andrew Mellon Faculty Fellowship at Harvard University (1987–1988), the VCU College of Humanities and Sciences Lecturer Award (1993), and the Council of Editors of Learned Journals' Phoenix Award for Distinguished Editorial Achievement (1996). His publications include *Hermeneutic Desire and Critical Rewriting: Narrative Interpretation in the Wake of Poststructuralism* (1992), *Violence and Mediation in Contemporary Culture* (coedited with Ronald Bogue, 1995), and *Narrative Innovation and Cultural Rewriting in the Cold War Era and After* (forthcoming this year).

Patricia Harkin . . .

Patricia Harkin is Associate Professor of English at the University of Illinois at Chicago, where she teaches cultural studies and rhetorical theory. She is the author of *Acts of Reading: An Introduction to Literary and Cultural Studies* (Prentice Hall 1998), coauthor, with John Schilb, of *Contending with Words: Composition and Rhetoric in a Postmodern Age* (MLA 1991), and chair of the College Section of NCTE. Her writings have appeared in *College English, Rhetoric Review, JAC,* and other journals.

Marguerite Helmers . . .

Marguerite Helmers is Associate Professor of English at the University of Wisconsin Oshkosh, where she teaches courses in writing, literature, and literary criticism. She is the author of *Writing Students* (SUNY 1995) and articles appearing in *College English, JAC, Enculturation, Bad Subjects, The Writing Instructor,* and elsewhere. She is the editor of *WPA: Writing Program Administration* with Dennis Lynch. In 1998, she was awarded the Distinguished Teaching Award for UW Oshkosh and in 2001, she was announced Provost's Leadership Fellow. She is currently working in the area of visual cultural studies.

Charles A. Hill . . .

Charles A. Hill is an Associate Professor and director of the first-year seminar program at the University of Wisconsin Oshkosh. He teaches writing and rhetoric courses, including technical writing and computers and writing. His current research interests are in visual rhetoric, writing instruction, and online communication. Hill has published articles in *TEXT Technology*, the *Journal of Computer Documentation*, *Written Communication*, and *Computers and Composition*, and has published book chapters on the teaching of writing and argumentation. He is currently editing, with Marguerite Helmers, *Defining Visual Rhetorics*, an introduction to the theory and practice of reading images.

George Kalamaras . . .

George Kalamaras is Associate Professor of English at Indiana University-Purdue University Fort Wayne, where he teaches courses in creative writing and composition theory. He is the author of *Reclaiming the Tacit Dimension: Symbolic Form in the Rhetoric of Silence* (SUNY Press 1994) and articles *in International Journal of Hindu Studies*, *College Composition and Communication*, *Composition Studies*, and others. He spent several months in India in 1994 on a Fulbright Indo-U.S. Advanced Research Fellowship. He has also widely published poetry, including his award-winning collection, *The Theory and Function of Mangoes* (Four Way Books 2000), and poems in *Best American Poetry 1997*, *Sulfur*, *TriQuarterly*, and elsewhere.

Kathleen McCormick . . .

Kathleen McCormick is Professor of Literature and Pedagogy and Director of Writing at Purchase College, SUNY. McCormick's most recent textbook is *Reading Our Histories, Understanding Our Culture* (Allyn and Bacon 1999). Her previous book, *The Culture of Reading and the Teaching of English* (Manchester UP and NCTE 1994), won the Mina Shaughnessy Award in 1995. McCormick is the coeditor of the MLA volume on *Approaches to Teaching Joyce's Ulysses* (1993); and the coauthor of *Reading-to-Write: Exploring a Cognitive and Social Process* (Oxford 1990) and the textbook *Reading Texts* (Heath, 1987). She is also a contributor to a number of volumes linking theory and pedagogy including *Critical Theory and the Teaching of Literature* (NCTE 1996) and *Pedagogy is Politics* (Illinois, 1992).

Lizabeth Rand . . .

Lizabeth Rand is Assistant Professor of Rhetoric in the Rhetoric Department of Hampden-Sydney College in Farmville, Virginia. She received her PhD from the University of Nebraska-Lincoln in 2002. Her dissertation was an ethnographic study of an evangelical Seventh-day Adventist community in the Midwest. Her other research interests include exploring representations of women in sports with a particular focus on women in competitive bodybuilding. She is also interested in studying the illness narratives of women writers. Publications include essays in *College Composition and Communication*, *Middle-Atlantic Writers Association Review*, and *College Language Association Journal*.

Mariolina Salvatori

Mariolina Rizzi Salvatori teaches and does research in the areas of hermeneutics, composition, literacy, and pedagogy. She is particularly interested in exploring the transactions of knowledge, and the relations between teachers, students, and texts that different theories of reading make possible. Her publications include: "Conversations with Texts: Reading in the Teaching of Composition," "The Personal as Recitation," "On Behalf of Pedagogy," "Pedagogy in the Academy: 'The divine skill of the born teacher's instincts'," and *Pedagogy: Disturbing History 1819–1929*, "porque no puedo decir mi cuento: Mexican Ex-Votos' Iconographic Literacy." In 1999 she was selected as Carnegie Scholar by the Carnegie Foundation for the Advancement of Teaching for her work on "pedagogy of difficulty." She is editor of *READER*, with Paul Kameen.

James J. Sosnoski

James Sosnoski is Professor of English at the University of Illinois at Chicago. His teaching includes courses in technology and pedagogy, rhetorical and literary theory. Sosnoski is the author of *Modern Skeletons in Postmodern Closets: A Cultural Studies Alternative* (Virginia 1995) and *Token Professionals and Master Critics: A Critique of Orthodoxy in Literary Studies* (SUNY 1994). Sosnoski is the author and Web manager of UIC's Virtual Harlem project, a collaborative learning network whose purpose is to study the Harlem Renaissance through the construction and use of scenarios developed in Virtual Reality <http://www.evl.uic.edu/cavern/harlem/>.

Ann Woodlief

Ann Matthews Woodlief is an Associate Professor of English (American Literature) in the English department at Virginia Commonwealth University in Richmond, where she has taught since 1972. Her degrees in English are from Wake Forest University and the University of North Carolina at Chapel Hill. Academic areas of research interest include nineteenth-century literature, nature writing, American women writers, reader-oriented literary theory, and the use of computers, especially hypertext, for teaching. She has published articles and done a number of presentations on Thoreau, Emerson, and teaching with the computer; some are published online at http://www.vcu.edu/engweb.

Author Index

Subject Index

Frankenstein (Shelley), 145
Free will, evangelical readers and, 66
Friends, 33
Front Page, 170
Functional literacy, 36
Fundamentals of Cognition (Ashcraft), 114

G

Galileo (Brecht), 37–38
Gaps, closing, 108, 113, 222
Gender, xiv
  critical reading of media texts and, 32, 34
  difficulties with reading and, 28
  influence on reader's response, 110
  literacy and, 57
Gender and Reading (Schweickart), xiv
Gender roles
  images and, 134, 136
  symptomatic reading of, 43–44
Gender stereotyping, 35
General education requirement, creative writing as, 178, 180. *See also* First-year composition courses
Generalization, 85
Genre(s), 85
  in classical oral reading, 73
  in classroom, 173–174, 179
  composing in literary, 181–182
  diversity of, 182–183
  drama as master, 90
  of talk, 183, 184–186
Genre theory, 104
Getting Personal (Miller), 210
Give Attendance to Reading (Cobb), 55–56
Goals, student, 219–225
God words, 133
"A Good Man Is Hard to Find" (Flannery), 163–164
Gourmet, 23n2
Grammar, 74
Grammar of Motives, A (Burke), 114–115
Grammaticus, 74, 97n7
Graphicacy, 124
GUIDE, 159, 168, 170

Gutenberg Elegies, The (Birkerts), 20, 24n5
Gymnasmata, 75–76, 96n5, 98n9

H

Hermeneutic Desire and Critical Rewriting (Cornis-Pope), 154
Heroic reader, 23n2
Hidden in Plain View (Tobin & Dobard), xiv
Hidden meanings, reading for, 42, 44
Historical analysis, x–xi, 36–39, 45
History, oral reading of, 73
History of Reading, A (Manguel), 5
Horizon of expectations, 161
How to Read and Why (Bloom), 5, 18
"How to Recognize a Poem When You See One" (Fish), 109
Hybrid text, 145–146, 224
Hypertext, xii–xiii, 20, 88, 154, 171
Hyper/Text/Theory (Landow), 153
Hypertextual critical writing, 169–171
Hypertextual criticism, 154, 169, 223
Hypertextual reading, 157–171
  first readings, 160–164
  hypertextual critical writing, 169–171
  rereadings, 165–169
Hypertextual writing, online examples, 171
Hypertrails, 159

I

Icons, 132
Ideal readers, 23n2, 107
Identification, 114–115
Identificatory reading, 220–221
Identity themes, 104, 108
Ideology
  bias and, 113–114
  cultural analysis and, 39–41, 45
  dominant, xi, 39–41
  making meaning and, 65
  reading and cultural, 30, 34–35, 102
  symptomatic reading and, 42–43